International Insolvency Law

Elina Moustaira

International Insolvency Law

National Laws and International Texts

Springer

Elina Moustaira
School of Law
National and Kapodistrian University of Athens
Athens, Greece

ISBN 978-3-030-04449-7 ISBN 978-3-030-04450-3 (eBook)
https://doi.org/10.1007/978-3-030-04450-3

Library of Congress Control Number: 2018962737

This Springer imprint is published by the registered company Springer Nature Switzerland AG
The registered company address is: Gewerbestrasse 11, 6330 Cham, Switzerland

To my parents' memory

Preface

During the last decades, international insolvencies have often been the focus of courts and scholars, obviously because of their multiplication. Books and articles have been written, trying to explain issues or/and offer solutions.

The way I chose to present some of the issues that might arise in an insolvency case that has repercussions in more than one country is a "personal" approach, solidified by many years of reading, writing and teaching international insolvency law.

Obviously, this book has no ambition to present every issue of international insolvency law or detailed international insolvency regulations in the various countries of the world. This was not my aim and, in any case, it would need several tomes of an encyclopedia.

My aim was to isolate the most crucial issues that arise in international insolvency cases and try to find out and present how the national laws and the international texts perceive them and what solutions they offer, if any.

Many pages are dedicated to U.S. insolvency law and U.S. cases—even when the central issues might appear as ones of other countries. The reasons are obvious: (a) most cases were tried there; and (b) the legal transplanting is, not surprisingly, rather almost exclusively one way, that is, from USA to other countries, mostly non-common law countries. So, we need to understand the why and how of these transplants.

International insolvency law is probably very complicated—not least because of the different solutions adopted by the national laws and the international instruments—but at the same time is a challenging field of law that demands hard work and thorough attention, since many interests are at stake.

Once again, I would like to thank Springer and especially Dr. Brigitte Reschke, Springer Executive Editor Law, for her support and confidence.

Athens, Greece | Elina Moustaira

Contents

Chapter 1
Introduction

1.1 General Comments

Which is the principal aim of the insolvency proceedings? Is it the best possible satisfaction of the creditors or is it the protection/survival of the debtor?[1] Both are aims of the insolvency proceedings; but which one of the two should be considered as the main target? Not all countries follow the same path. In fact, there are many differences between the insolvency laws of the world. Further, even in the frame of one and the same country, there might exist different opinions regarding the answer to the above question; answers that may influence the trajectory of each country's insolvency law.

Do pre-insolvency proceedings have the same aims, the same priorities? Do rescue (insolvency or pre-insolvency) proceedings have a different procedural aim than liquidation proceedings? Some say yes; others deny that, arguing that restructuring is only a means to the best possible satisfaction of the creditors.

Do international insolvencies have the same aims as the restricted in one country insolvency proceedings? Is cooperation, at whatever level possible between the debtor and its creditors, or between the administrator and the creditors, or—in case there are parallel insolvency proceedings in more than one country—between the administrators of the insolvency proceedings, or between the courts, or between the courts and the administrators, or between all of them? Are courts of countries that share the same legal traditions and fundamental principles of law, more able to cooperate?[2]

---

[1] Landfermann (2017), pp. 408–409.

[2] Peacock (2015), p. 564.

E. Moustaira, *International Insolvency Law*,
https://doi.org/10.1007/978-3-030-04450-3_1

1.2 History of Bankruptcy Law: Bankruptcy Stigma

Under Roman law, when the debtor did not repay or could not repay his debt towards his creditor and no one was willing to give him some financial aid then the creditor had the right to punish him corporeally.[3] The debtor's body was the only security that he could offer to his creditor.[4]

Later, at the Italian cities' open markets, a creditor who had not been repaid, would go and crash his debtor's table, publicly, so that everyone could see that he was not a worthy person. The stigma followed him through life.

It is argued that the study of the underlying sources of bankruptcy stigma must begin from the relation of religion and law, since the earliest references on moral code and conviction are traced in this relation. The moral codes of all the world's major religions, Judaism, Christianity, Islam and Hinduism, state that their followers must avoid becoming a debtor and, if by chance they do become a debtor, that it is very important to repay their financial obligations.[5]

"Resorting to bankruptcy is a form of sin."[6] In Islam, the fulfillment of contractual obligations is ranked in the Quran "with the highest achievements and the noblest virtues".[7] This influences Muslims and deters them from filing bankruptcy to avoid debt repayment.[8] Hindus also place great value on debt repayment and consider the failure to do so, a sin.[9] Most Jewish jurists consider paying one's debts an affirmative biblical injunction.[10]

The bankruptcy stigma survived until recently—if it ever really disappeared. However, the situation is very different, at least in some countries, which influence others. Examples of the bankruptcy laws' trajectory, laws that influenced and still influence many others, are the following.

---

[3] Korobkin (2003), p. 2134.

[4] For the reasons of this cruelty, see Nietzsche (1887/1991), pp. 55–56: "Die Äquivalenz ist damit gegeben, daß an Stelle eines gegen den Schaden direkt aufkommenden Vorteils (also an Stelle eines Ausgleichs in Geld, Land, Besitz irgendwelcher Art) dem Gläubiger eine Art *Wohlgefühl* als Rückzahlung und Ausgleich zugestanden wird – das Wohlgefühl, seine Macht an einem Machtlosen unbedenklich auslassen zu dürfen, die Wollust "*de faire le mal pour le plaisir de le faire*", der Genuß in der Vergewaltigung …".

[5] Efrat (1998), pp. 162–167.

[6] Sousa (2013), p. 446.

[7] Habachy (1962), p. 465.

[8] Hamoudi (2011), p. 513.

[9] Sousa (2013), p. 447.

[10] Resnicoff (2011), p. 557.

1.2.1 UK

The first modern bankruptcy[11] statute was an English statute (*An Act Against Such Persons As Do Make Bankrupts* 1542 or 1543). It contained elements of Roman Law and it imposed harsh punishments on those who tried to avoid paying their debts.[12] It established the principle of seizing and distributing debtors' assets, but it did not institute an administrative or judicial process for that purpose. Therefore, its practical utility was almost inexistent.[13]

Debtors were considered criminals; the mischief for which they were punished was the fraud of which they were seen to be capable. The [above] Act was aimed against 'absconding debtors', that is, persons who:

> ... craftily obtaining in their own hands great substance of other men's goods, do suddenly flee to parts unknown, or keep their houses, not minding to pay or restore to any their creditors their duties, but at their own wills and pleasures consume debts and the substance obtained by credit or other men, for their own pleasure and delicate living, against all reason, equity and good conscience.[14]

Bankruptcy continued to be seen as stigma until relatively recently. During the Victorian period, there was much and widespread agitation against specifically imprisonment but also generally the inadequacy of the system.

It is interesting that, by the nineteenth century, Ireland had a much more sophisticated and efficient system than the system of England's. According to the first, a jury of independent and impartial neighbors of the debtor fixed the amounts and dated for debts to be paid by installments. Debt recovery had a much better rate there.[15]

The *Bankruptcy Act 1603* provided for the public examination of debtors and their economic situation. The *Bankruptcy Act 1623* provided that any debtor who would hide assets from creditors could be 'set upon the pillory in some public place ... and have one of his ears cut off'. Obviously, the stigmatization of debtors was the main aim.

1.2.2 USA

When the first U.S. bankruptcy law was enacted in April 4, 1800 ("a roughly three-year experiment that began in 1800 and ended in 1803", when the law was repealed[16]), Congress copied the English legislation. Consequently, the bankruptcy

[11] The words "bankruptcy" and "insolvency" are used interchangeably throughout this book. Eidenmüller (2017), mentions that: "Bankruptcy law" is the term more used in the US, while "insolvency law" is more common elsewhere in the world, especially in the UK.

[12] Ali et al. (2015), p. 1579.

[13] Levinthal (1919), p. 15.

[14] Rajak (2008), p. 12.

[15] Rajak (2008), p. 14.

[16] Pardo (2018), p. 1171.

laws of the two countries share many similarities; however, there are also many differences between them.

In 1841, after almost four decades of non-existence of any bankruptcy law, a new Bankruptcy Act was enacted (again: it was repealed in 1843). It was considered so radical that there was a controversy involving the leading politicians of that epoch.[17]

During the late eighteenth century and throughout the nineteenth century, there was an ideological struggle over the future of the country, mirrored also on the disagreement between the Federalists who believed that commerce was the most important element for USA's future and that bankruptcy law should be federal and the Jeffersonian Republicans who called for a more agrarian future and questioned whether a federal bankruptcy law was needed. The Bankruptcy Act of 1998 was the first federal law on bankruptcy.

During the nineteenth century, there was also the expansion of the railroads as the country's first big corporations. This growth—together with other reasons—brought with her the default of many railroads on their obligations. The U.S. courts developed a judicial reorganization technique, the equity receivership, which technique became the basis for modern corporate reorganization.[18]

In USA, the idea of bankruptcy as moral failure was early transformed into one of economic failure. States abolished imprisonment for debt, starting from 1821. Until 1842 it had been done by Kentucky, Vermont, New York, Ohio, Michigan, Alabama, Tennessee, New Hampshire, Pennsylvania, Connecticut, Maine, Massachusetts and South Carolina. In 1839, the USA abolished imprisonment for debt for all people in federal courts in states which had acted to do so. The Supreme Court upheld the constitutionality of such laws.

Generally, bankruptcy/insolvency in the U.S. is not really considered as the End, but as a means to another, healthier end. As it is declared: "Bankruptcy law in the United States is unique in the world. Perhaps most startling to outsiders is that individuals and businesses in the United States do not seem to view bankruptcy as the absolute last resort, as an outcome to be avoided at all costs."[19]

U.S. Insolvency law is considered debtor-friendly, debtor-centric[20]; the reorientation that shifted the focus away from its origins primarily as a creditor-collection device to a mechanism for debtor relief took place with the enactment of the Bankruptcy Act of 1841. Of course, access to that relief was not easy (for example, because of the court fees and attorney's fees[21]), however the 1841 Act provided that a bankrupt discharge encompassed all pre-bankruptcy debts, something that has changed over time: Congress has dramatically reduced the scope of bankruptcy discharge.[22]

[17] Tabb (1991), p. 350.

[18] Skeel Jr (2001), pp. 3–4.

[19] Skeel Jr (2001), p. 1.

[20] Bernardo (2012), p. 827.

[21] Pardo (2016), pp. 1123–1124.

[22] Nash and Pardo (2012), pp. 937–939.

An interdisciplinary approach of the bankruptcy system there (and elsewhere), may give more accurate conclusions than a strictly legal approach. For example, one cannot ignore that the U.S. bankruptcy law is the product of three forces, three "political determinants": creditor groups, pro-debtor interests, and bankruptcy professionals. The balance of power between these political determinants has been destabilized by several facts/reasons, one of which was the periodic price shocks.[23]

As it is pointed out, several characteristics of the U.S. Bankruptcy/Insolvency Law make it far friendlier to debtors than are other national insolvency laws.

One very important characteristic, that also makes U.S. Insolvency law much more different to other national laws, is the fact that the debtor who files for bankruptcy can keep the control of the whole situation: he/she can either turn his/her assets over the court and have his/her obligations immediately discharged (liquidation), or keep his/her assets and make payments to his/her creditors under a rehabilitation (reorganization) plan. The choice for which procedure to file, is his/hers.

1.2.3 Australia

Australia's first bankruptcy laws followed English laws of the time. The "frequent economic shocks" of the nineteenth century, due mainly to "rampant speculation" had, as a consequence, the bankruptcy of many people, not necessarily dishonest.[24]

In 1841, New South Wales enacted a new statute, the *Debtors' Relief Act 1840* (NSW), which adopted a lenient approach to bankruptcy. On the other hand, it rather seems that as in the UK and the US, the colonies' lenient bankruptcy regime coexisted with the mentality of people, who continued to see bankruptcy as a stigma. English and colonial attitudes towards certain issues kept on having strong bonds between them. Consequently, the influence exerted by the English law to the colonies' law was very strong.

In 1901, the six Australian colonies federated to become the Commonwealth of Australia, comprising six States—Queensland, New South Wales, Victoria, Tasmania, South Australia and Western Australia—and two internal Territories—the Australian Capital Territory, which is the seat of the national capita Canberra, and the Northern Territory.

Under the Australian Constitution, section 51 (xvii), the Federal Parliament was granted a specific power, to be exercised concurrently with the States, to legislate on "bankruptcy and insolvency".

The personal bankruptcy and insolvency laws continued to apply until comprehensive federal bankruptcy legislation came into effect in 1928. The law that currently applies to the insolvency of natural persons is the Bankruptcy Act 1966.

---

[23] Skeel Jr (2001), p. 16.

[24] Ali et al. (2015), p. 1585.

Australia was following—and still is—the English approach in many legal issues, insolvency included.[25] That is the reason why Australia too, following the example of England, includes the regulation of corporate insolvency in various Companies Acts.[26]

It is the federal Parliament, based in Canberra, the one that is responsible for legislating on both personal and corporate insolvency.

Individual insolvency administrations are regulated by the Australian Financial Security Authority (AFSA) while corporate insolvency administrations are regulated by the Australian Securities and Investments Commission (ASIC). AFSA and ASIC have signed a Memorandum of Understanding to facilitate liaison, cooperation, assistance and the exchange of information between the agencies in performing their regulatory functions.[27]

Furthermore, different government departments are responsible for policy and law reform for personal (the Commonwealth Attorney-General) and corporate (The Treasury) debtors.[28]

The most recent reform of Australia's insolvency law is the *Insolvency Law Reform Act 2016 (Cth)* (ILRA), the last step of which was taken on September 1, 2017.[29]

1.3 Human Rights and Insolvency Law

Human Rights considerations have played an important role in the two recent decades—and will undoubtedly do the same in the decades to come, especially regarding the natural persons, whether they are debtors or creditors.[30]

In relation to England and Wales, it has been stated:

> …[t]he Human Rights Act 1998 has necessitated a comprehensive review of the operation of the insolvency law and procedure in the light of the requirements of the European Convention of Human Rights, as the validity of established domestic provisions comes to be challenged with increasing frequency before the courts.[31]

---

[25] See Steele et al. (2018), p. 142: "A comparison between the UK and Australia is also justified due to the similarity between the profiles of the corporate insolvency markets in those jurisdictions."

[26] Mason (2015), pp. 200–201.

[27] Available at: https://download.asic.gov.au/media/2225959/afsa-mou-published-1-october-2014.pdf.

[28] Mason (2015), p. 202.

[29] Australian Insolvency Law Reform—Expectations for the future (2017) Clifford Chance. Available at: https://www.cliffordchance.com/briefings/2017/09/australian_insolvencylawreform-expectation.html.

[30] The latter would mainly refer to the employees and their rights in case of their employer's insolvency.

[31] Fletcher (2002), p. vii.

In South Africa, a mixed jurisdiction, the legal system of which has elements of both Roman-Dutch law and English law,[32] the 1996 Constitution with its Bill of Rights brought about significant changes to the country's jurisprudence and its legal system, including its insolvency law.[33] As it is pointed out:

> Human rights considerations now permeate every aspect of the law, including insolvency law and debt enforcement procedures, which are required to conform to constitutional imperatives. Statutory provisions and well-established principles and practices may now be challenged constitutionally.[34]

1.4 Concluding Comments

During the twentieth century, credit, especially consumer credit reached big heights. The mass adoption of consumer credit[35] contributed to a change of attitudes (or was the result of change…). From being a source of shame, it almost became a status symbol and the inability to pay one's debts was attributed to "external, uncontrollable events" and not to bad individual management.[36] This in turn led to a change of attitudes, so that people, mainly in the Western world, stopped seeing bankruptcy as a stigma.[37]

Not all empirical studies—most of which have been carried out in the U.S.[38]—agree to that, though. According to certain ones, American bankrupts now have higher debts relative to their incomes, because when in financial distress, they are "more reluctant" to file for bankruptcy, due to bankruptcy's (possibly) increasing stigma[39]

References

Ali P, O'Brien L, Ramsay I (2015) 'Short a Few Quid': bankruptcy stigma in contemporary Australia. Univ N S W Law J 38:1575–1613

Bernardo PJF (2012) Cross-border insolvency and the challenges of the global corporation: evaluating globalization and stakeholder predictability through the UNCITRAL model law on cross-border insolvency and the European Union insolvency regulation. Ateneo Law J 56:799–833

[32] On mixed jurisdictions, see Moustaira (2003), pp. 113–121. On South Africa, as a mixed jurisdiction, see Moustaira (2004/2012), pp. 79–83.

[33] Steyn (2004), pp. 1–2.

[34] Boraine et al. (2015), p. 60.

[35] The book does not refer to consumer's bankruptcy, though.

[36] Efrat (2006a), p. 495.

[37] Sousa (2013), pp. 453–455.

[38] Efrat (2006b), p. 365.

[39] Sullivan et al. (2006), p. 242.

Boraine A, Evans R, Roestoff M, Steyn L (2015) The pro-creditor approach in South African insolvency law and the possible impact of the constitution. Nottingham Insolv Bus Law e-J 3:59–91
Efrat R (1998) The moral appeal of personal bankruptcy. Whittier Law Rev 20:141–167
Efrat R (2006a) Bankruptcy stigma: plausible causes for shifting norms. Emory Bankruptcy Dev J 22:481–519
Efrat R (2006b) The evolution of bankruptcy stigma. Theor Inq Law 7:365–393
Eidenmüller H (2017) Comparative corporate insolvency law. Oxford Legal Studies Research Paper No. 30/2017. Available at: https://ssrn.com/abstract=2799863
Fletcher I (2002) The law of insolvency, 3rd edn. Sweet & Maxwell, London
Habachy S (1962) Property, right, and contract in Muslim law. Columbia Law Rev 62:450–473
Hamoudi HA (2011) The surprising irrelevance of Islamic bankruptcy. Am Bankruptcy Inst Law Rev 19:505–522
Korobkin DR (2003) Bankruptcy law, ritual, and performance. Columbia Law Rev:2124–2159
Landfermann H-G (2017) Die Befriedigung der Gläubiger im Insolvenzverfahren – bestmöglich und gleichmäßig! In: Paulus/Wimmer-Amend (Hrsg.) Festschrift für Dr. Klaus Wimmer. Nomos, Baden-Baden, pp 408–445
Levinthal LE (1919) The early history of English bankruptcy. Univ Pa Law Rev 67:1–20
Mason R (2015) Insolvency specialists and government enquiries: a unique opportunity to contribute to the public good. In: Parry R, Omar PJ (eds) International insolvency law: future perspectives. INSOL Europe, Nottingham/Paris, pp 199–219
Moustaira EN (2003) Milestones in the course of comparative law. Theses and antitheses [in Greek]. Ant.N. Sakkoulas Publishers, Athens/Komotini
Moustaira EN (2012) Comparative law [in Greek]. Nomiki Bibliothiki, Athens
Nash JR, Pardo RI (2012) Does ideology matter in bankruptcy? Voting behavior on the courts of appeals. William Mary Law Rev 53:919–985
Nietzsche F (1887/1991) Zur Genealogie der Moral. Eine Streitschrift. Insel taschenbuch, Frankfurt am Main/Leipzig
Pardo RI (2016) Taking bankruptcy rights seriously. Wash Law Rev 91:1115–1191
Pardo RI (2018) Bankrupt slaves. Vanderbilt Law Rev 71:1071–1166
Peacock LL (2015) A tale of two courts: the novel cross-border bankruptcy trial. Am Bankruptcy Inst Law Rev 23:543–570
Rajak H (2008) The culture of bankruptcy. In: Omar P (ed) International insolvency law. Themes and perspectives. Routledge, London and New York, pp 3–25
Resnicoff SH (2011) Jewish and American bankruptcy law: their similarities, differences and interactions. Am Bankruptcy Inst Law Rev 19:551–584
Skeel DA Jr (2001) Debt's dominion. A history of bankruptcy law in America. Princeton University Press, Princeton and Oxford
Sousa MD (2013) Bankruptcy stigma: a socio-legal study. Am Bankruptcy Law J 87:435–482
Steele S, Wee MS, Ramsay I (2018) Remunerating corporate insolvency practitioners in the United Kingdom, Australia, and Singapore: the roles of courts. Asian J Comp Law 13:141–172
Steyn L (2004) Human rights issues in South African insolvency law. Int Insolv Rev 13:1–25
Sullivan TA, Warren E, Westbrook JL (2006) Less stigma or more financial distress: an empirical analysis of the extraordinary increase in bankruptcy filings. Stanford Law Rev 59:213–256
Tabb CJ (1991) The historical evolution of the bankruptcy discharge. Am Bankruptcy Law J 65:325–370

Chapter 2
Insolvency: International Insolvency

2.1 Juridical Nature and Aim of Insolvency Proceedings

Insolvency laws often—if not always—reflect the times and the conditions of life in every part of the world. Economy has an important role to play in insolvency law's structure and choices,[1] nowadays—or had it always? The particularities of countries and their legal cultures are also reflected in their insolvency laws.

Insolvency is a multidimensional phenomenon and not only economic, it is rightly stated.[2] Insolvency is also an economic phenomenon rather complicated, since, to interpret certain exteriorized facts, one has to consider various elements, such as the personal quality of the debtor, his/her access to credit, his/her assets and debts, the market conditions, his/her productive capacity.[3]

To access and verify those elements, one needs sufficient information about important details of the business entity, that usually are covered by the principle of confidentiality. Thus, one could easily say that insolvency is an indeterminate legal concept that can be more or less verified on the basis of certain elements.[4]

In our days, things change with a tremendous rapidity. The influence of Law and Economics on insolvency law is big—even for countries which do not necessarily try to adapt their legal system to the "orders" of this theory (and praxis). Sometimes, declarations about insolvency have a cynical color:

> However, insolvency *per se* is not necessarily negative, since economic growth in general requires certain non-profitable activities to be phased out, in order to spare up room for new

---

[1] Paulus (2016), p. 1657.

[2] Altman (2011), p. 463.

[3] Frade (2012), p. 45.

[4] Pérez Ragone and Martínez Benavides (2015), p. 95.

E. Moustaira, *International Insolvency Law*,
https://doi.org/10.1007/978-3-030-04450-3_2

> ones and therefore, failing projects and the replacement of non-profitable firms has to be seen as a fundamental element of economic growth.[5]

it is stated.

2.2 Private International Law Meets Insolvency Law

Insolvency is a collective proceeding. Essential elements of insolvency, in each national law, are the orderly identification of the debtor's property, the verification of creditors' claims and the distribution of the debtor's divisible property in satisfaction of those claims, the promotion of commercial morality.

Individual private rights of parties, in case of liquidation they are transformed into an opportunity to participate in a collective administration and in case of reorganization they affect a creditor's position in the collective approval of a plan.[6] Party autonomy, of debtor and creditor law, gives its place to collective impartiality of insolvency law.

In case of an international insolvency, issues of private international law appear: Choice of forum (international jurisdiction), recognition and enforcement, choice of law (applicable law). The answers/solutions given by the various national laws often differ enormously. These—perhaps unavoidable—differences are probably the main reason for the huge problems that are created in international insolvency cases.

Unifying, harmonizing national insolvency laws had been proved rather impossible. Harmonization of private international law rules have been considered as "easier" task. It seems that this not absolutely true. Few are the examples of "successful" international instruments that managed, after many years of failures, to harmonize some such rules, providing at the same time for several exceptions. Further, even then, the interpretation of the harmonized rules by the national courts often gave different results.

It seems that the castles of [international] insolvency laws are not willing to open their gates.

2.3 Universalism: Territorialism

Cross-border insolvencies, international insolvencies, are not easy to handle, as it is already mentioned and as it will be several times repeated. Opposing theories are proposed, the theory/approach of universalism and the theory/approach of territorialism.[7]

Universalism goes together with unity of bankruptcy, insolvency: one proceeding for each insolvent debtor, wherever its creditors and/or assets are located.[8] A

---

[5] Kammel (2008), p. 61.

[6] Mason (2008), p. 32.

[7] About these principles, see Moustaira (1992), pp. 61–64.

[8] Fletcher (2005), p. 11.

single court would administer a cross-border insolvency proceeding, applying the *lex fori concursus*,[9] that is, its own rules to govern the commencement, conduct, administration, and conclusion of the insolvency proceedings[10] and all decisions would be effective in all countries where assets of the debtor are located.[11]

The main advantages of universalism are increased predictability, reduced transaction costs and risks[12] as well as guaranteed equal protection of all creditors.

Territorialism goes together with plurality of insolvency proceedings: as many insolvency proceedings for each insolvent debtor, as the countries where its assets may be located. Each proceeding only includes and administers the assets and aspects located in its territory,[13] it applies its own insolvency law and, in its purest form, accepts the participation of only the local creditors, "with little or no regard for foreign proceedings regarding the same debtor".[14]

Territorialism emphasizes the importance of differences between national legal insolvency regimes, and points out that interference with domestic policies, such as the application of a formal universalist law would be, might be, considered as an insult to state sovereignty.[15]

The universalism versus territorialism debate seems to be a never ending one,[16] with an unusual intensity. Nevertheless, the situation is not the same as it used to be some decades ago.

Universalism promotes the goals of insolvency law, that is, efficiency and fairness as well as equal treatment of similarly situated creditors. To promote efficiency and fairness under the universalist model, countries should surrender sovereignty in international insolvency cases,[17] something very difficult.

Pure universalism would not be feasible, without an international convention, it is (rather rightly) pointed out.[18] It would be unworkable in the current world circumstances, it is also suggested.[19] An ideal universalism "may take decades, however, or even centuries", it is argued. "The issue is what to do while we are waiting for the "new world" society – essentially, a world government – to arrive …".[20]

Territorialism seems insufficient to address the special problems of international insolvencies. On the one hand "it could actually prove counter-productive for reor-

---

[9] Westbrook (1991a), p. 458.

[10] Westbrook (2007), pp. 1021–1022.

[11] Mevorach (2018a), p. 3.

[12] Guzman (2000), pp. 2179, 2181; Rasmussen (2000), p. 2255.

[13] Bufford (2005), p. 108.

[14] Mevorach (2018a), p. 4.

[15] LoPucki (2000), p. 2216; Tung (2001), p. 31.

[16] Rasmussen (2007), p. 983.

[17] Says Mevorach (2018a), p. 7. Her analysis is imbued with terms of law and economics: "It is the essence of universalism that it resolves the collective action problem that creates a 'prisoners' dilemma' and a race to collect, translating the insolvency principle of collectivity to the global level." *Id.* p. 8.

[18] Anderson (2000), p. 682.

[19] Kipnis (2008), p. 173.

[20] LoPucki (2000), p. 2217.

ganization or efficient liquidations of an entire international company if each jurisdiction involved handles a fraction of the case"[21] and on the other hand the plurality of procedures increases the costs and makes it difficult to achieve a package sale or a restructuring of the business as a whole.

2.4 Secondary Proceedings: Local Priorities?

"Why allow secondary proceedings?", it is often asked. The principal reasons put forth are: respect of local courts that have jurisdiction over locally situated assets, or/and fulfill the expectations of local creditors that their rights would be governed by domestic insolvency law.[22] Secondary proceedings are needed, it is argued, to impede an offence to the sovereignty of other states, by the court/state of the main proceeding.[23]

Universality has as one of its consequences, the application of *lex fori concursus* everywhere. Its rules about distribution of the assets of the insolvent debtor may not be considered by creditors in other countries from the one where the insolvency proceeding has been opened as favorable to their claims. They often invoke their belief that their claims, in case of their debtor's insolvency, would be satisfied according to the respective local laws.

Thus, the pressure for allowing parallel proceedings is often intense. As it is very clearly stated, "secondary proceedings owe their existence in large part to the persistence of the territorialism-fomenting priority differences between domestic bankruptcy systems."[24]

It is often difficult, if not impossible, for states to accept that the insolvency law of some other state (being that law the *lex fori concursus*) will set the priorities of the claims of the insolvent estate, wherever these claims are "situated". Many states (and their courts) find it difficult to change their old attitude towards international insolvencies ("like an adolescent struggling with clothes that no longer fit"[25]), they are unwilling to accept that local priorities will not be applied in distributing local assets.

Why would states insist on "localism"[26]—applying local priority rules to locally seized assets? And why would scholars speak in favor of localism and of localist models?

Although many answers may be given, probably this question will never really want to be answered.

---

[21] Mevorach (2014), p. 230.

[22] Pottow (2011), p. 581.

[23] Pottow (2006), p. 1915.

[24] Pottow (2005), pp. 1011–1012.

[25] Westbrook (2011), p. 602.

[26] Westbrook (2011), p. 602.

2.5 Modified Universalism

Modified (or mitigated or …) universalism seems to be the dominant approach almost everywhere, nowadays, for addressing international insolvency.[27] It soothes the "injuries" of territorialism and it avoids the hurdles of universalism.

It was the tendency that the works for a European Insolvency Convention had ultimately taken (Convention of 1995—never in force—finally a EC Regulation).[28] It was the way chosen by the UNCITRAL Model Law 1997 on Cross-Border Insolvency.[29] It was proposed by American scholars, almost 20 years ago, as the best interim solution in the way to the optimal solution, the "true universalism".[30]

Other proposals, other "modes of thinking" about cross-border insolvency, have been brought up, during the last years. One of them is the "universal proceduralism".[31] This universal proceduralism is based on choice-of-law principle that his proponent calls "virtual territoriality".[32]

According to this proposal, "the goal is to facilitate a bankruptcy case administered at the debtor's center of main interest that is procedurally global, but substantively territorial."[33] Universal proceduralism is less concerned with equality of distribution across borders and more concerned with the respect of local priorities.

The supporters of modified universalism disagree with those of universal proceduralism about the importance of respecting local priorities.[34] The first believe in a regime of "one case under one law", while the latter believe in a regime of "one case under many laws".[35]

In the modified universalism, the choice of law gives as applicable law the *lex fori concursus*, a rule with some exceptions.[36]

One can hardly understand why the supporters of universal proceduralism accuse modified universalism for "asymmetric comity". They argue that it is a one-way street and that, according to that approach, the courts in an ancillary jurisdiction must defer to the home court, even if the creditors would receive substantially different treatment there.[37] By contrast, they say, the court in the main jurisdiction will only apply its law and that it will do nothing to minimize the outcome differences.[38]

---

[27] Mevorach (2018b), p. 1403.

[28] See *infra*, Sect. 2.5.

[29] See *infra*, Sect. 5. See also Berends (1998), p. 309.

[30] Westbrook (2000), p. 2276.

[31] His proponent is Janger (2007), p. 819.

[32] Janger (2010), p. 408.

[33] Janger (2011), p. 442.

[34] Westbrook (2010), p. 517.

[35] Janger (2011), p. 442.

[36] Clark and Goldstein (2011), p. 515 and note 7.

[37] Westbrook (1998), pp. 28–31.

[38] Janger (2011), p. 447.

But this is a paradoxical argument. This is not about "do ut des". Respect of the main proceeding by applying comity does not mean that the ancillary jurisdiction courts give something to get something in return. It means that they contribute to an orderly bankruptcy administration and that in analogous cases they expect that the other countries' courts will do the same—although such an implicit expectation of reciprocity is not a formal requirement; it is only a hope.

Nor is it really clear why modified universalism creates "a choice of law vicious circle". It rather seems that the accusation has as its aim the traditional choice of law, which operates neutrally and according to which, the applicable law in certain issues would be a foreign one—and in the case of bankruptcies, not necessarily the *lex fori concursus*, which of course will be the generally applicable—with certain exceptions—law.

Of course, modified universalism works best if by chance the bankruptcy regimes of the interested countries are harmonized.[39] However, that is not easy to happen. But to say that "modified universalism itself creates an incentive for jurisdictional differentiation and the seeds of its own undoing"[40] is really an exaggeration. It would mean that bankruptcy regimes would change out of fear that they would have to cooperate according to the principle of modified universalism, in case of an international insolvency. The arguments brought to convince us for that, are not really convincing, they seem kind of sophistry.

On the other hand, there are other voices too that speak harshly about modified universalism. Thus, it is argued that by allowing ancillary courts to retain their right to apply their own law and protect their own local creditors, modified universalism is territorialist in its nature and that that is its downfall. The predictability that pure universalism guarantees, is sacrificed when modified universalism governs because the "regime or regimes that will ultimately distribute the debtor's assets may depend on the country in which the assets are located at the time of bankruptcy."[41]

Furthermore, it is pointed out that modified universalism does not resolve the problem of forum shopping, that is considered as one of the main evils of pure universalism.[42]

So, another approach has been proposed, that of "cooperative territorialism". Under this approach, each country may open and administer its own bankruptcy case, applying each its own law. None of these cases may be considered a main case or an ancillary case.

As stated, "[n]o nation need recognize foreign authority over domestic assets or sacrifice the interests of local debtors or creditors in particular cases. The elimination of that universalist tension provides the foundation for cooperation among courts and representatives that will be mutually beneficial in each case."[43]

---

[39] Westbrook (1991b), p. 517; Moss (2007), p. 1018.

[40] Janger (2011), p. 447.

[41] LoPucki (1999), p. 728.

[42] See infra, Sect. 2.7, about forum shopping in insolvency.

[43] LoPucki (1999), p. 750.

Although cooperative territorialism might have some advantages, as for example that it solves the "home" country problem and that it provides greater predictability to lenders",[44] it seems too optimistic an approach, given the fact that the regime that it promotes *does not require* cooperation.

2.6 Is Modified Universalism Becoming Customary International Law?

It has been supported that modified universalism, from a transitory approach could become customary international law.[45] Could it? Should it? It seems doubtful.

It is argued that "we are witnessing a gradual reunification of private and public international law in both theory and practice".[46] But, really, are we? It is also pointed out that this is not a question of merger of private international law and public international law but that it is about an "internationally oriented mission of private international law" which "should continue to evolve"[47] and learn from public international law,[48] seek guidance from foreign law through the notion of the law of nations (*ius gentium*).[49]

Still, one wonders whether this would be something new. In continental European countries, at least, private international law was never really nationally oriented, since the traditional choice of law rules were and are neutral and the application of a foreign law was and is almost always guaranteed, when the private international law rules point to that. The exception of public policy is only in specific circumstances activated. On the contrary, in common law countries (with many variations between them, of course), private international law or, as it is mostly called there, conflict of laws/choice of law very often points to lex fori, as the applicable law.[50]

The different approaches to choice of the applicable law obviously are determined by the different legal traditions. When the applicable law is rarely a foreign law, then it is obviously very difficult, if not impossible, to accept such a solution in the case of an international bankruptcy/insolvency, where the stakes are extremely high.

But even in European continental countries, before the Regulations' entry in force,[51] there were differences, regarding the application of a foreign law in the case of an insolvency that was not limited in one country.

---

[44] Clark and Goldstein (2011), p. 520.

[45] Mevorach (2018a), pp. 80 ff.

[46] *Id*, p. 105.

[47] *Id*, p. 105.

[48] Michaels (2008), pp. 137–138.

[49] Waldron (2006), pp. 135–138.

[50] About that, see Moustaira (1996).

[51] See *infra*, Sect. 4.4.

For example, France and Germany (and other countries) wanted their insolvency judgments to have universal effect but refused such effect to foreign insolvency judgments and, consequently, refused to recognize them and apply a foreign law, e.g. by rendering assets located in their territory to the foreign administrator, according to the rules of the foreign *lex fori concursus*. They were universalists and territorialists, regarding the domestic and the foreign insolvencies, respectively.

On the contrary, Greece was among the (rather few) countries which were willing to recognize a foreign insolvency and consequently apply the foreign *lex fori concursus*. Obviously, modified universalism is rather a drawback for these countries: their private international law did have an internationally oriented mission that gradually—and obligatorily, because of the governing European Regulations and the adoption of a law incorporating the UNCITRAL Model Law[52]—was restricted.

2.7 Bankruptcy Forum Shopping

"Is there such a thing as "good" forum shopping?",[53] it is asked. All kind of answers have been given, both positive and negative. Those that are hostile to it, argue that "in non-contractual setting, forum shopping is problematic because it leads to forum selling"[54] or that it carries dangers.[55] Those that are in favor of its use argue that it is beneficial; they speak about the "unappreciated virtues of global forum shopping".[56]

Nevertheless, arguments against forum shopping are getting stronger and stronger.

Especially when the forum shopping is abusive, that is when by being more favorable to one party, possibly has adverse effects on other parties, it may harm the insolvency proceedings in numerous ways, it is argued. Further, this would reduce the legal certainty of the proceedings, since the applicable law might be changed.[57]

The lack of legal certainty has given the opportunity to the debtors themselves or the directors of distressed companies to resort to abusive forum shopping, because of the differences between the various insolvency laws. By selecting jurisdiction and consequently the [most favorable to their own interests[58]] applicable law, it is very possible that certain creditors may be harmed by this choice, since the applicable law might not be favorable to them[59]—it might cause them unexpected monetary expenses and liabilities[60] or it might discriminate between domestic and

[52] See *infra*, Sect. 5.

[53] Block-Lieb (2018), p. 2.

[54] Klerman and Reilly (2016), p. 242.

[55] McCormack (2009), p. 181.

[56] Bookman (2017), p. 579.

[57] McCormack (2014), p. 815.

[58] Szydlo (2010), p. 253.

[59] Almaskari (2016), p. 12.

[60] Coburn (2012), p. 8.

foreign creditors, or it might not guarantee the equal protection of creditors, or the payoff might altered,[61] etc.

Forum shopping could also be considered abusive when debtors put the creditors at excessive procedural disadvantage or when directors of a debtor company select a jurisdiction that enables them to avoid personal liability or delay the proceedings.[62]

Two main forum shopping strategies are presented as the mostly used. The first one is when the debtor seeks to move its registered office (principal place of business or habitual residence, when the debtor is a natural person) and, sometimes, certain additional operations, to another country. The second strategy is when the corporate debtor moves its effective head office functions abroad, but keeps its registered office behind.[63]

In USA, bankruptcy forum shopping seems to have become a custom: "Beginning in 1990, the bankruptcy forum shopping produced an unexpected dynamic ... within six years, nearly 90 percent of all large public companies filing bankruptcy in the US filed in Delaware."[64].

When a court is prepared to accept an insolvency filing from a debtor who has only a limited connection with the forum jurisdiction and this court applies its own insolvency law to all issues connected with this insolvency, one may speak about a "denationalized" insolvency.[65]

2.8 Forum Non Conveniens: *Similar Legal Traditions*

The reasons invoked by courts to justify the cooperation between those and foreign courts, in insolvency matters, sometimes are close to the ones used in cases of application of the *forum non conveniens* rule/doctrine.[66] Obviously, this may only happen when the considering courts belong to common law countries.

2.8.1 Case McGrath v. Riddell ("HIH")

An interesting case, in which such a reason was brought forth (although nobody mentioned literally the *forum non conveniens* rule) was the case *McGrath v. Riddell* (*"HIH"*), that reached the House of Lords.[67]

[61] Mucciarelli (2013).

[62] Almaskari (2016), p. 13.

[63] Ringe (2017), pp. 41–42.

[64] LoPucki (2005), p. 16.

[65] Westbrook (2015), p. 7.

[66] About *Forum Non Conveniens*, see Moustaira (1995).

[67] *McGrath v. Riddell* (*In re HIH Cas. & Gen. Ins. Ltd.*), [2008] UKHL 21, 1 W.L.R. 852 (H.L.).

The House of Lords had to decide on an appeal from the lower courts refusing to remit the assets of Australian insurance companies that were in United Kingdom, to the Australian insolvency procedure that had been opened.

The "problem" was that under United Kingdom law, insurance claimants/creditors in an insolvency share *pari passu* with other unsecured creditors against the insolvent estate, while in Australia insurance claims take priority over the claims of other unsecured creditors.

The facts were the following:

An insolvency procedure had been opened in Australia against companies belonging to an Australian insurance group of companies—HIH Casualty & General Insurance. Substantial assets of those companies were in the United Kingdom. Those assets were mainly reinsurance claims corresponding to reinsurance policies taken out in the London market.[68]

A request was sent to England asking for those assets to be remitted to the Australian liquidators for distribution. According to § 562A of the Corporations Act 2001, there is a priority in favor of insurance creditors.

In the first instance, the English court considered that the priority that Australian law was giving would result in a prejudice to English unsecured creditors. It rejected the Australian request, stating that it had no power to order a transfer if the *pari passu* rule of the principal jurisdiction were not substantially the same as that under English law.[69]

After differing judgments in previous instances, the House of Lords agreed to remit the assets to the Australian insolvency proceedings, in spite of the differences in distribution schemes.[70] Applying the universality principle of international insolvency, it considered that since the Australian courts had jurisdiction over the insolvency of the insurance companies, it was *appropriate* that the Australian ranking of claims was applied to all assets of the company, wherever they might be situated:

> There should be a unitary bankruptcy proceeding in the court of the bankrupt's domicile which receives world-wide recognition and it should apply universally to all the bankrupt's assets.[71]

The first judgment was delivered by the High Court on October 7, 2005. The final judgment was delivered by the House of Lords on April 9, 2008. During the period in which the English proceedings progressed from the High Court, via the Court of Appeal, to the House of Lords, the U.K. law concerning the treatment of creditors' claims against insolvent insurers had been amended in accordance with E.U. Directive 2001/17/EC.

Thus, by the time of the final judgment of the House of Lords, U.K. law was closely similar to the respective Australian law which was initially considered as

---

[68] Garrido (2011), p. 461.

[69] *McMahon v. McGrath (In re HIH Cas. & Gen. Ins. Ltd.)*, [2005] EWHC (Ch) 2125.

[70] Garrido (2011), p. 462.

[71] *McGrath v. Riddell* (*In re HIH Cas. & Gen. Ins. Ltd.*), [2008] UKHL 21, 1 W.L.R. 852 (H.L.).

unacceptable to English public policy for the assets to be remitted for distribution under those, Australian, rules.

It must be noted, though, that the judgments of the English courts in the case were delivered on the basis of the law as it was at the time the proceedings were commenced.[72]

2.8.2 *In re National Bank of Anguilla (Private Banking Trust) Ltd*

Recently, on January 29, 2018, the U.S. Bankruptcy Court for the Southern District of New York stayed litigation commenced in a chapter 11 case, on grounds of *forum non conveniens* and comity. It was the case *National Bank of Anguilla (Private Banking Trust) Ltd.*[73]

National Bank of Anguilla (Private Banking Trust) Ltd. and Caribbean Commercial Investment Bank Ltd. ('the debtors') were Anguillan offshore banks.

Having severe problems, following the 2008 financial crisis, the debtors' parent banks were placed into conservatorship in 2013 by the regulator of Anguilla's banking system. The parent banks' boards were replaced by conservator directors pending the preparation of rescue plans.

The conservator directors, having concluded that certain funds had been commingled between the debtors and their parent banks, directed the debtors to transfer about $23 million to U.S. accounts maintained by the parent banks and caused the parent banks to transfer more than $210 million to the Anguillan bank regulator.

The regulator placed the parent banks into receivership in 2016 and transferred their banking operations and deposits to a newly formed bank owned by the government of Anguilla.

In February 2016, the Anguilla High Court placed by order the operations of the debtors under administration.

In May 2016, the debtors sued the parent banks and the successor bank in the Anguilla Court, alleging that the conservator directors and the bank regulator had breached their fiduciary duties by directing the transfers to the parent banks. The Anguilla Court dismissed the action on the ground (among others) that the receivership stayed litigation against the parent banks.

On May 26, 2016 and October 11, 2016, the Administrator filed separate petitions in the U.S. Bankruptcy Court on behalf of the debtors (PBT and CCIB), seeking recognition of the Anguillan Administrations under Chapter 15 of the U.S. Bankruptcy Court.[74] By orders dated June 17, 2016 and November 15, 2016,

---

[72] Fletcher (2011), p. 491 note 6.

[73] *In re National Bank of Anguilla (Private Banking Trust) Ltd*, 580 B.R. 64 (Bankr. S.D.N.Y. 2018).

[74] See *infra*, Sect. 5.2.1.1.

the U.S. Bankruptcy Court granted the petitions as to PBT and CCIB, respectively, recognizing the Anguilla Administrations as foreign main proceedings and the Administrator as the Debtor Banks' foreign representative.

Subsequently, PBT and CCIB filed chapter 11 petitions on June 22, 2016 and October 11, 2016, respectively, having as purpose to file federal avoidance actions against the Defendants. On December 16, 2016 and May 1, 2017, PBT and CCIB filed these Adversary Proceedings. The two Complaints were almost identical and were seeking identical relief. They asserted claims to

(a) avoid and recover intentional or constructive fraudulent transfers under applicable provisions of the Bankruptcy Code, New York law and Anguillan law;
(b) recover the avoidable transfers from NCBA and ECCB as subsequent transferees;
(c) disallow claims of the Parent Banks, NCBA, and ECCB under section 502(d) of the Bankruptcy Code; and
(d) impose liability against ECCB for breach of fiduciary duty, gross negligence, and aiding and abetting breach of fiduciary duty.

All defendants sought dismissal under *forum non conveniens*. Some defendants, independently, sought dismissal on other grounds too, such as: foreign sovereign immunities act, lack of personal jurisdiction, international comity, non-extraterritoriality of the provisions of Bankruptcy Code, etc.

All defendants asserted that the adversary proceedings should be dismissed on grounds of *forum non conveniens*. The main reasons that they invoked were that the parties were Anguillan entities and Anguilla was the most convenient forum for the Plaintiffs' claims. They argued that the debtor banks were merely *forum shopping* by filing their claims in the U.S. Bankruptcy Court to avoid constructive fraudulent transfers under the Bankruptcy Code, a claim not recognized under Anguillan law.

In response, the plaintiffs argued, *inter alia*, that the adversary proceedings should not be dismissed, since many of the transfers at issue had occurred in New York and the Anguillan High Court had authorized the plaintiffs to commence actions in foreign jurisdictions and had stayed the Judicial Review Application that had been filed in it, pending the outcome of the U.S. adversary proceedings.

The court, discussing the *forum non conveniens* motion, referred to the three-step process that courts in the Second Circuit apply to determine whether to dismiss an action on this ground or not, quoting phrases from Second Circuit's cases:

(1) The court must determine the degree of deference properly accorded to the plaintiff's choice of forum;
(2) after determining whether the plaintiff's choice is entitled to more or less deference, the court must determine whether an adequate alternative forum exists;
(3) the court must then balance a series of factors involving the private interests of the parties in maintaining the litigation in the competing fora and any public interests at stake.

In determining the degree of deference accorded to a foreign plaintiff's choice of a United States forum, courts consider various factors to ascertain whether the plaintiff's forum choice was motivated by convenience or instead by the desire to forum shop.

(1) In this case, the U.S. court found that the plaintiff's choice of forum was not motivated by convenience. The debtor banks were incorporated in Anguilla, were not operating in the United States (they only had accepted U.S. dollar deposits that were deposited in the parent banks' New York bank account) and their administrator were residing in England. The Conservator Directors were residing in Anguilla, the Eastern Caribbean or London, all of the evidence and witnesses for these cases were located in the Eastern Caribbean or elsewhere, but not in the United States, and, finally, the defendants were amenable to suit in Anguilla.

Considering all the above, it seemed that the choice of a New York venue was not at all accidental; on the contrary it was an exercise in forum shopping.

(2) Regarding the existence of an adequate alternative forum, the U.S. court found that Anguilla was such a forum for the litigation of the subject matter of the dispute, for the following reasons:

First, the parties did not contest, and the U.S. Court had previously found, that the Anguillan courts are competent to adjudicate disputes.

Second, although Anguillan law does not recognize a claim to avoid and recover a constructive fraudulent transfer, this did not render the Anguillan forum inadequate.

Third, other causes of action that had been asserted by the plaintiffs in the Anguillan initial proceedings, also provide the same remedy that the plaintiffs were seeking in this (the US) Court—the recovery of the up-streamed funds and transferred property.

(3) Balancing the private and public interest factors,[75] the U.S. Court said the following:

(a) Regarding the private interest factors:

The majority of the relevant evidence was located or accessible in Anguilla but not in New York. None of the witnesses, in particular the Conservator Directors, were located in the United States or within the U.S. Court's subpoena power.

The records of the debtor banks and the parent banks were presumably located in Anguilla, but were certainly not located in USA.

The testimony of the Conservator Directors and of ECCB was considered crucial to the adversary proceedings before the U.S. Court but it would be difficult, if not impossible to procure their attendance in this Court.

(b) Regarding the public interest factors:

[75] About the private and public interest factors, see Moustaira (1995), pp. 40–49.

Among them is the fact that there is a parallel litigation arising out of the same or similar facts already pending in the foreign jurisdiction,[76] said the U.S. Bankruptcy Court, citing a previous judgment of the same court.[77]

In this case, parallel litigations were already pending in Anguilla, although the Anguilla initial proceeding had been stayed against the parent banks.

The legality of the actions taken by the Conservator Directors, including the up-streaming of customer deposits and the transfer of other property owned by the debtor banks to the parent banks, and ultimately, to NCBA and possibly ECCB, should be determined in accordance with the ECCB Act and applicable Anguillan law.

The need to apply foreign law alone is not sufficient to warrant dismissal, however it may be considered as part of the balancing equation.

There was also an issue of immunity from suit of the Conservators Directors and the defendants, according to an article of ECCB Act, that is, Anguillan law; an issue that had already been a focal point of litigation in the Anguillan proceedings, not resolved until the U.S. Court had to decide on the motion for dismissal on the ground of *forum non conveniens*. The U.S. Court stated that only the Anguillan courts were authorized to speak definitively on these issues, therefore deference to those proceedings were appropriate.

Also about the legality of the transfers connected to the Anguillan rescue plan, the U.S. Court said that Anguilla had an overwhelming and stronger interest in determining the legality of those actions and the extent of the defendants' liability.

The U.S. Court concluded that *forum non conveniens* supported staying (and not dismissing) the adversary proceedings before it, in favor of the courts in Anguilla.

It also discussed additional requests by certain defendants, for dismissal or stay of the cases, among which was international comity.[78]

It first quoted the words about comity that had been used in the leading case *Hilton v. Guyot*:

> Comity, in the legal sense, is neither a matter of absolute obligation, on the one hand, nor a mere courtesy and good will, upon the other. But it is the recognition which one nation allows within its territory to the legislative, executive or judicial acts of another nation, having due regard both to international duty and convenience, and to the rights of its own citizens or of other persons who are under the protection of its laws.[79]

It pointed out that the adjudicative comity or comity among courts is "a discretionary act of deference by a national court to decline to exercise jurisdiction in a case properly adjudicated in a foreign state"[80]

---

[76] In civil law countries, foreign litispendence, if recognized, leads to a stay of the local proceedings.

[77] *Argus Media Ltd. v. Tradition Fin. Servs. Inc.*, No. 09 Civ. 7966 (HB), 2009 WL 5125113 (S.D.N.Y. Dec. 29, 2009).

[78] On comity/comitas gentium, see Moustaira (1992), pp. 215–220.

[79] *Hilton v. Guyot*, 159 U.S. 113, 163-64 (1895).

[80] *Official Comm. of Unsecured Creditors v. Bahrain Islamic Bank (In re Arcapita Bank B.S.C.(C))*, 575 B.R. 229, 238 (Bankr. S.D.N.Y. 2017).

The Court concluded that comity among courts also supported a stay of the proceedings before it, in deference to the main insolvency proceedings in Anguilla. As it had been said in another case, "[f]ederal courts generally extend comity whenever the foreign court had proper jurisdiction and enforcement does not prejudice the rights of the United States citizens or violate domestic public policy" and "deference to the foreign court is appropriate so long as the foreign proceedings are procedurally fair and ... do not contravene the laws or public policy of the United States."[81]

The Court also mentioned that, to be certain about the procedural fairness of the foreign proceedings, the U.S. courts usually look to the following nonexclusive factors:

(1) whether creditors of the same class are treated equally in the distribution of the assets;
(2) whether the liquidators are considered fiduciaries and are held accountable to the court;
(3) whether creditors have the right to submit claims which, if denied, can be submitted to a bankruptcy court for adjudication;
(4) whether the liquidators are required to give notice to the debtors potential claimants;
(5) whether there are provisions for creditors meetings;
(6) whether a foreign country's insolvency laws favor its own citizens;
(7) whether all assets are marshaled before one body for centralized distribution; and
(8) whether there are provisions for an automatic stay and for the lifting of such stays to facilitate the centralization of claims.[82]

References

Almaskari BJ (2016) Towards legal certainty: European cross-border insolvency law and multinational corporate groups. Thesis submitted for the degree of Doctor of Philosophy at the University of Leicester School of Law. Available at: https://lra.le.ac.uk/bitstream/2381/39163/1/2016AlmaskariBJPhD.pdf

Altman J (2011) A test case in international bankruptcy protocols: the Lehman brothers insolvency. San Diego Int Law J 12:463–495

Anderson K (2000) The cross-border insolvency paradigm: a defence of the modified universal approach considering the Japanese experience. Univ Pa J Int Econ Law 21:679–779

Berends AJ (1998) UNCITRAL model law on cross-border insolvency: a comprehensive overview. Tulane J Int Comp Law 6:309–400

Block-Lieb S (2018) Reaching to restructure across borders (without over-reaching), even after brexit. Am Bankruptcy Law J 92:1–52

[81] *CT Inv. Mgmt. Co., LLC. V. Cozumel Caribe, S.A. de C.V. (In re Cozumel Caribe, S.A. de C.V.)*, 482 B.R. 96, 114 (Bankr. S.D.N.Y. 2012).

[82] *Finanz AG Zurich v. Banco Economico S.A.*, 192 F.3d 240, 249 (2d Cir. 1999).

Bookman PK (2017) The unsung virtues of global forum shopping. Notre Dame Law Rev 92:579–635
Bufford SL (2005) Global venue controls are coming: a reply to Professor LoPucki. Am Bankruptcy Law J 79:105–141
Clark LM/Goldstein K (2011) Sacred cows: how to care for secured creditors' rights in cross-border bankruptcies. Tex Int Law J 46: pp. 513-558
Coburn A (2012) The growth of bankruptcy tourism in the United Kingdom. Insolv Intell 25:8–11
Fletcher IF (2005) Insolvency in private international law. Oxford University Press
Fletcher I (2011) *"L'enfer, c'est les autres"*: evolving approaches to the treatment of security rights in cross-border insolvency. Tex Int Law J 46:489–512
Frade C (2012) Bankruptcy, stigma and rehabilitation. ERA Forum 13:45–57
Garrido JM (2011) No two snowflakes the same: the distributional question in international bankruptcies. Tex Int Law J 46:459–488
Guzman A (2000) International bankruptcy: in defense of universalism. Mich Law Rev 98:2177–2215
Janger EJ (2007) Universal proceduralism. Brooklyn J Int Law 32:819–849
Janger EJ (2010) Virtual territoriality. Columbia J Transnatl Law 48:401–441
Janger EJ (2011) Reciprocal comity. Tex Int Law J 46:441–458
Kammel AJ (2008) The law and economics of corporate insolvency – some thoughts. In: Omar P (ed) International insolvency law. Themes and perspectives. Routledge, London and New York, pp 61–79
Kipnis AM (2008) Beyond UNCITRAL: alternatives to universality in transnational insolvency. Denver J Int Law Policy 36:155–189
Klerman D/Reilly G (2016) Forum selling. South Calif Law Rev 89: pp 241-314
LoPucki LM (1999) Cooperation in international bankruptcy: a post-universalist approach. Cornell Law Rev 84:696–762
LoPucki LM (2000) The case for cooperative territoriality in international bankruptcy. Mich Law Rev 98:2216–2251
LoPucki L (2005) Courting failure: how competition for big cases is corrupting the bankruptcy courts. University of Michigan Press, Ann Arbor, MI
Mason R (2008) Cross-border insolvency law: where private international law and insolvency law meet. In: Omar P (ed) International insolvency law. Themes and perspectives. Routledge, London and New York, pp 27–60
McCormack G (2009) Jurisdiction competition and forum shopping in insolvency proceedings. Camb Law J 68:169–197
McCormack G (2014) Bankruptcy forum shopping: the UK and US as venues of choice for foreign companies. Int Comp Law Q 63:815–842
Mevorach I (2014) Cross-border insolvency of enterprise groups: the choice of law challenge. Brooklyn J Corp Financ Commer Law 9:226–249
Mevorach I (2018a) The future of cross-border insolvency. Overcoming biases and closing gaps. Oxford University Press
Mevorach I (2018b) Modified universalism as customary international law. Tex Law Rev 96:1403–1436
Michaels R (2008) Private and public international law: German view on global issues. J Priv Int Law 4:121–138
Moss G (2007) Group insolvency – choice of forum and law: the European experience under the influence of English pragmatism. Brooklyn J Int Law 32:1005–1018
Moustaira EN (1992) The equality of creditors in international bankruptcy law [in Greek]. Ant.N. Sakkoulas Publishers, Athens/Komotini
Moustaira EN (1995) Forum Non Conveniens. Equity in the frame of legality [in Greek]. Ant.N. Sakkoulas Publishers, Athens/Komotini
Moustaira EN (1996) The evolution of private international law in the USA. Tradition – Revolution – Counter-Revolution [in Greek]. Athens

Mucciarelli F (2013) The unavoidable persistence of forum shopping in European insolvency law. CEFIN. Working Paper No 36. Available at: http://www.cefin.unimore.it/?q=webfm_send/186

Paulus CG (2016) Gutwetter-Insolvenzrecht vs. Schlectwetter-Insolvenzrecht: Über die ökonomischen Grundbedingungen des Insolvenzrechts. Zeitschrift für Wirtschaftsrecht:1657–1663

Pérez Ragone, Á.J./Martínez Benavides, P. (2015) Del sobreendeudamiento a la insolvencia: Fase de crisis del deudor desde el derecho comparado europeo. Revista Chilena de Derecho 42: pp. 93-121

Pottow JAE (2005) Procedural incrementalism: a model for international bankrutpcy. Va J Int Law 45:935–1015

Pottow JAE (2006) Greed and pride in international bankruptcy: the problems of and proposed solutions to "local interests". Mich Law Rev 104:1899–1949

Pottow JAE (2011) A new role for secondary proceedings in international bankruptcies. Tex Int Law J 46:579–599

Rasmussen R (2000) Resolving transnational insolvencies through private ordering. Mich Law Rev 98:2252–2275

Rasmussen R (2007) Where are all the transnational bankruptcies?: The puzzling case for universalism. Brooklyn J Int Law 32:983–1003

Ringe W-G (2017) Insolvency forum shopping, revisited. Hamburg Law Rev:38–58

Szydlo M (2010) Prevention of forum shopping in European insolvency law. Eur Bus Organ Law Rev 11:253–272

Tung F (2001) Is international bankruptcy possible? Mich J Int Law 23:31–102

Waldron J (2006) Foreign law and the modern *Ius Gentium*. Harv Law Rev 119:129–147

Westbrook JL (1991a) Theory and pragmatism in global insolvencies: choice of law and choice of forum. Am Bankruptcy Law J 65:457–490

Westbrook JL (1991b) Choice of avoidance law in global insolvencies. Brooklyn J Int Law 17:499–538

Westbrook JL (1998) Universal priorities. Tex Int Law J 33:27–45

Westbrook JL (2000) A global solution to multinational default. Mich Law Rev 98:2276–2326

Westbrook JL (2007) Locating the eye of the financial storm. Brooklyn J Int Law 32:1019–1040

Westbrook JL (2010) A comment on universal proceduralism. Columbia J Transnatl Law 48:503–518

Westbrook JL (2011) Breaking away: local priorities and global assets. Tex Int Law J 46:601–622

Westbrook JL (2015) The present and future of multinational insolvency. In: Parry R, Omar PJ (eds) International insolvency law: future perspectives. INSOL Europe, Nottingham/Paris, pp 1–16

References

Chapter 3
Influences: Legal Transplants

3.1 General Comments

National laws are shaped by many influences. History and culture are among the strongest influences.[1] National insolvency laws, including private international law rules on insolvency, follow the same path. Only here, the influence of economic theories (and of law and economics, during the last decades) is even stronger. Still, economic analysis of law may be considered as part of the culture, in the broad sense, where culture is the way of living of each society. Even jurists who deny the direct relation of law with culture cannot avoid searching for reasons that lead countries to different decisions about their laws, to different laws.

Many insolvency laws around the world have copied or transplanted or received foreign ideas or rules. This is something that first happened during the nineteenth century, when civil and commercial codes were created in Europe and, after that, countries in other parts of the world, usually former colonies of European countries, tried to form their own legal systems, unavoidably influenced by their former colonizers. It also happened through the judicial system of the English colonies, which applied common law and equity, in order, either to fill the gaps of the local laws or, explicitly, to form legal systems like the English.[2]

Examples of the above are many. Jurists of Latin America studied European Commercial Codes, before composing respective Codes for their countries. The *Código de Comercio* of Chile, of 1865, included rules on bankruptcy, which rules were obviously influenced by the French *Code de Commerce* of 1830 (with its amendments of 1838).[3]

[1] Martin (2005), p. 1.

[2] Indirect rule; see about that, Moustaira (2013), pp. 81–85.

[3] See Baeza Ovalle (2011), p. 37 and note 3, who points out that in the *Mensaje* that introduced the *Código de Comercio*, Gabriel Ocampo, its redactor, was expressing his confidence in the good functioning of the French law of June 8, 1838, that had already been applied for almost 30 years,

E. Moustaira, *International Insolvency Law*,
https://doi.org/10.1007/978-3-030-04450-3_3

Western jurists who have been imbued by the law and economics theory and try to explain everything on the basis of economic terms (that anyway could also be considered as laws' histories' terms, as it was above mentioned), such as efficiency/inefficiency or path dependency, often express the—anyway right—opinion that transplanted law does not always work as efficiently in the recipient country as it does in the country from which it was transplanted, because of the different legal traditions, cultural backgrounds and socioeconomic conditions that reign in the two countries. This is also something that the opponents of the legal transplants theory are saying, without however using economic terms such as efficiency.

Thus, the supporters of the economic analysis of law and of the comparative law and economics seek to persuade us that the success of a transplant depends on the "fit" between the imported rule and the host environment.[4] They insist that the transplant will achieve greater efficiency when it fits well the micro setting, that is the preexisting legal infrastructure in the host country, and the macro setting, that is the preexisting institutions of the political economy there.[5] On the contrary, a low level of either micro fit or macro fit will lead to inefficiency.[6]

Copying foreign insolvency rules is still an option—no rarely because countries are forced to do that (for example, to get loans[7] or to become members of countries' associations) or because they want to attract investments (and the investors want assurance that the law will be familiar to them).[8] Sometimes such a move, such a decision is baptized "a pragmatic move forward". It "happens" that this forward is meant to be a legal transplant from a common law country.

USA and UK have influenced many contemporary insolvency laws—probably USA more than UK. The "problem" is, as it is mentioned, that this country has a very different cultural attitude towards debt forgiveness. Still, this fact has not prevented many countries from "importing" its bankruptcy legal system, especially

---

hoping that the implementation of the Chilean *Código de Comercio* would manage to reduce "the number of bankruptcies, making difficult the success of the fraudulent plots that, approaching the fatal moment, suggests the perspective of misery, or of the punishable wish to become rich with other people's fortune." (*the translation is mine*).

[4] See also Smaliukas (2015), p. 379, who states that "Lithuanian insolvency law, company law and largo sensu its civil law was drafted using extensively the so called legal transplants: i.e. adopting the best regulatory examples (selected using comparative law methodology) from jurisdictions with more developed and sophisticated legal systems."

[5] Kanda and Milhaupt (2003), p. 891.

[6] Guseva (2014), p. 546.

[7] To give a loan to a country, International Institutions or big funds ask the country to change their insolvency law (or create one, in case they had not) so that it resembles to a model that they probably have made, which model is very much common law-oriented.

[8] Rwanda is one out of many examples of countries which reformed their legal systems, adopting many common law characteristics. Its move from the continental civil law (which was imposed to the county, while it was a colony of France) to a hybrid legal system, that is, with many elements of common law, "was not only necessitated by the country's membership of the East African Community (EAC) or the Commonwealth but also by the country's desire to increase local investment and improve the standard of living of the people." Rwanda joined the East African Community on July 1, 2007 and the Commonwealth in November 2009, see Leno (2015), p. 123 and note 6.

U.S. Bankruptcy Code's Chapter 11 which allows the reorganization of failing enterprises during which organization the existing management stays in place and manages the company.

But importing, copying a foreign regulation is often a failure, especially when it seems "strangely out of place",[9] since the institution of insolvency is influenced by the concrete social system of each country and countries often view debt differently, in philosophical terms too.[10] Sometimes, even sharing a common legal tradition does not have as a consequence similar rules.[11]

USA is also the leader in influencing other countries' laws, especially as regards the corporate reorganization. As it is stated, the "U.S. leads the world in its experience with reorganization of corporations through bankruptcy law."[12] U.S. jurists head the International Monetary Fund, the World Bank and other international organizations that, among other things, push countries for insolvency law reforms. Having had the U.S. insolvency law experience, these jurists have contributed "to make the global model for reform more or less resemble ... a one-size-fits-all solution".[13]

3.2 Iberoamérica

3.2.1 Argentina

Argentina is one of the few Latin American countries that regulate in detail the subject of international insolvency. Sources of law are, on the one hand the national one, La Ley de Concursos y Quiebras No 24.522, de 1995, and on the other hand, international Conventions, more specifically the Montevideo treaties, of 1889 and of 1940.[14]

The Montevideo Treaties constitute a "grandiose codification work", according to most jurists. Specifically, on international insolvency, they include "avant-garde" rules, at least for the time they were concluded.

The first Montevideo Treaty of International Commercial Law (*Tratado de Derecho Comercial Internacional*), of 1889, had been signed by Argentina, Bolivia, Brazil, Chile, Paraguay, Perú and Uruguay and ratified by Argentina, Paraguay,

---

[9] Martin (2005), pp. 2–3.

[10] See Ciuro Caldani (1994), p. 31, who points out that the bankruptcy, in its (various) systems of preferences or equivalences for the satisfaction of creditors, shows the values that the capitalism in crisis wants to save.

[11] See Martin (2003), pp. 403–410, who states that even in countries that share a common legal tradition, such as USA, England, Canada, and Australia, there are marked differences in governing business and personal bankruptcies.

[12] Halliday and Carruthers (2007), p. 1187.

[13] Gao and Wang (2017), p. 140.

[14] On the Montevideo Treaties, see Moustaira (1992), pp. 292–295.

Perú, Uruguay and Bolivia. Colombia too adhered, in 1933. In this Treaty, the Title X "De las falencias" (arts. 35–48) is included.

The second Montevideo Treaty of International Commercial Terrestre Law (*Tratado de Derecho Comercial Terrestre Internacional*), of 1940, had been signed by Uruguay, Brazil, Colombia, Bolivia, Argentina, Perú and Paraguay and ratified by Argentina, Uruguay and Paraguay. In this Treaty, the Title VIII "De las quiebras" (arts. 40–53) is included.[15]

Legal scholars, in Argentina, have repeatedly recommended that the country adopts the UNCITRAL Model Law of 1997.[16] On the initiative of the "Comisión Redactora para el Examen y Preparación de Enmiendas a la Legislación de Insolvencia Internacional" that had been created by the Ministry of Justice and of Human Rights in 2002, a draft law was presented before the Argentinian Parliament, largely based on the UNCITRAL Model Law. However, it seems that the initiative had no result whatever.[17]

Nevertheless, Argentinian jurists still support the idea of bringing back that draft law and enact it.

The general characteristics of that draft law of 2002, according to its *Exposición de Motivos*, are[18]:

1. It is conscientious of the tendency of many countries' legislation to be open and willing to coordinate between each other and of the fact that the excessive territorialism disappears in favor of an effective reciprocity and common rules the adoption of which benefits the transparency and the basic identity of the international insolvency solutions.
2. The adoption of a text elaborated in a neutral and high international level forum secures the place of Argentina among the countries that offer the best actual solutions.
3. An effective insolvency law can play a critical role in numerous areas, augmenting the enterprises' competitiveness, making easier the access to credit and the development of the capital market.
4. The adoption of a harmonious, modern and foreseeable regime will diminish the risk rate of the country and will fortify the possibilities of the Argentine enterprises in distress, when they take refuge to the insolvency regime seeking to achieve a reorganization and the maintenance of employments.
5. The fraudulent operations of insolvent debtors, having as aim to hide or transfer assets to foreign jurisdictions, constitute a frequent problematic fact and it gets easier to concretize because of the actual interrelation of the transactions world. The mechanisms that are proposed in the Draft Law have as aim to fight this international fraud.

[15] Scotti (2006), p. 136.

[16] See *infra*, Sect. 5.

[17] Scotti (2007), p. 156.

[18] Miguens (2018), pp. 75–77.

6. Between the two dominant theoretical models in this matter—territoriality and universality—the bridge is a qualified universality: the international cooperation oriented towards the coordination of the proceedings. The result presupposes a central forum localized in one country and complemented by proceedings localized in other country or countries.
7. This implies a realist solution of the conflicts that universality and territoriality have as a consequence and combines both principles maximizing their advantages and minimizing their disadvantages. The draft is based on the Model Law of UNCITRAL and permits to direct the local insolvency according to the *lex fori concursus*, in coexistence with different proceedings in an international insolvency.
8. In order for a foreign proceeding to enter the ambit of application of the Draft Law, it must have certain qualities: to have been opened in accordance with the local insolvency law of the country of origin, to provide a collective representation of the creditors and the debtor, to have the control or the supervision of the assets or business/transactions of the debtor, a tribunal or other official organ, and to have as aim the reorganization or liquidation of the debtor's business. In any case the general principle is that the tribunal must aim at the cooperation and the coordination [of the proceedings].
9. In the works of the Comisión Redactora, it has been pointed out that each defect of communication and coordination between the tribunals and the administrators of the interested jurisdictions favors la dispersion or the fraudulent hiding of the assets or [favors] the liquidation, preventing thus the previous exploration of other solutions that might be more advantageous. Consequently, not only the probabilities that the creditors get paid but also that enterprises economically or financially viable are bought, saving thus employments.
10. As it was pointed out in the Working Group of UNCITRAL, every provision/rule of the local/national law that permits to coordinate the administration of international insolvencies opens ways to the adoption of reasonable solutions that can interest both the creditors and the debtor, for which reason this type of mechanisms in the local law of a country is perceived as an advantageous factor for every inversion/investment or commercial operation in this country.
11. The *Draft Law* follows closely the Model Law of UNCITRAL in the parts the Model Law does not leave expressly at the discretion of the States that adopt it. This explains its writing technique that, as it is habitual in international instruments, among other things incudes the definition of the used terms.
12. The *Draft Law* preferred to not change the language of the official Spanish version of the United Nations because changes of this type can create perplexities and because one can attribute to these changes juridical intentions that the legislator did not have.
13. The sanction of this Draft Law constitutes an important step in the modernization process of the Argentinian bankruptcy legislation.
14. It has been taken care to subject the application of the uniform law to reciprocity conditions so that the interests at stake be suitably protected in a realm of international equilibrium. Likewise, rules have been drafted for the cases in which there is no such reciprocity.

In the actual Ley de Concursos y Quiebras No 24.522, de 1995, there are certain rules that have been the cause of controversies among the legal scholars.

For example, Article 2.2 states that debtors domiciled abroad may be declared bankrupt in Argentina as regards their property that exists in the country.

The reasons that have been brought in defense of this provision are: protection of the local creditors' interests, principle of State sovereignty, or the possibility of liquidation of those assets in favor of the credits that are payable in the country.[19]

There are various private international law problems, though. It is argued that it is not necessary that the property situated in Argentina, constitutes an establishment nor that it constitutes an important part of the total property.

On the other hand, it is pointed out that while immovable property can be easily traced, it is more difficult to say whether movable property "exists" in the country. For example: merchandise that is in the country to be transported or sold, where does it "exist"? If the characterization of the rules that attribute international jurisdiction is done according to the *lex fori*, as the Cámara Nacional de Apelaciones en lo Comercial has stated on December 9, 1992, in the case "*Transportadora Coral S.A. s/concurso preventivo*", which law will say where that merchandise exists: the law of the domicile of the proprietor (as says the Argentinian private international law rule for the movables) or the *lex fori*? The answer is: the *lex fori*.

Another issue that has been discussed is what would happen in the cases that while there would be property in Argentina, of a debtor domiciled and declared insolvent abroad, there would not be any local creditors, that means creditors whose claims are payable in Argentina. It seems that the answer is that in this case, the debtor could not be declared bankrupt in Argentina, because the rule of international jurisdiction should be interpreted as demanding the simultaneous existence of property and creditors in the country.

3.2.2 Venezuela

The national legislation of the country does not contain anything referring specifically to the international insolvency. Because of that, one can only have recourse to the general rules of insolvency, in the Commercial Code of 1919.

Furthermore, the above general rules do not say anything about reorganizing/restructuring a business entity; they only have measures leading to the traditional bankruptcy/liquidation.

Given the absence of specific rules about international insolvency, in case a foreign decision, opening an insolvency proceeding, seeks to be recognized in Venezuela, the only remedy is to apply the general rules about the *exequatur* of foreign decisions.

These rules may be found in the Law of 6.8.1998—the Venezuelan Private International Law. One of the conditions for the recognition and enforcement of a

[19] Scotti (2007), p. 165.

foreign decision is that it does not touch real rights on immovable property situated in the country. Obviously, it is a consecration of the principle of *lex rei sitae*: the applicable law to the property is the law of the country in which the property is situated.[20]

As far as rules on international insolvency, of international/conventional origin, are concerned, the only such instrument that exists in Venezuela, is the Código Bustamante (Código de Sánchez de Bustamante y Sirvén) de 1928.[21]

3.2.3 Brazil

The transnational aspects of bankruptcy law were, for the first time in Brazil, provided in the *Decreto* 6.982/27.6.1878. The rules of that decree were only applicable where there was not a bilateral or multilateral treaty on the enforcement of foreign civil or commercial judgments (Art. 22), that is, the Decree's application was subsidiary to a treaty.[22]

The currently in force Brazilian Federal Bankruptcy and Reorganization Law 11.101/2005 was enacted in February 2005 and was influenced by the United States Bankruptcy Code but also by the French insolvency law's principles.

The prior bankruptcy regime was favoring liquidation, while the new insolvency system is designed to rescue distressed but viable enterprises.[23] Under the prior bankruptcy law, secured creditors' claims had limited safeguards and they were ranked lower than labor claims and tax claims.[24]

Under the prior regime, the only possibility for distressed companies to reorganize was under the procedures of *concordata*, which prescribed fixed repayment plans to unsecured creditors and in which tax and labor creditors could not be included in the restructuring plan.[25] These proceedings were often accused of leading potentially viable companies to have high default rates and, as a result, to end up in liquidation.[26] The new law introduced an extra-judicial procedure, with many similarities to U.S. pre-packs, and a judicial reorganization, *recuperação judicial*, proceeding with many similarities to Chapter 11 of the U.S. Bankruptcy Code.[27]

---

[20] Vásquez and Darío Acevedo-Prada (2014), p. 110.

[21] See *infra*, Sect. 3.2.4.

[22] de Assumpção Alves and da Fonseca Rocha (2016), p. 46.

[23] Colombo et al. (2017).

[24] Labor claims were of first priority and tax claims, of second priority.

[25] Locatelli (2016), p. 31.

[26] Anapolsky and Woods (2013), pp. 399–400.

[27] According to Telles (2010), p. 466, the French insolvency law's influence is evident in the fact that, although the Brazilian insolvency law favors the reorganization of a viable enterprise, it does not provides for the U.S. insolvency law's possibility of *cram down*, according to which a court can approve a rescue plan, if it is reasonable and viable, without any payment to the creditors.

However, neither the prior regime contained nor the law of 2005 contains any provision on international insolvencies. It does not contain any rule that would refer to the effects in Brazil of an insolvency proceeding opened in some other country. It does not say anything about the rights of the foreign creditors nor foresees any specific category or rank for the foreign claims. However, it does not distinguish local or foreign creditors and the law's text speaks about "any creditor" (*cualquier acreedor*) or "all the creditors" (*todos los acreedores*).[28] It does not establish any condition for the recognition of a foreign insolvency proceeding nor asks for reciprocity. Also, it does not have any rule that would permit the possibility of parallel insolvency proceedings in more countries,[29] nor has any rules about cooperation or coordination of insolvency proceedings.[30]

The result is that international insolvency issues are decided in Brazil on a case by case basis,[31] mostly following the principle of territoriality.[32] This general adherence of Brazil to the territoriality principle together with its lack of cross-border provisions is considered by some commentators as a significant gap in its current restructuring regime,[33] bringing uncertainty and unpredictability to the cross-border cases that involve Brazil.[34]

A narrow exception to the country's adherence to the principle of territoriality in cross-border insolvency cases, are insolvency proceedings in which the Código Bustamante is applicable. It is pointed out, though, that the application of the Código Bustamante has been almost inexistent because the main flow of investment is from other countries—or is legally connected to other countries—, rather than from the countries in which Código Bustamante is in force.[35]

3.2.4 *Código Bustamante*

El *Código de Bustamante y Sirvén* or *Código de Derecho Internacional Privado*, that had been adopted in La Habana, on February 20 de 1928, in the frame of the Sixth American International Conference,[36] is in force in Bolivia, Brazil, Chile,

[28] See Locatelli (2016), p. 34, whom states that a foreign creditor is entitled to file a petition in a Brazilian court, asking that it opens an insolvency proceeding in Brazil; this proceeding will be restricted to the assets located in Brazil.

[29] Scotti (2006), p. 178.

[30] Locatelli (2016), p. 35.

[31] Roux Azevedo and Fragoso Bauch (2017).

[32] Locatelli (2008), p. 338.

[33] Campana Filho (2009), p. 150.

[34] Kargman (2012), p. 10.

[35] Locatelli (2016), p. 35.

[36] Moustaira (1992), pp. 295–298.

Costa Rica, Cuba, Ecuador, Guatemala, Haiti, Honduras, Nicaragua, Panama, Peru, República Dominicana, Salvador, Venezuela.[37]

Two articles speak about international jurisdiction.

Article 328 states that in the bankruptcies, where the debtor is voluntarily present in the country of his/her domicile, the judge of that country shall have competence.

Article 329 states that in the bankruptcies that are opened upon a petition by the creditors, shall have competence the judge of whichever country in which the creditors might have filed petition, with a preference, if it is among those countries, for the country of the debtor's domicile, where he/she or the majority of creditor have so asked.

The Title "*De la quiebra o concurso*", divided in three chapters, adopts a system of regulation of the international insolvency that does not differ from the one adopted by the Montevideo Treaties.

Chapter I, titled "*Unidad de la quiebra o concurso*", has only one article, 414, in which it states that when the insolvent debtor does not have more than one civil or merchant domicile, then there can only be one proceeding either preventive of bankruptcy, or bankruptcy for all the debtor's assets and obligations in the contracting States.

Chapter II "Universalidad de la quiebra o concurso y sus efectos" has five articles that refer to various extraterritorial effects of the bankruptcy declaration.

Article 416 states that the judgment that declares the debtor bankrupt has extraterritorial effects in the Contracting States after the accomplishment of the registry or publication formalities that the legislation of each State demands.

According to the Article 417, the bankruptcy judgment that has been issued in one of the contracting States, is enforced in the other States in the way that this Code establishes for the judicial decisions. However, it will produce the effects of a judgment from the moment that it will become final.

The Article 418 establishes that the functions of the syndics that are appointed in one of the contracting States according to the Bustamante Code's rules will have extraterritorial effect in the other States, without needing to follow any local rules.

The Article 419 speaks about the retroactivity of the bankruptcy declaration and the annulation of certain acts because of that declaration, and states that they will be determined by the governing law and they will be applicable in the territory of the other contracting States.

The last article of the Chapter II, Article 420, contains the classic exception according to which the actions regarding real rights, notwithstanding the declaration of bankruptcy, will continue to be subjects to the lex rei sitae and to the jurisdiction of the courts of that situs.

Chapter III "Del convenio y la rehabilitación" has two articles.

The Article 421 states that the agreement between the creditors and the (bankrupt) debtor shall have extraterritorial effects in the other contracting States, except

---

[37] Scotti (2006), p. 184.

as regards the real right action of the creditors that would not have accepted the agreement.

Finally, the Article 422 provides that the rehabilitation of the bankrupt debtor will also have extraterritorial effect in the other contracting States from the moment the judgment that so disposes becomes definitive, and according to its terms.[38]

3.3 China

3.3.1 Interregional Cooperation

China's legal system has undergone many radical changes during the twentieth and the twenty-first centuries. Confucianism and Legalism still "compete" between each other and coexist in that country.[39] After 1949, year of the PRC's establishment, the new government used the Soviet Union model as a reference to create its new system.[40] During the last decades, China has copied, has transplanted several Western legal rules, especially in commercial law. It had already copied—or, was forced to receive—Western legal rules during the upheaval times, end of nineteenth century/beginning of twentieth century, but the communist regime during Mao era had changed almost everything.

Following the reunification of the Mainland China with Macao, Hong Kong and Taiwan, the basic formula that the Mainland has adopted is the "one country, two systems" principle. It was declared by Deng Xiaoping, became a constitutional principle crafted for the reunification of Hong Kong with China in the early 1980s[41] and was written into the Sino-British Joint Declaration and Sino-Portuguese Joint Declaration.

The Mainland and the SARs (Special Administrative Regions) entered into a set of legal cooperation arrangements. Among them were arrangements concerning recognition and enforcement of judgments in civil and commercial matters.

In 2006, the Mainland and Hong Kong SAR entered into the Arrangement on Reciprocal Recognition and Enforcement of Judgments in Civil and Commercial Matters by the Courts of the Mainland and of the Hong Kong Special Administrative Region Pursuant to Choice of Court Agreements between Parties Concerned.[42]

It was adopted on June 12, 2006 and it took effect on August 1, 2008. It only applies to civil and commercial matters and it requires a choice of jurisdiction agreement—to be in either Hong Kong or China.[43] It has been pointed out that this

[38] Scotti (2006), p. 185.

[39] About China's legal system, see Moustaira (2012), p. 9396.

[40] Gong (2018), p. 14.

[41] Lee (2015a), p. 262.

[42] Zhang and Smart (2006), p. 553.

[43] Lee (2015b), p. 336.

restrictive requirement could encourage forum shopping because it would enable "a party to seize the Chinese court with the purpose to avoid a jurisdiction clause concluded by it" and thus would "invalidate many jurisdiction clauses which might be valid under the law of other countries."[44]

Also, in 2006, the Mainland and Macao SAR entered into the Arrangement Between the Mainland and the Macao Special Administrative Region on the Mutual Recognition and Enforcement of Civil and Commercial Judgments. This Arrangement is improved, compared to the Mainland—Hong Kong Arrangement: (1) it has a wider scope and (2) it does not require a choice of court agreement.

In 2009, the Mainland and Taiwan entered into the Agreement between Both Sides of the Taiwan Strait on Jointly Fighting against Crimes and Mutual Judicial Assistance. In the same year, the Supreme People's Court promulgated the Supplementary Provisions of the Supreme People's Court on the People's Courts' Recognition of Civil Judgments of the Relevant Courts of the Taiwan Region.[45]

3.3.2 Cross-Border Insolvency [Different] Systems of China and Hong Kong

3.3.2.1 China: Mainland

Before 2006, China's bankruptcy system was not homogeneous. State-owned enterprises (SOEs) were subject to the 1986 law, while non-SOEs were subject to the 1991 PRC Civil Procedure Law as well as other regulations, decrees and interpretations on insolvency laws.

Several were the reasons that led to the reform of its bankruptcy law. In the years that followed, there was a fast growth of the private economy that called for a bankruptcy law that could address that growth. Also, the 1997 Asian Financial Crisis was undoubtedly a "significant precipitating event",[46] although it did not had serious repercussions in China as it had in other Asian countries which also started reforming their insolvency laws.[47]

The insolvency law reform, in this country, as in many other countries' insolvency laws' reforms before and after, was in many respects the result of Western influences.[48] Jurists, either Chinese or/and foreigners, who had studied in Western universities and worked with Western lawyers sat on the board that drafted the new Chinese Enterprise Bankruptcy Law, and the drafts were given for comments to international organization experts.[49]

---

[44] Tang (2012), p. 464.

[45] Gong (2018), pp. 16–25.

[46] Gao and Wang (2017), p. 153.

[47] Arner et al. (2007), p. 550.

[48] Gao and Wang (2017), p. 140.

[49] Carruthers and Halliday (2006), pp. 561–568.

The actual insolvency law, the Enterprise Bankruptcy Law (EBL) of Mainland China, a "patchwork of the U.S. Chapter 11 and English Administration",[50] was promulgated on August 27, 2006 and came into effect on June 1 2007.[51] It consists of 12 chapters with 136 articles.[52]

It was considered "a significant step forward" for the country's legislation. It replaced the administrative process of bankruptcy with a judicial process of bankruptcy.

Contrary to the previous law, the EBL applies to "enterprise legal persons". This definition covers SOEs, non-SOEs, private enterprises and foreign-invested enterprises; it excludes partnerships and individual-owned businesses.[53]

It is argued that this law presents "an alternative perspective" which "diverges significantly from the global mainstream".[54]

Nevertheless, it constitutes "a drastic revision of the old Law" and "is praised by many scholars", according to some other opinion.[55] Obviously, it contributes to the development of China's market economy,[56] since insolvency as an institution is part of that economy.

It is pointed out that the legal framework of China's Bankruptcy Law is composed of two parts: the Enterprise Bankruptcy Law and the judicial interpretations consecutively issued by the Supreme People's Court having as aim to coordinate with the implementation of the EBL.

The EBL provides for three bankruptcy procedures: liquidation, reorganization and conciliation (or settlement or composition[57]). According to the jurists' experience (although not yet official statistics, there are no consolidated official data available), the main focus of proceedings to date has been liquidation, with only about 20% of the cases being reorganization cases and very few settlement cases.[58]

It is pointed out that the reorganization regime of the Chinese EBL shares many common characteristics with Chapter 11 of the U.S. Bankruptcy Code. However, there are also differences between them.

One of them is that only debtors and receivers have the right to propose a reorganization plan under the Chinese EBL,[59] while under Chapter 11 "any party in interest" may file a plan when the debtor's plan is not accepted within the time limit.

Another very important characteristic of the EBL is that it puts great emphasis on the protection of employees' rights. Thus, to apply for a court's confirmation of a

[50] Qi (2008), p. 13.

[51] Godwin (2007), p. 755.

[52] Lee (2011), p. 940.

[53] Lee and Ho (2010), p. 149.

[54] Godwin (2012), p. 179.

[55] See Lin (2018), p. 79.

[56] Arsenault (2008), p. 45.

[57] The translation of legal terms is very important and sometimes very difficult, since the terms used may not correspond to the reality.

[58] Steele et al. (2017), p. 7.

[59] Ren (2011), p. 181.

reorganization plan, the employees' claims must be fully satisfied. In U.S. Chapter 11, a plan may be crammed down even if an employee's claim is impaired, provided the classification of claims does not discriminate unfairly.

In case of a reorganization where a reorganization plan[60] has to be submitted (by the debtor) and approved by all of the creditors' groups, the court can use its power to cram-down the reorganization plan, that is, force the creditors to accept the plan, even if they do not want to.[61] It is argued that the wide use of the cram-down by the courts[62] has contributed to the low repayment rate for the creditors.[63]

It is argued that bankruptcy law in China is not well designed for creditors' interests[64]; various reasons are mentioned, such as that the procedural requirements for initiating a bankruptcy procedure are complex enough or that the Chinese bankruptcy law is rather "manager-displacing" than "manager-friendly", since it provides for a court-appointed administrator to take over as soon as the bankruptcy procedure is opened by the court. But the latter argument does not seem convincing, given the fact that many are the national bankruptcy laws that follow the same way. The fact that U.S. law for example allows, in Chapter 11 cases, directors to continue being in charge of the company in debt, while in a United Kingdom administration procedure a court-appointed administrator takes over the power and the responsibilities,[65] does not mean that the first system is better designed for the creditors' interests than the other.

In any case, the numbers of bankruptcy proceedings in China, following the legislative reform, were initially very low, for various reasons, among which was the high level of discretion that courts have as to whether to accept them or not.[66] Things seem to change, however it is rather early to say.

As it is pointed out, the concept of cross-border insolvency, of international insolvency did not exist in Chinese national legislation before the enactment of the EBL 2006. This does not mean that there were no cross-border insolvency cases in China, then; it means that there was no nationwide legislation concerning cross-border insolvency in the Mainland. The opening up policies in 1978 also led to such cases the solution of which was territorial and based on civil procedure laws.[67]

Article 5 of the EBL 2006 is the first—and only—Chinese provision to address cross-border insolvencies—there are no rules governing international jurisdiction or choice of law. It consists of two paragraphs, respectively concerning the universal

---

[60] That the reorganization system is inspired by the U.S. Chapter 11, see Lee (2011), p. 941.

[61] Except if employees' claims are not fully satisfied.

[62] Tomasic and Zhang (2012), p. 315.

[63] Wei and Chen (2018), p. 115.

[64] Wei and Chen (2018), pp. 112–116.

[65] Armour et al. (2002), p. 1699.

[66] Jiang (2013), p. 559.

[67] Parry and Gao (2018), pp. 7–8.

ambitions of Chinese insolvency proceedings and the modified universalist (or, rather, territorialist) approach to foreign insolvency proceedings in China.[68]

The first paragraph says that insolvency procedures commenced in accordance with this Law are binding on the debtor's property located outside the territory of the People's Republic of China.

The second paragraph sets out the criteria for recognition of foreign insolvency proceedings. Therefore, for an insolvency proceeding opened outside Mainland China to be recognized and enforced, the conditions are that:

(1) relevant international treaties between the country concerned and Mainland China have been concluded; or
(2) reciprocal relations between the country concerned and Mainland China have been established;
(3) the insolvency proceeding shall not violate the basic principles of the laws of the PRC;
(4) the insolvency proceeding shall not jeopardize the sovereignty and security of the State or public interests;
(5) the insolvency proceeding shall not undermine the legitimate rights and interests of creditors within Mainland China.[69]

Regarding the first condition, we are informed that from 1987 until today, China has signed over 30 mutual civil and commercial judicial assistance treaties or agreements. Some of them exclude recognition of insolvency proceedings, while some others only apply to recognition of arbitral awards. In any case, the existence of a relevant bilateral treaty is considered a concrete foundation for the recognition by the Chinese court of a foreign insolvency proceeding.

If there is no mutual civil and commercial judicial assistance treaty, the foreign insolvency proceeding will probably not be recognized.[70] Thus, a (Mainland) Chinese court refused to recognize a UK judgment that had opened insolvency proceedings of Lehman Brothers International Europe (LBIE),[71] on the basis that no treaty had been concluded between the UK and China; on the contrary, Chinese courts have recognized French and Italian insolvency proceedings on the basis that bilateral judicial cooperation treaties have been concluded between China and those countries.[72]

---

[68] Parry and Gao (2018), pp. 10–17.

[69] Gong (2018), p. 40.

[70] See Gong (2018), p. 41 and note 73, who refers to a case of 2011, related to the Lehman Brothers collapse—see *infra*. In *Hua An Funds v Lehman Brothers International Europe*, a fund management firm of Mainland China filed petitions to the High People's Court of Shanghai Municipality based on the fund product cooperative agreement, claiming damage of US$96.4 million and sought an attachment of the assets of the defendant within the territory of the Mainland China, soon after the Lehman Brothers collapse in 2008 and the insolvency proceeding in UK. The judge did not recognize the UK insolvency proceeding, because there was no relevant international treaty between UK and China. Finally, the dispute was settled by mediation.

[71] About that case, see *infra*, Sect. 6.4.2.

[72] Gong (2013), pp. 240–241.

3.3.2.2 Hong Kong

Hong Kong's insolvency system is modeled after the UK's Insolvency Act of 1986.

As it is mentioned, there seems to be no prospect of Hong Kong adopting the UNCITRAL Model Law on Cross-Border Insolvency 1997 in the near future.[73]

It is now settled that foreign representatives appointed in the place of incorporation of the debtor can, based on traditional PIL rule, be recognized and assisted in Hong Kong without entering into local ancillary winding up proceedings. Under some circumstances, such recognition and assistance can be obtained even without going through any court proceeding.[74]

In the case *The Joint Official Liquidators of A Company v. B and Another* [*Re A Company*], it was held that:

> …if a person in Hong Kong receives a request or instruction from a liquidator of a foreign corporation, with which if it had come from the board of directors of that foreign corporation he would have complied, he should once he is satisfied that the liquidator was properly appointed in the place of incorporation act upon the request or instruction.[75]

The holding in *Re A Company* was confirmed and restated in the case *Bay Capital Asia Fund, LP (In Official Liquidation) v. DBS Bank (Hong Kong)* [*Bay Capital*].

The judge considered that DBS's refusal to cooperate without being presented a recognition order issued by a Hong Kong court was an "unattractive exercise in obtuseness, which served no other purpose than to run up costs."[76]

3.3.2.3 China–Hong Kong: A Sui Generis Relation

"One Country, Two Systems", as it was mentioned above, is the rubric used for the parallel operation of two judicial systems within one country—here, of Mainland China and Hong Kong.[77] Hong Kong was returned to Chinese sovereignty in 1997. Article 8 of the Basic Law, the Constitution of Hong Kong, provides that the "laws previously in force in Hong Kong, that is, the common law, rules of equity, ordinances, subordinate legislation and customary law shall be maintained, except for any that contravene this Law, and subject to any amendments by the legislature of the Hong Kong Special Administrative Region."[78]

On December 19, 1984, the *Joint Declaration of the Government of the United Kingdom of Great Britain and Northern Ireland and the Government of the People's*

---

[73] Li and Tu (2018), pp. 33–34.

[74] Li and Tu (2018), p. 37.

[75] *The Joint Official Liquidators of A Company v. B and Another* HCMP 902/2014 [2014] 4 HKLRD 374.

[76] See *Bay Capital Asia Fund, LP (In Official Liquidation) v. DBS Bank (Hong Kong) Ltd* HCMP 3104/2015.

[77] Gong (2011), p. 58.

[78] Ng (2009), p. 9 note 12.

Republic of China on the Question of Hong Kong[79] announced that the colony of Hong Kong would be returned to China as the HKSAR on July 1, 1997. China guaranteed the HKSAR's freedoms and pluralism under the rule of law for 50 years, beginning on the date of return.[80]

Since 1997, Hong Kong has had a bilingual common law system. Chinese language[81] and English language share equal status within Hong Kong's system, both are official languages of the law. Article 9 of the Basic Law, provides that "[in] addition to the Chinese language, English may also be used as an official language by the executive authorities, legislature and judiciary of the Hong Kong Special Administrative Region."

It is pointed out that each of the two language structures "maintains its own standards and limits of pragmatic effectiveness; that English is the language of business, politics, and other public activities and that Cantonese is the language of the family, the mass media, and the street."

How many purposive alternatives can be tolerated in one legal system?[82] How easily can two systems in one country survive?

And what about the judicial recognition and assistance in insolvency cases that cross the border of Hong Kong and Mainland China?

3.3.2.4 Cooperation on a Regional Level in Insolvency Matters

Interregional insolvency could be considered as having the same characteristics with international insolvency: they both cross borders, although these borders are not similar. It is about a regional conflict of laws or private interregional law on insolvency matters.[83]

---

[79] Available at: http://www.legislation.gov.hk/blis_ind.nsf/CurAllEngDoc/034B10AF5D3058DB482575EE000EDB9F?OpenDocument.

[80] Lee (2015c), p. 442.

[81] See Ng (2009), pp. 5, 9 and notes 3, 4, 9, who points out that the people of Hong Kong use Cantonese in the oral context and Standard Modern Chinese in the written context. He mentions that many of the spoken words in Cantonese have no standardized written characters; that, when the people of Hong Kong must write down words, they often write in homophones. He states that more often, people write in Standard Modern Chinese, which is the written form of Putonghua, that is, Mandarin. The author claims that the fact that both languages are used as languages of law in this British ex-colony, is a rarity among British ex-colonies, since English remains the sole language of the law in many other former British colonies, "from India and Singapore in Asia to Kenya and Nigeria in Africa, not to mention former settler colonies such as Australia and New Zealand."

[82] Ruskola (2000), p. 1599.

[83] Zhu (2002), pp. 626–627, argues that conflict of laws between the HKSAR and Mainland China cannot be regulated by analogy of general conflict of laws rules because it "is seen in a vertical sense". According to the same way of thinking, a conflict of laws between the HKSAR and a province of Mainland China or another autonomous region would be seen in a horizontal sense. It does not seem a convincing argument.

Unfortunately, there is no legislation either in the Mainland or in the other regions, which would provide for recognition of insolvency proceedings of the other regions or/and for coordination of rules or of parallel insolvency proceedings. This, at times, has awkward results.

Thus, when in 2011 the High Court of Beijing, upon a request for recognition of the Hong Kong winding-up proceeding concerning *Norstar Automotive*, referred a question to the Supreme People's Court in order to clarify whether the winding-up order rendered by the High Court of Hong Kong could be recognized in the Mainland, the Supreme People's Court gave the following (seemingly extreme, however typically right) reply:

> In accordance with the Article 1 of Arrangement of the Supreme People's Court between the Mainland and the Hong Kong SAR on Reciprocal Recognition and Enforcement of the Decisions of Civil and Commercial Cases Pursuant to Choice of Court Agreements between Parties Concerned, the winding-up order in dispute does not fall within the ambit of the enforceable final judgment under the Arrangement and thus the Arrangement is irrelevant to this case. The Article 265 of the Civil Procedure Law and the Article 5 of the Enterprise Bankruptcy Law, which provide rules on recognition and enforcement of judgments rendered by the foreign courts, cannot be applied to this case, either. The decision of your court that in accordance with the aforementioned legislation, recognition of the winding-up order in dispute can be granted, is groundless.[84]

So, what would be the possible solutions?

Comity, has been suggested, would be one such solution. However, comity does not create an absolute obligation nor is it a mere courtesy or goodwill gesture by a foreign country.[85] The differences between the two systems of insolvency law could be an obstacle to the application of this principle and, consequently, the recognition of the insolvency judgments of the Mainland by Hong Kong or of the Hong Kong by the Mainland.

For example, according to the Chinese insolvency law the debtor company must be insolvent to file a plan for reorganization.[86] In Hong Kong, under the Companies Ordinance this requirement of insolvency is not so strict.[87]

Also, the differences between the two systems regarding the priority rankings of creditors could deter the courts in Hong Kong or China from granting recognition or assistance to the foreign party.[88]

What should be stressed is that Hong Kong, while before 1997 was regarded as a foreign jurisdiction to China, after the Handover it cannot anymore be considered as such. That means, among other things, that no bilateral treaty may be concluded between the Mainland and Hong Kong, about the mutual recognition and assistance in cross-border insolvency cases.

Perhaps an Arrangement could be a solution?

---

[84] Gong (2018), p. 3.

[85] *Hilton v Guyot* 159 US 113 (1895) at 163–164.

[86] The EBL, Chapter 8.

[87] Hong Kong Companies Ordinance (Cap 32), s 166.

[88] Lee (2015a), p. 263.

References

Anapolsky JM, Woods JF (2013) Pitfalls in Brazilian bankruptcy law for international bond investors. J Bus Technol Law 8:397–450

Armour J, Cheffins B, Skeel D Jr (2002) Corporate ownership structure and the evolution of bankruptcy law: lessons from the United Kingdom. Vanderbilt Law Rev 55:1699–1785

Arner DW, Booth CD, Lejot P, Hsu BFC (2007) Property rights, collateral, creditor rights, and insolvency in East Asia. Tex Int Law J 42:515–559

Arsenault S (2008) The westernization of Chinese bankruptcy: an examination of China's new corporate bankruptcy law through the lens of the UNCITRAL legislative guide to insolvency law. Penn State Int Law Rev 27:45–87

Baeza Ovalle JG (2011) Naturaleza juridical del proceso concursal. Revista Chilena de Derecho 38:33–56

Campana Filho PF (2009) The legal framework for cross-border insolvency in Brazil. Houst J Int Law 32:97–151

Carruthers BG, Halliday TC (2006) Negotiating globalization: global scripts and intermediation in the construction of Asian insolvency regimes. Law Soc Inq 31:521–584

Ciuro Caldani MA (1994) Notas para la compresión capitalista del Derecho Comercial (aportes para la Filosofía del Derecho Comercial). Revista de Filosofía Jurídica y Filosofía Social 18:31–32

Colombo G, Kaye R, Tamer Langen J, Lutkus S, Shirley J, Turetsky D (2017) Cross-border insolvency in Brazil: a case for the model law. Available at: www.uncitral.org/pdf/english/congress/Papers_for_Congress/117-COLOMBO_KAYE_LANGEN_LUTKUS_SHIRLEY_and_TURETSKY-_Cross_Border_Insolvency_in_Brazil.pdf

de Assumpção Alves AF, da Fonseca Rocha RV (2016) Insolvência Transnational e Direito Falimentar Brasileiro. Revista EMERJ, Rio de Janeiro 19:9–65

Gao S, Wang Z (2017) The U.S. reorganization regime in the Chinese mirror: legal transplantation and obstructed efficiency. Am Bankruptcy Law J 91:139–176

Godwin A (2007) A lengthy stay? The impact of the PRC enterprise bankruptcy law on the rights of secured creditors. Univ N S W Law J 30:755–773

Godwin A (2012) Corporate rescue in Asia – trends and challenges. Sydn Law Rev 34:163–187

Gong X (2011) When Hong Kong becomes SAR, is the Mainland ready? Problems of judgments recognition in cross-border insolvency matters. Int Insolv Rev 20:57–73

Gong X (2013) To recognise or not to recognise? Comparative study of Lehman brothers cases in Mainland China and Taiwan. Int Corp Rescue 10:240–247

Gong X (2018) China's insolvency law and interregional cooperation. Comparative perspectives from China and the EU. Routledge, London and New York

Guseva Y (2014) KGB's legacy: transplanting efficient financial infrastructures without efficiency. Univ Pa J Int Law 36:525–649

Halliday TC, Carruthers BG (2007) The recursivity of law: global norm making and national lawmaking in the globalization of corporate insolvency regimes. Am J Soc 112:1135

Jiang Y (2013) The curious case of inactive bankruptcy practice in China: a comparative study of U.S. and Chinese bankruptcy law. Northwest J Int Law Bus 34:559–582

Kanda H, Milhaupt CJ (2003) Re-examining legal transplants: the director's fiduciary duty in Japanese corporate law. Am J Comp Law 51:887–902

Kargman ST (2012) Emerging economies and cross-border insolvency regimes: missing BRICs in the international insolvency architecture (Part I). Insolv Restruct Int 6:8–15

Lee EH (2011) The reorganization process under China's corporate bankruptcy system. Int Lawyer 45:939–974

Lee EH (2015a) Comparing Hong Kong and Chinese insolvency laws and their cross-border complexities. J Comp Law 9:259–280

Lee EH (2015b) Legal pluralism, institutionalism, and judicial recognition of Hong Kong-China cross-border insolvency judgments. Hong Kong Law J 45:331–350

Lee EH (2015c) Problems of judicial recognition and enforcement in cross-border insolvency matters between Hong Kong and Mainland China. Am J Comp Law 63:439–465
Lee EH, Ho K (2010) China's new enterprise bankruptcy law – a great leap forward, but just how far? Int Insolv Rev 19:145–177
Leno ND (2015) Rwanda legal framework on insolvency: problems and proposals for reform. Int Insolv Rev 24:122–139
Li X, Tu G (2018) Recent developments in recognition of and assistance to foreign insolvency representatives under the Hong Kong Common Law. Int Insolv Rev 27:32–57
Lin S (2018) The empirical studies of China's enterprise bankruptcy law: problems and improvements. Int Insolv Rev 27:77–109
Locatelli F (2008) International trade and insolvency law: is the UNCITRAL model law on cross-border insolvency an answer for Brazil? (An economic analysis of its benefits on international trade). Law Bus Rev Am 14:313–345
Locatelli F (2016) International insolvency and economic law. The legal and economic benefits of the UNCITRAL model law for international trade & Brazil. Lambert Academic Publishing, Saarbrücken
Martin N (2003) Common-law bankruptcy systems: similarities and differences. Am Bankruptcy Inst Law Rev 11:367
Martin N (2005) The role of history and culture in developing bankruptcy and insolvency systems: the perils of legal transplantation. Boston Coll Int Comp Law Rev 28:1–77
Miguens HJ (2018) El derecho internacional privado de la insolvencia en Argentina. Propuestas de reforma "de lege lata" y "de lege ferenda" para Argentina y el MERCOSUR. Editorial Académica Española, Mauritius
Moustaira EN (1992) The equality of creditors in international bankruptcy law [in Greek]. Ant.N. Sakkoulas Publishers, Athens/Komotini
Moustaira EN (2012) Comparative law [in Greek]. Nomiki Bibliothiki, Athens
Moustaira EN (2013) Juridical influences in the frame of comparative law. Sakkoulas Publications, Athens/Thessaloniki
Ng KH (2009) The common law in two voices. Language, law & the post-colonial predicament in Hong Kong. Stanford University Press, Stanford, CA
Parry R, Gao N (2018) The future direction of China's cross-border insolvency laws, related issues and potential problems. Int Insolv Rev 27:5–31
Qi L (2008) The corporate reorganization regime under China's new enterprise bankruptcy law. Int Insolv Rev 17:13–32
Ren Y (2011) The "control model" in Chinese bankruptcy reorganization law and practice. Am Bankruptcy Law J 85:177–194
Roux Azevedo LA, Fragoso Bauch LA (2017) Limitations of Brazilian law regarding cross-border insolvency. Financier Worldwide. Available at: https://www.financierworldwide.com/limitations-of-brazilian-law-regarding-cross-border-insolvency/#.WbOcCNSLTs0
Ruskola T (2000) Conceptualising corporations and kinship: comparative law and development theory in a Chinese perspective. Stanford Law Rev 52:1599–1729
Scotti L (2006) Armonización legislativa en materia de insolvencia internacional de los grupos económicos: ¿una asignatura pendiente para el MERCOSUR? (Tesina de Maestría) Argentina: Universidad de Buenos Aires. Available at: www.derecho.uba.ar/investigacion/investigadores/scotti-insolvencia-internacional-de-los-grupos-economicos.pdf
Scotti L (2007) La Insolvencia Internacional a la Luz del Derecho internacional privado Argentino de Fuente Interna. Revista del Instituto de Investigaciones "Ambrosio L. Giorgia" Universidad de Buenos Aires 1:156–191
Smaliukas A (2015) Insolvency of group of companies in the scope of the new EIR: Lithuanian perspective. Int Insolv Law Rev:379–382
Steele S, Godwin A, Jin C, Han C, Ren Y, Chi W (2017) Trends and developments in Chinese insolvency law: the first decade of the PRC *Enterprise Bankruptcy Law*. Available at https://ssrn.com/abstract=3049685

Tang ZS (2012) Effectiveness of exclusive jurisdiction clauses in the Chinese courts – a pragmatic study. Int Comp Law Q 61:459–484

Telles J (2010) Breve estudio comparativo del derecho concursal Español y Brasileño. Anuario Facultad de Derecho – Universidad de Alcalá III:463–475

Tomasic R, Zhang Z (2012) From global convergence in China's enterprise bankruptcy law 2006 to divergent interpretation: corporate reorganization in China. J Chin Leg Stud 12:295–332

Vásquez MV, Darío Acevedo-Prada R (2014) Análisis de la regulación sobre insolvencia transfronteriza en América Latina: Argentina y Venezuela. Revista de investigaciones en Derecho y Ciencias Políticas Universidad La Gran Colombia:104–114

Wei C, Chen Y (2018) The predicament of bank creditors in Chinese bankruptcy and the way out. Int Insolv Rev 27:110–134

Zhang X, Smart P (2006) Development of regional conflict of laws: on the arrangement of mutual recognition and enforcement of judgments in civil and commercial matters between Mainland China and Hong Kong SAR. Hong Kong Law J 36:553–584

Zhu G (2002) Inter-regional conflict of laws under "One Country, Two Systems": revisiting Chinese legal theories and Chinese and Hong Kong Law, with special reference to judicial assistance. Hong Kong Law J 32:615–676

Chapter 4
European Union

4.1 General Comments

European Union Member States' legal orders differ between them in many insolvency law issues; among them, the moment and the prerequisites that must be met for a debtor to be declared in state of economic crisis, in state of insolvency.[1] Liquidation and rescue proceedings are coexisting in most of them, also with many differences between them. The latter were "substantially modernized"[2] in EU Member States—Germany, Belgium, Spain, France, Denmark, Portugal, Italy, Greece, Poland—following the 2008 worldwide crisis. There had already been reforms in other EU Member States—UK, Ireland, Finland, France, the Netherlands, Slovakia, Spain—in the early 2000s. The US law influence in that sector too, was undoubted.[3]

Definitions in national laws often differ, however there are certain common elements.

The old classic bankruptcy perhaps is the institution that has most similarities in all countries. So, for example, according to the definition that Finnish insolvency law gives to bankruptcy—and which could be easily be given by other national laws too—, "Bankruptcy is a form of insolvency proceedings covering all the liabilities of the debtor, where the assets of the debtor are used in payment of the claims in bankruptcy. In order to achieve the objective of the bankruptcy, the assets of the debtor shall in the beginning of bankruptcy become subject to the authority of the creditors. An estate administrator appointed by the court shall see to the management and liquidation of the assets of the debtor and to the other administration of the bankruptcy estate."[4]

[1] Pérez Ragone and Martínez Benavides (2015), p. 93.

[2] Ghio (2017), p. 66.

[3] Gant (2016), p. 72.

[4] Available at: http://www.finlex.fi/en/laki/kaannokset/2004/en20040120.pdf.

E. Moustaira, *International Insolvency Law*,
https://doi.org/10.1007/978-3-030-04450-3_4

Insolvency is closely connected to the liquidity of the entity. It seems that European Member States follow one of three models, which models are: (1) the laws that relate insolvency to the cessation of payments; (2) the laws that relate insolvency to the incapacity, impossibility of payments; and (3) the laws that combine the two previous alternatives.

Notwithstanding the differences of the EU Member States' insolvency laws, there was a desire/ambition, since the beginning, of creating a European instrument that would establish common rules of jurisdiction and choice of law in civil and commercial matters, bankruptcy/insolvency matters included. The way would be long for insolvency. The differences between national laws in private international approach to insolvencies were very big. As it is very clearly stated, "when one examines Member States' private international law rules on insolvency, it is apparent that the conflicting views are even more deeply rooted than in any other types of conflict of laws."[5]

4.2 EEC Draft Convention

In 1960, a committee was formed to draft a Convention on the recognition and enforcement of judgments in civil and commercial matters. It was decided that bankruptcy presented special difficulties, so a second committee was constituted in 1963 to draft a Convention on the recognition and enforcement of judgments in bankruptcy matters. The basis for both projects was Article 220 of the Treaty of Rome, of 1957, under which EEC Member States had committed to negotiate, for the benefit of their nationals, "the simplification of formalities governing the reciprocal recognition and enforcement of judgments of courts and tribunals and of arbitration awards."[6]

Both committees also considered rules on the assumption of jurisdiction by EEC Member States' courts. The first committee was very successful, creating the Brussels 1968 Convention on jurisdiction and enforcement of judgments in civil and commercial matters. The bankruptcy committee produced a preliminary draft convention also in 1968 which was followed by a revised draft in 1970, accompanied by a detailed explanatory report.[7]

The ambitious intention of the Draft Convention was to apply the principle of universality of bankruptcy proceedings; to establish a single jurisdiction that would decide on cross-border insolvency issues. *Lex fori concursus* would apply to most procedural and substantive matters, with limited exceptions. Most importantly, the judgments in the course of bankruptcy proceedings would be recognized and enforced in the other Member States.[8]

---

[5] Ghio (2017), p. 64.

[6] van Zwieten (2016).

[7] Noel and Lemontey (1970).

[8] Omar (2003), p. 151.

One of the main problems of that Draft Convention was that it was designed to be applied only with the parallel introduction of a uniform law. There were other points that made the Member States hesitant to adopt in. Furthermore, United Kingdom became member of the European Communities in 1973, and commentators there, were stressing the fact that certain (draft) convention terms were reflecting the underlying views of civil law systems and consequently English law would have big difficulties to adopt—or to be harmonized with—such terms.[9]

The Committee continued its work and the result was a second Draft, transmitted to the Council in 1980 and published in the *Official Journal* in 1982. Unity and universality remained as reigning principles. Uniform rules on jurisdiction for opening proceedings (at the debtor's "centre of administration") were adopted and the *lex fori concursus* remained dominant with limited exceptions.[10]

After a failure to reach a consensus on the second Draft, the Committee's work was suspended in 1985.

4.3 European Convention on Insolvency Proceedings 1995

In 1990, the Istanbul Convention on Certain Aspects of Bankruptcy, that had been prepared under the auspices of the Council of Europe, was opened for signature by the Member States of the organization. It had a very limited scope—only bankruptcies—and was never adopted.[11] It was the first text ever that included the concept of "Center of Main Interests" (COMI). Article 4 stated that:

> The courts or other authorities of the party in which the debtor has the centre of his main interests shall be considered as being competent for opening the bankruptcy. For companies and legal persons, unless the contrary is proved, the place of the registered office shall be presumed to be the centre of their main interests.[12]

In 1991, the European Communities Working Group for insolvency matters was reformed. After a preliminary draft, in 1991, an Explanatory Memorandum, in 1991 too, and a final discussion draft, in 1994, there came the version that the Council of Ministers were to approve.

In 1995, a compromise text had been completed and was presented to the Member States for their signature. It was followed by an explanatory report ("Virgos/Schmidt Report").[13]

(1) It established jurisdictional rules for the opening of insolvency proceedings within European Community: main proceeding in the Member State in which

---

[9] See Omar (2003), pp. 152–153, for a detailed presentation of the situation, then.

[10] About the trajectory of works until (1985), see Moustaira (1992), pp. 299–322.

[11] It was only by Cyprus ratified.

[12] Tirado (2015), p. 693.

[13] Virgós and Schmidt (1996).

the debtor's center of main interests (COMI) was located and secondary proceedings in Member States in which the debtor had an establishment.
(2) It provided for the automatic recognition of the opening of main and secondary proceedings in all other Member States and for the enforcement of decisions entered in such proceedings.
(3) It also created uniform conflict of law rules governing in insolvency proceedings.

As it is above mentioned, in November 1995, the simpler and less rigid than its attempted predecessors Convention, which was applying a modified or mitigated universalism,[14] was finalized and ready to enter into force after it would have been signed by the Member States: a period was opened for Member States to adhere by signature from 23 November 1995 to 23 May 1996.[15]

However, the United Kingdom did not sign it by the required deadline.[16] Therefore, the Convention never became law.

4.4 European Insolvency Regulations

Germany and Finland reintroduced the failed 1995 Convention as the European Union Council Regulation on Insolvency Proceedings 1346/2000. That initiative converted the unsuccessful Convention into a regulation that bound all European Union Member States, except Denmark.[17]

Most probably, Europe has been the most advanced, the most successful region in the development of cross-border insolvency frameworks. Both the EC Regulation 1346/2000 on Insolvency Proceedings, that entered into force on May 31, 2002 and the Recast EU Regulation 848/2015 (which applies from June 26, 2017—with some exceptions) managed to square the circle[18]: they follow the modified universalist approach[19]—or, according to another [perhaps sincerer] opinion, they provide for a territorialist scheme with universalist pretentions.[20]

They provide a comprehensive framework, covering all private international law issues that are related to insolvency. Nevertheless, not all articles of the Regulations contain rules on conflict of laws.[21] Some of them constitute in reality real rules of

[14] Virgós and Garcimartín (2004), p. 17.

[15] Omar (2003), p. 161.

[16] Either UK was furious because of the European Commission's ban on the export of British beef, or it was a political issue behind the scenes: the conflict between Spain and UK about the situation of Gibraltar.

[17] DeLaughter (2016), p. 400.

[18] Ortega Rueda (2016), p. 231.

[19] Mevorach (2018), p. 38.

[20] Tung (2001), p. 77.

[21] Dal Maso (2013), p. 202.

uniform substantive law, by which, it is argued, the Regulations have tried to create an autonomous discipline that is incorporated in the national legal orders and takes the place of previous rules.[22]

Such an example is the Article 5 of the EC Regulation 1346/2000—Article 8 of the Recast Regulation 848/2015.

This rule intends to preserve the rights in rem that have been constituted on property items situated in a Member State as a guarantee for the future payment by the debtor when an insolvency proceeding is opened in a different Member State. Thus, the rule has a double effect, as it is pointed out: on the one hand it obliges the insolvency proceeding to recognize the valid constitution of the right in rem on an asset situated in a different Member State according to the law that is applicable to that constitution of the right in rem; and on the other hand, it permits the creditor to be repaid by an enforcement procedure on this asset without concurring with the other creditors.[23]

4.5 EC Insolvency Regulation 1346/2000

One of the most important—and problematic—issues in the application of the EC Insolvency Regulation 1346/2000 was the concept of the center of the debtor's main interests (COMI), as a ground for opening main insolvency proceedings according to Article 3(1).[24]

The use of the COMI test in international instruments has been described as a "multilateralist" choice of law rule, because it recognizes that there might be several countries that would be interested in the insolvency proceeding, so it attempts to locate the one that would be most connected to the insolvency with foreign elements.[25]

It must be stressed that the concept of COMI in the Regulation has been created as an autonomous European Law concept.[26] COMI was not defined in this first Regulation.[27] Recital 13 furnished a sort of definition:

'The "centre of main interests" should correspond to the place where the debtor conducts the administration of his interests on a regular basis and is therefore ascertainable by third parties.'[28]

---

[22] Daniele (2002), p. 33.

[23] Bariatti (2004), p. 841.

[24] Torremans (2008), p. 173.

[25] Pottow (2005), p. 971.

[26] Tirado (2015), p. 695.

[27] van Calster (2015).

[28] Benedetelli (2011), p. 126, mentions that the range of meanings that has been attributed to the notion of COMI in the case law of the Member States is quite varied: it has been held to be located within the Member State of (1) the debtor's "administrative seat/central administration"; (2) the debtor's "administrative seat/central administration" but only if the debtor also carries out entre-

Recital 13 repeated unchanged the explanation that had been given to the concept of COMI in the Virgos/Schmidt Report, where it was stated:

> The concept of "centre of main interests" must be interpreted as the place where the debtor conducts the administration of his interests on a regular basis and is therefore ascertainable by third parties. The rationale of this rule is not difficult to explain. Insolvency is a foreseeable risk. It is therefore important that international jurisdiction (which, as it will be seen, entails the application of the insolvency laws of that Contracting State) be based on a place known to the debtor's potential creditors. This enables the legal risks which would have to be assumed in the case of insolvency to be calculated.[29]

As it is pointed out, EU Member States may give a definition to COMI in their legislation, but this definition would only have internal effects; regarding the application of the Regulation, judges could freely interpret the concept of COMI in a different way than that of the internal definition.

The Regulation contains a presumption according to which a company's COMI is located at its registered office. This presumption is rebuttable; it may be proved that the real company's COMI is its real seat, the country where the company carries out the administration of its main interests on a regular basis, something that can be ascertainable by third parties.

The European Union Court of Justice (CJEU) case law on companies, though, points to the incorporation theory. Given the fact that choice of law rules in company law are not harmonized, there is often a danger of non-coincidence between the COMI and a company's registered office.

The probably ensuing non-coincidence between *lex societatis* and *lex fori concursus* may result in the over-protection or the under-protection of creditors.[30] That is mainly the reason why certain scholars have advocated replacing COMI with the country where the registered office is located.[31]

On the other hand, it has been pointed out by other scholars that using as a jurisdictional basis the registered office would also foster insolvency forum shopping, since it would allow shareholders and directors to choose the incorporation law which would be more favorable to their interests[32] or to transfer their registered office, if they were considering more favorable the new incorporation law.

"Freedom of migration" is considered by the CJEU as one of the foundational principles of the European Union. On the other hand, CJEU has repeatedly admitted

---

preneurial activities with third parties there; (3) the debtor's "principal place of business"; (4) the "administrative seat/central administration" of the holding company of the debtor, if the debtor belonged to a group of companies; (5) the residence/domicile of the main creditors of the debtor; (6) the residence/domicile of the members of the board of directors of the debtor; (7) the place where the majority of the employees of the debtor work; (8) the law governing the main commercial contracts of the debtor; (9) the citizenship of the members of the board of directors of the debtor company; and (10) the place of incorporation of the sole shareholder of the debtor.

[29] Virgós and Schmidt (1996).

[30] Carballo Piñeiro (2014), p. 209.

[31] Eidenmüller (2013), pp. 13–17.

[32] Westbrook (2007), pp. 1028–1035.

that insolvency scholarship was "built on the shoulders of this corporate law doctrine".[33]

This interaction of freedom of migration with cross-border insolvency forum shopping within the EU has been commented by several authors.[34] It seems that many are open to the idea of shopping among fora, where there is no fraudulent or abusive activity involved.[35]

In *Eurofood*,[36] the CJEU emphasized that the facts that lead to the determination of a debtor's COMI should be "readily ascertainable" to its creditors. It repeated and clarified this, in *Interedil*.[37]

Certain commentators argue that, in case of a company's "migration", what is most important is whether the creditors had consented to the move, whether this move benefitted them by maximizing the debtor's net assets, appearing thus the movement not as abuse but as a socially beneficial "free choice".[38]

Secondary proceedings can be opened only where the debtor has an establishment, that is, a place of operations where the debtor carries out a "non-transitory economic activity with human means and goods." (Article 2(h))

The liquidator in the secondary proceedings is attributed exclusive power on the assets that are situated in that member state. This does not mean that main and secondary proceedings are completely separated. On the contrary, they are interdependent proceedings and the liquidator in the secondary proceedings is under the dominance of the main liquidator.[39]

4.6 EU Recast Insolvency Regulation 848/2015

The reform of the European Insolvency Regulation was considered necessary,[40] on the one hand to codify the Court of Justice of the European Union's case law and on the other hand to incorporate into the EC Regulation 1346/2000 the developments undergone by national insolvency laws in recent years.

---

[33] Block-Lieb (2018), p. 6.

[34] Enriques and Gelter (2006), p. 417.

[35] Eidenmüller (2009), p. 1; Mevorach (2013), p. 523.

[36] *Eurofood IFSC Ltd* C-341/04 (2006) ECR I-3813.

[37] *Interedil Srl, in liquidation v Fallimento Interedil Srl and Intesa Gestione Crediti SpA* C-396/09 (2011) ECR I-9915.

[38] Eidenmüller (2005), pp. 428–429.

[39] de Boer and Wessels (2008), p. 207.

[40] Weiss (2015), p .192.

Thus, the Regulation (EU) 2015/848 of the European Parliament and of the Council of 20 May 2015 (Recast Regulation) was adopted[41] and it is applicable to insolvency proceedings opened after 26 June 2017.[42]

Emphasis was given to business restructuring rather than liquidation. The new approach to business failure and insolvency aims at economic recovery and thus is favorable to a second chance for entrepreneurs instead of promoting their liquidation/extinction.[43]

Not everybody is satisfied with the amendments to the previous Regulation[44]; certain scholars believe that the steps taken were hesitant and that the ambitions of the Commission did not really run in parallel with the needs of business in difficulties.[45] Most scholars, though, believe that the Recast Regulation is a significant improvement regarding the functioning of cross-border insolvency proceedings.[46]

The substantive scope of application of the Recast Regulation is described in its Article 1(1). According to this article, the Regulation is applicable to

> public collective proceedings, including interim proceedings, which are based on laws relating to insolvency and in which, for the purpose of rescue, adjustment of debt, reorganization or liquidation: (a) a debtor is totally or partially divested of its assets and an insolvency practitioner is appointed; (b) the assets and affairs of a debtor are subject to control or supervision by a court; or (c) a temporary stay of individual enforcement proceedings is granted by a court or by operation of law, in order to allow for negotiations between the debtor and its creditors, provided that the proceedings in which the stay is granted provide for suitable measures to protect the general body of creditors, and where no agreement is reached, are preliminary to one of the proceedings referred to in point (a) or (b).

The insolvency proceeding, to fall under the scope of application of the Recast Regulation, must comply with the requirements of Article 1.1 and to be listed in Annex A.

The fact that it does not only apply to insolvency proceedings in the traditional sense, but that it also extends to preventive, hybrid or pre-insolvency proceedings, is considered as one of the main innovations of the Recast Regulation. Many Member States, during the last years, have enacted laws[47] that aim to the rescue of the distressed debtor who may be still economically viable.[48]

Further, it only applies to public proceedings of insolvency or pre-insolvency, that is, to proceedings that are submitted to publicity. Thus, the creditors get informed of the proceedings and they can exercise their procedural rights: contest the jurisdiction of the court that opened the proceeding, or lodge his/her claim.

---

[41] OJ L 141, 5.6.2015.

[42] Article 84 Recast EIR. Some exceptions are noted in Article 92 Recast EIR.

[43] Carballo Piñeiro (2014), p. 207.

[44] McCormack (2016), p. 121.

[45] McCormack (2014), p. 41.

[46] Castelló Pastor and Gómez Fonseca (2017), p. 21.

[47] About the Greek pre-insolvency procedures, see Michalopoulos (2013).

[48] Schürmeyer (2018), p. 77.

Publicity is facilitated by an exhaustive list of insolvency registers, included in the Recast EIR (Articles 24 et seq).[49]

The Recast EIR contains seven chapters.

The first chapter includes the foundations of the regulation as well as international jurisdiction (Article 3 *et seq.*) and applicable law (Article 7 *et seq.*).

The second chapter is about the recognition of foreign insolvency proceedings and their effects (Article 19 *et seq.*).

The third chapter refers in a detailed way to the secondary insolvency proceedings (Article 34 *et seq.*).

The fourth chapter contains the rules about the rights of creditors (Article 53 *et seq.*).

The fifth chapter contains rules on group insolvency (Article 56 *et seq.*).

The sixth chapter contains rules on data protection during insolvency proceedings (Article 78 *et seq.*).

Finally, the last, seventh chapter addresses administrative and transitional issues.[50]

Regarding COMI, it had been decided to improve it rather, but not transform it drastically. Voices had been heard, supporting its elimination,[51] since many were its defaults and the problems that it was creating, but not all were agreeing and no one could ever dare to do that: eliminate the concept from the text of the Regulation.

It has been "characterized as a vague and indeterminate compromise formula"[52] that creates legal uncertainty. Legal certainty will be restored, it is argued, by the courts, especially by the CJEU.[53] Many national courts have initiated preliminary ruling proceedings before CJEU, asking it to resolve the COMI enigma. Still, even the decisions of CJEU have not totally clarified the picture.

Significant amendments of COMI's regulation may be considered the following:

(a) Courts of the Member States must examine on their own motion whether the COMI is in their jurisdiction.
(b) A definition of COMI was expressly introduced in the Article 3(1) of the Regulation: " … *The centre of main interests shall be the place where the debtor conducts the administration of its interests on a regular basis and which is ascertainable by third parties.*"
(c) The Recitals of the Recast Regulation incorporated rules for COMI's interpretation, that were derived from case law, national and European.[54]

[49] Castelló Pastor and Gómez Fonseca (2017), p. 27.

[50] Bork (2017), pp. 249–250.

[51] Eidenmüller (2013).

[52] Gruber (2017), p. 41.

[53] Fehrenbach (2013), pp. 361 ff.

[54] Tirado (2015), p. 710.

Let it be mentioned here, that the problem of forum shopping still remains and that it is rather unclear whether the EIR Recast wants to resolve it, or not. For example, it is stated in Recital 29 that "the Regulation should contain a number of safeguards aimed at preventing fraudulent or abusive forum shopping". Would that mean that the Regulation admits the existence of a "positive forum shopping"?

In the Recast Regulation too, modified universalism has been preferred over other models.[55] The absolute universalism, that is, a single insolvency proceeding with universal effects (recognized everywhere), would theoretically be the perfect, most efficient model. However, it has been proved unrealistic since many countries wish to apply their insolvency law to protect local creditors, local priorities.[56]

Thus, secondary insolvency proceedings are permitted and are regulated by the articles of Chapter III of the Regulation.[57]

Coordination between main and secondary proceedings is strengthened.[58] Furthermore, according to the totally new Article 38, a court in which a request for the opening of a secondary insolvency proceeding has been filed, must immediately notify the insolvency administrator or the debtor in possession in the main insolvency proceedings and give them the opportunity to be heard on the request.

The Recast Regulation generally increased the duties of communication and cooperation that courts and insolvency practitioners have. The Regulation 1346/2000 contained only one article (Art. 31), while the Recast Regulation contains several such articles: Article 41 'Cooperation and communication between insolvency practitioners', Article 42 'Cooperation and communication between courts', Article 43 'Cooperation and communication between insolvency practitioners and courts' and Article 44 'Costs of cooperation and communication'.

Obviously, the influence of the common law tradition led to that choice of policy. Common law courts were much more accustomed to the idea of cooperation and their systems permits that, while civil law courts are constrained by cultural and legal obstacles to do so, in cross-border insolvency cases.[59] The latter is not a matter of unwillingness; it is rather a matter of sovereignty that could be offended. By the way, the "why" of this only one direction influence may never be explained. Although it is awkward that a common law traditional element reigns in this Regulation (as are other common law traditional elements in other European Regulations), at a moment when one of the two common law countries makes her exit from the European Union.[60]

In any case, it seems that the ideal of a unitary insolvency proceeding within the EU has not been fully given up, since there is an interest in avoiding the commencing of secondary proceedings and furthermore it is shown that concentrating the

[55] See *supra*, Sect. 2.5.

[56] McCormack (2012), p. 325.

[57] Carruthers (2017), p. 65.

[58] De Miguel Asensio (2015), p. 5.

[59] Mangano (2017), p. 315.

[60] See *infra*, Sect. 4.8.2.3, about Brexit.

insolvency of a group of companies[61] in a single country (member state) is feasible,[62] on the condition that its courts have national and local jurisdiction over all companies concerned.[63]

4.7 Avoidance Rules in European Union Insolvencies

4.7.1 General Comments

A most important element of administering the affairs of an insolvent debtor is for the insolvency administrator to accumulate all, if possible, assets owned by the debtor to augment the insolvent estate. In this process, there are rules (in probably all national insolvency laws) that permit the avoidance of transactions that took place before the opening of insolvency proceedings.[64]

The reasons of the existence of these avoidance provisions are several insolvency law policies.[65]

First and probably most important policy is the equal treatment of the creditors,[66] the fair distribution of the insolvent's property,[67] subject to any statutory exceptions.

Second policy, considered very important during the last decades, is the prevention of the dismemberment of the insolvent's estate that could occur because of those pre-insolvency transactions. Loss of assets would result to the loss of chances for the debtor's restructuring.

As it is pointed out, the origin of the avoidance of transactions in insolvency law is rather the Roman law, in which there were four legal processes that could be used to recover property: the *actio pauliana*, *interdictum fraudatorium*, the action *in factum* and the action *in integrum restitutio*.

The first one, the *actio pauliana*, has survived to the present day,[68] in many European laws, in often very different ways. The divergence is a consequence of many factors, such as the sources of each law, the history of each country, the [legal] culture, the [legal] tradition of each country.

---

[61] About groups of companies, see *infra*, Sect. 7.

[62] See *infra*, Sect. 7.3.

[63] In favor of the consolidation of a group of companies' insolvencies in one jurisdiction, Mevorach (2008), p. 427.

[64] McCormack et al. (2016), p. 137.

[65] Keay (1996), p. 56.

[66] Moustaira (1992).

[67] Warren (1993), p. 353.

[68] See Keay (2017), p. 82, who mentions that there has been some dispute about this action's nature and that there might have been more than one kind of *actio pauliana*.

Besides the differences, there are several similarities regarding the legal consequences of these avoidance rules,[69] the most characteristic one being that they provide for the setting aside of transactions that were entered into by the insolvent before the advent of insolvency proceedings and that are considered suspect from an insolvency law perspective.[70]

In some Member States' insolvency legislation, it is stated that avoidance actions may be taken against transactions that are detrimental to the creditors' interests. When the transactions have been made at undervalue, they are presumed to be detrimental.

Another aim of law's provisions against voidable transactions is that the latter often lead to the dismemberment of the insolvent debtor's estate.[71] The loss of assets might reduce the chances of the debtor to continue doing business and perhaps be restructured, since the value of assets might be bigger when employed in a going concern than when disposed of independently.[72]

4.7.2 International vis attractiva concursus: Article 6(1)

The EC Regulation 1346/2000 does not directly address the issue whether the courts of the Member State where the insolvency proceedings have been opened have international jurisdiction over also all actions arising from the insolvency.[73] It provided for the recognition and enforcement of judgments "deriving directly from the insolvency proceedings and which are closely linked to them", however it does not address the issue of jurisdiction.

The issue was resolved by the CJEU in its decision in *Seagon v Deko Marty Belgium NV*,[74] which case was about a transaction avoidance action brought under German insolvency law. It was held that Article 3 of the Regulation had to be interpreted as conferring jurisdiction in actions directly deriving from and closely connected to the insolvency proceedings.[75]

[69] *Christopher Seagon v Deko Marty Belgium NV* C-339/07 [2009] ECR I-767.

[70] Keay (2017), p. 82.

[71] McCormack et al. (2016), p. 139.

[72] Mucciarelli (2013), p. 179.

[73] Fabok (2017), p. 298.

[74] *Christopher Seagon v Deko Marty Belgium NV* C-339/07 [2009] ECR I-767.

[75] According to the CJEU case law, insolvency related actions are the following: "avoidance actions, actions on the personal liability of directors based on insolvency law, lawsuits relating to the admission or the ranking of a claim, disputes between the liquidator and the debtor on whether an asset belongs to the bankrupt's estate and disputes related to the exercise of the powers of the liquidator, including the related liability issues", see Fabok (2017), p. 297.

In a following case that came before it, *Schmid v Hertel*,[76] the CJEU, held that even if the transaction avoidance action was brought against a person based in a non-member state (in that case, Switzerland), it would suffice if the insolvency proceedings, a result of which would be the annex proceedings, were opened in a member state.

Following the CJEU case law, Article 6(1) of the EU Recast Regulation provides that:

> The courts of the Member State within the territory of which insolvency proceedings have been opened in accordance with Article 3 shall have jurisdiction for any action which derives directly from the insolvency proceedings and is closely linked with them, such as avoidance actions.[77]

According to its wording, Article 6(1) does not set a requirement that a main insolvency proceeding (Article 3.1) is opened. So, the annex jurisdiction of a Member States' courts also exists when a secondary insolvency proceeding (Article 3.2) is opened in that Member State.

Furthermore, Article 32(1)(1) and (2) provides that the automatic recognition system of the Recast Regulation (Article 19 regarding the judgments opening insolvency proceedings) extends to annex judgments too.

It is argued that the Recast Regulation follows the model of the "limited" *vis attractiva concursus*, that is, only insolvency-related actions belong to the jurisdiction of the Member State opening insolvency proceedings and no other commercial actions.[78] In any case, the Recast Regulation does not specify the criteria for assessing whether an action "derives directly" from an insolvency proceeding.[79]

Some Member States' courts and some commentators consider the international jurisdiction in annex cases as exclusive,[80] while others are of the contrary opinion. It seems that CJEU has given no conclusive answer to that.

It must also be pointed out that the wording of Article 6(1) does not clarify whether there would be annex international jurisdiction in case the avoidance action was brought against a person based in a non-member state. If the answer is negative, that would mean that the article has taken a distance from the CJEU's position[81] in the *Schmid* judgment.

---

[76] CJEU case C-328/12 *Schmidt v. Hertel* ECLI:EU:C:2014:6.

[77] Wimmer et al. (2016), p. 99.

[78] Fabok (2017), p. 298.

[79] Mucciarelli (2016), p. 23.

[80] Brinkmann (2013), p. 372; Lennarts (2010), p. 110.

[81] Wimmer et al. (2016), p. 100.

4.8 Specific Issues

4.8.1 *The Influence of EU Regulations on Member States' Autonomous International Insolvency Laws*

The long trajectory of European [Communities, before] Union's works on a European text that would deal with international jurisdiction, choice of law and recognition and enforcement of foreign insolvency proceedings, seems to have influenced some Member States' respective legislative works on their autonomous international insolvency laws. Three of these Member States are Germany, Austria and Spain.[82]

According to the autonomous German international insolvency law the recognition of foreign insolvency proceedings is contained in §§ 343 ff. Insolvenz Ordnung (InsO). German international insolvency law is always enforced, when the [insolvency] proceeding is opened in a third state or when the European Insolvency Regulation cannot be applied, because it does not cover the subject matter of the case.

§ 343 par. 1 abs. 1 says: "The opening of a foreign insolvency proceeding shall be [is] recognized". The German legislator has decided to stipulate the automatic recognition of foreign insolvency proceedings and to enforce the principles of universality and unity in international insolvency cases.

According to § 343 InsO, the recognition of a foreign insolvency proceedings is only then refused, when (1) the court that opened the insolvency proceedings is not considered as having had [indirect] jurisdiction to do so, or (2) the recognition would offend the German *ordre public*. This is the main difference between the German recognition procedure and the EU Insolvency Regulation recognition procedure: In the second case, the indirect jurisdiction is not being examined, while according to the German autonomous international insolvency law, this one of the few requirements for the recognition of a foreign insolvency.

The foreign insolvency proceeding must be a validly opened one. It must correspond, functionally, to a German insolvency proceeding.[83]

It could be said that Germany, not only has reverted her previous negative stance towards foreign insolvencies,[84] but has created perhaps the best structured private international law (lato sensu, including international procedural law) rules regarding

---

[82] Not only Member States' insolvency rules have been influenced by the European Regulations, but other countries insolvency rules have also been influenced. Such an example is Norway: On April 1, 2016, the Ministry of Justice and Public Security proposed new rules on cross-border insolvencies and on June 17, 2016, the Parliament unanimously adopted the proposal. The new rules adopt the concept of the "center of main interests" (COMI), in accordance with Article 3 of the Regulation 848/2015. Sections 161 and 163(1)(a) of the new rules implicitly refer to the European concept, see Ali and Røsæg (2015–2016), p. 388.

[83] Strickler (2017), p. 230.

[84] See Moustaira (1992), pp. 40–51 and 177–183, about §§ 237 and 238, respectively, of the Konkursrdnung that was in force until 1999.

insolvency in the whole European Union, by legislating in detail about recognition of foreign insolvencies not covered by the EU Regulations. The rules in both circumstances have many similarities; perhaps one could say that Germany's national rules of private international law regarding insolvency proceedings are a "creative legal transplanting"—and a successful one—of EU Regulations' rules.

According to the autonomous Austrian international insolvency law, the recognition of foreign insolvency proceedings is contained in § 240 IO. The Austrian legislator has decided to apply rules like the ones contained in the EU Insolvency Regulation, also in cases of insolvencies opened in third States. According to the Insolvenzrechtsnovelle (IIrG 2003), foreign insolvency proceedings are recognized, under certain requirements, *ipso iure*, that is without a specific recognition procedure.[85]

The Spanish Insolvency Act of 2003, for the first time in Spanish legal history, as is stated, refers to cross-border insolvencies.[86] It contains rules on international jurisdiction, on applicable law and on recognition and enforcement of foreign insolvency proceedings.[87] These rules apply only to situations falling outside the scope of Regulation (then 1346/2000 and now 848/2015).

The rules on international jurisdiction and applicable law are drafted in line with the respective articles of the Regulation 1346/2000. The rule on recognition of foreign non-community insolvency proceedings could not be in line with the Regulation, it is argued, since those insolvency proceedings are "opened outside the harmonized legal framework"[88] developed by the Regulation.

Thus, according to Article 220 of the Insolvency Act, foreign judgments opening an insolvency proceeding shall be recognized in Spain following the exequatur proceeding that the Spanish Civil Procedure Act of 1881 foresees. The recognition depends upon the fulfillment of several conditions and in certain cases it may be modified or revoked.

4.8.2 The Special Case of United Kingdom

As it is pointed out, the UK has four simultaneous legal regimes for cross-border insolvency cases:

(a) With regard to other EU Member States, the European Insolvency Regulation applies—the 1346/2000 until 25.6.2017 and the Recast afterwards. Brexit will influence that.[89]

---

[85] Strickler (2017), p. 269.

[86] Barona Vilar and Esplugues Mota (2011), p. 74.

[87] Esplugues Mota (2006), p. 9.

[88] Barona Vilar and Esplugues Mota (2011), p. 84.

[89] See *infra*, Sect. 4.8.2.3.

(b) With regard to Commonwealth states, section 426 of the Insolvency Act 1986 applies.
(c) With regard to all other states, the provisions of the Cross-Border Insolvency Regulation 2006 which incorporated the UNCITRAL Model Law 1997[90] into English insolvency law apply.
(d) English common law imposes duties of cooperation.[91]

Under the English common law, English courts have the power to assist foreign courts and help a foreign representative, pursuant to the principle of comity, to act in United Kingdom according to domestic English law.

Far back in 1764, English courts recognized for the first time extraterritorial effects of a foreign bankruptcy—and particularly in England. In *Solomons v Ross*,[92] "trustees in bankruptcy appointed in Amsterdam were allowed to collect assets in England which had been garnished by an English creditor shortly before the trustees were appointed in Amsterdam."[93]

The reasoning of the court in that case was not clear. Subsequent references, though, to that case considered it as based on the idea of "comity of nations". So, in *Alivon v Furnival*, a case of 1834, *Solomons v Ross* was cited in support of the court's reasoning:

> The property in the effects of the bankrupt does not appear to be absolutely transferred to these [French] syndics in the way that those of a bankrupt are in this country; but it should seem that the syndics act as mandatories or agents for the creditors; the whole three or any two or one of them having the power to sue for and recover the debts in their own names. This is a peculiar right of action, created by the law of that country; and we think it may by the comity of nations be enforced in this, as much as the right of foreign assignees or curators, or foreign corporations, appointed or created in a different way from that which the law of this country requires.[94]

In the recent case *Agbaje v Akinnoye-Agbaje*, the UK Supreme Court described comity as follows:

> 52. First, comity is sometimes used not simply in the sense of courtesy to foreign states and their courts, but also in the sense of rules of public international law which establish the proper limits of national legislative jurisdiction in cases involving a foreign element. In that sense it will be contrary to comity for United Kingdom legislation to apply in a situation involving a foreign country when the United Kingdom has no reasonable relationship with the situation. …
>
> 53. The second relevant sense in which comity is used is that a court in one country should not lightly characterize the law or judicial decisions of another country as unjust.
>
> 54. The third sense in which comity may be relevant is that it is said to be the basis for the enforcement and recognition of foreign judgments.[95]

---

[90] See *infra*, Sect. 5.

[91] Bork (2017), p. 247; Bowen (2013), p. 121.

[92] (1764) 1 HBI 131.

[93] According to Nadelmann (1946), p. 154, this is "the leading case on the effect in England of bankruptcy declared abroad."

[94] *Alivon v Furnival* (1834) 149 ER 1084. See about this Godwin et al. (2017), pp. 7–8.

[95] *Agbaje v Akkinoye-Agbaje* [2010] 1 AC 628, 650–651.

British influences on the original EU Insolvency Regulation were important, but it seems that even more important was the British impact, after that Regulation went into effect.[96]

According to an opinion, the reason was the British imperial history. British courts were very experienced in coordinating foreign insolvency proceedings with domestic ones or, rather, in recognizing foreign insolvency proceedings especially when those "foreign" proceedings were arising within the British Empire. Thus, in 1914 there had been enacted an Insolvency Act that governed insolvency proceedings opened anywhere in the Empire.[97]

So, the country was following since then the principle of universalism of insolvencies, specifically for the proceedings opened in the Empire, though; it was an "Imperial universalism". The country continued to enforce this principle even after the fall of British Empire, after WWII, and in a way codified it in the Insolvency Act of 1986.[98]

4.8.2.1 Schemes of Arrangement: Pre-insolvency Initiatives

This is an English, unique until recently[99] among EU Member States procedure, that allows financially distressed companies to work out problematic bank or bond debt without having to commence an insolvency proceeding.[100] Schemes of arrangement often bind dissenting creditors to a financial restructuring whose aim is to avoid an insolvency proceeding.[101]

It is one of the oldest restructuring procedures available in the United Kingdom.[102] It was initially created with the Companies Act of 1862.[103] The need for court sanction was introduced in the Joint Stock Companies Arrangement Act 1870, s 2. Back then, schemes of arrangement were permitted only between the company and its creditors and classes of creditors. Companies Act 1900, s 24 permitted schemes of arrangement with members and classes of members too. The essential statutory regime of today is the same as the one enacted in the Companies Act 1929, ss 153 & 154.[104]

---

[96] So it was a kind of revenge, from UK's part, since when the country adhered to European Communities, back in 1973, it could not accept the Draft Bankruptcy Convention that had been proposed, claiming that the influence of civil law was too big.

[97] Hoffman (1995–1996), pp. 2510–2512.

[98] Block-Lieb (2017), pp. 1393–1394.

[99] There is a Dutch proposal for a scheme of arrangement "Dutch Style", see Renssen (2017), pp. 214–215.

[100] Payne (2013), p. 563.

[101] Block-Lieb (2018), p. 12.

[102] Kastrinou and Jacobs (2016), p. 97 and note 38.

[103] Companies Act 1862 (25 & 26 Vict. C.89), at § 126.

[104] Bailey (2015), p. 350.

The current provisions are found in Part 26 of the Companies Act (CA) of 2006.[105] They are distinct from both purely contractual workouts and reorganization proceedings.

The popularity of this very flexible procedure is steadily rising over the last decades and so are the corporate migrations from other countries to take advantage of this procedure.

British courts keep a positive stance towards these corporate migrations and courts of other European countries have not reacted negatively towards them.[106]

The scheme is a compromise or arrangement between the company and its creditors or any class of them or between the company and its members, or any class of them. Four are the steps that the process involves:

(1) The 'Convening Hearing': (a) the company or (b) any creditor or member of the company or (c) the liquidator or administrator (if the company is already in formal insolvency proceeding) makes an application to the court, for a meeting to be summoned to achieve the above compromise or arrangement (CA 2006, s. 896).
(2) Summoning the meeting: a notice of the meeting together with a statement that explains the effect of the compromise or arrangement is sent to all creditors and members of the company (CA 2006, s. 897).
(3) Approving the proposal: the compromise or arrangement must be approved by 75% of the creditors or members who are present and voting at the meeting either in person or by proxy (CA 2006, s. 899).
(4) The 'Sanction Hearing': if the compromise or arrangement is approved at the meeting an application must be made to the court for the compromise or arrangement to be sanctioned (CA 2006, s. 899).[107]

The court may not sanction a scheme even where it has received the approval of creditors, if it is not satisfied that the classes of creditors were fairly represented by the parties who attended the meeting and that the terms of the scheme are fair. It also may not sanction a scheme if it is not convinced that all procedural requirements have been complied with.[108]

Once an arrangement becomes binding under the scheme, it binds all creditors, including the dissenting ones.[109]

[105] Companies Act 2006, at § 895.

[106] Hermanns (2013).

[107] Bailey (2015), pp. 351–352.

[108] See Renssen (2017), p. 215, who states that according to the proposed in the Netherlands regulation of schemes of arrangement (there are differences between this and the English respective procedure), "[t]he court will refuse to adopt a scheme in the following cases: • The interests of one or more creditors or shareholders would be damaged disproportionally by adopting the scheme. • The compliance of the scheme is not sufficiently guaranteed. • The scheme is based on deception. Other material reasons give grounds for refusing to adopt the scheme."

[109] Kastrinou and Jacobs (2016), pp. 97–99.

The problem is that these schemes of arrangement are not included in the EU Insolvency Regulation's list of procedures,[110] either because the British delegation explicitly asked that or because the definition of "insolvency proceedings" in the EU Regulation is far narrower.[111]

Not being included in the EU Insolvency Regulation's list of procedures means that neither the jurisdictional bases nor the rules about automatic recognition and enforcement of the Regulation may be applied—or, at least, it is a matter of dispute, whether they may.

So, the question is: how such a scheme of arrangement, either of an English company or of a foreign company would be enforceable against creditors residing in EU Member States?[112]

English courts have referred to academic opinion letters offered as evidence which letters argue in favor of the application of the Brussels I Regulation—whether the original 44/2000 or the revised 1215/2012.

This is doubtful, though. Both Regulations identically state that the "Regulation shall not apply" to "bankruptcy, proceedings relating to the winding-up of insolvent companies or other legal persons, judicial arrangements, compositions and analogous proceedings."[113] Furthermore, Brussels Regulation refers to defendants, its scope is mainly adversarial proceedings,[114] and does not really suit to the non-adversarial, multi-party structure of the schemes of arrangement.[115]

There has also been discussed whether the Rome Regulation on the law applicable to contractual obligations would have something to say, in these issues, since Article 12 provides that the governing law of the contract should also govern the various ways of extinguishing obligations and prescriptions and limitations on actions in relation to the contract. Others deny that, considering Article 1(2)(f) of the Rome Regulation, which states that questions governed by the law of companies are excluded from the ambit of the Regulation.

It seems that according to several expert opinions that were given by, among others, German, Dutch, Spanish to English courts, the latter were convinced that their orders sanctioning foreign schemes of arrangement would be likely enforced somehow in the other EU Member States.[116]

A notable exception to the generally positive—or non-negative—reaction of the courts of the EU Member States towards these English courts' scheme orders is the

---

[110] United Kingdom did not want that the Schemes of arrangement be included in the substantive scope of the Insolvency Regulation. See Iodice (2015), p. 1093; De Cesari (2015), p. 1026.

[111] Eidenmüller (2018).

[112] Kortman and Veder (2015), p. 251.

[113] Article 1(2)(b).

[114] Kuipers (2012), p. 225.

[115] See Block-Lieb (2018), p. 20, who suggests that "[t]his requirement may be met where there is at least one defendant-creditor residing in England, but given modern debt structures the residence of the company's creditors may not be easy to determine."

[116] Block-Lieb (2018), p. 22.

case of *Equitable Life*, before the *Bundesgerichtshof* (the German Federal Supreme Court) in 2012.[117]

The German Court upheld an intermediate appellate court decision that had refused to recognize an English court's order sanctioning creditor approval of a scheme of arrangement that involved Equitable Life, a mutual life assurance company incorporated in the United Kingdom.

The German policy holders had voted against the English scheme of arrangement, but they were too few and too small in value, so that although dissenting they could not preclude the English court's order that bound them to the arrangement.

In the litigation that followed in German courts, the latter held that the English scheme of arrangement could not invoke either the EU insolvency Regulation or the Brussels Regulation. The Equitable Life scheme of arrangement involved an insurance company. The Brussels Regulation has specific jurisdictional requirements for insurance cases: the insurer has to bring proceedings in the courts of the EU Member States in which its creditors are domiciled, whether the creditors are policyholders, insured persons or beneficiaries of a company domiciled in another EU Member State.[118] Considering the above said, the German Court stated that the German policyholders were not bound by the English court's order.[119]

What is perhaps more interesting is the fact that often U.S. scholars (hypothetically of similar or at least relative legal mentality) are hostile to the recognition of the British schemes of arrangement.[120]

Nevertheless, it seems that several such schemes have been approved by U.S. courts, under Chapter 15,[121] as "foreign proceedings". It is even more interesting that such schemes have been recognized by U.S. bankruptcy courts in cases of companies that could not have direct access to U.S. bankruptcy jurisdiction—for example insurance companies. Thus, U.S. bankruptcy courts have held that solvent insurers' schemes of arrangement may be recognized under Chapter 15, although neither a domestic nor a foreign insurance company could otherwise access US bankruptcy jurisdiction.[122] And thus, as it is pointed out, once recognized, the schemes become binding in the two leading financial jurisdictions.[123]

4.8.2.2 Codere Case: Good Forum Shopping?

A case that shows exactly the popularity of this pre-insolvency procedure among not only British companies is the *Codere case*.[124]

---

[117] Der Bundesgerichtshof 15 Februar 2012, IV ZR 194/09.

[118] Brussels Regulation 2000, Article 12; Brussels Revised Regulation 2012, Article 14.

[119] Block-Lieb (2018), p. 22.

[120] Johnston (2007), p. 6.

[121] See *infra*, Sect. 5.2.1.1.

[122] Morton (2006), p. 1312.

[123] Couwenberg and Lubben (2015), p. 726.

[124] Block-Lieb (2018), pp. 8–9.

A Spanish corporation, Codere SA, engaged in gaming services in Spain, Italy, and several countries of Latin America, had financial difficulties since many years. It (the group of companies) wanted to avoid insolvency proceedings in Spain or in any other country and so it formed Codere Finance (UK) Ltd. to be able to take advantage of the above British pre-insolvency procedure.

The new, British, subsidiary assumed most of the debt of the Codere group—which group had initially borrowed by Codere Finance (Luxembourg) SA. The assumed debt was governed by New York law, guaranteed by the Spanish parent company Codere SA and other group companies and it was subject to an English law inter-creditor agreement that had originally been made in 2005.

Codere Finance (UK) Ltd. convened a meeting of creditors for consideration of a proposed scheme of arrangement. Creditors were convinced that the scheme of arrangement would be much more favorable to them than a Spanish insolvency proceeding, which could be very risky for their claims, so they—"with claims totaling more than 98 percent of the value of the outstanding indebtedness"—voted in favor of the scheme.

A London High Court was asked to sanction the *Codere* scheme of arrangement. The court approved the scheme, acknowledging that the group had engaged in forum shopping, however it said that in this case, the forum shopping should be forgiven, because it was "good forum shopping", since Codere had not acted in bad faith, but on the contrary it had worked in tandem with its creditors and had elected the scheme of arrangement solution to maximize the repayment of creditors.[125]

So, may it be concluded that there is a "good forum shopping", a "good forum selling" in the case of foreign schemes of arrangement[126] and perhaps in other cases too? Or is it just a cynical stance of the big "players", entrepreneurs, which tends to be consecrated?

4.8.2.3 Brexit: What Next?

Brexit means that United Kingdom will become a simple "Third State". There will be neither freedom of establishment of companies in European Union nor recognition of other Member States' insolvency proceedings—nor the opposite. On an English insolvency proceeding, that will want to be recognized in a European Member State normally it will be the national rules of that State that will be applied and not the Article 16 of the European Insolvency Regulation. Therefore, the recognition—or not—will depend on whether the general private international law of insolvency of that country applies the universality or the territoriality principle.[127]

[125] *Re Codere Finance (UK) Ltd.* [2015] EWHC 3778 (Ch.).

[126] Klerman (2007), pp. 1182–1183.

[127] Weller et al. (2016), p. 2382.

As it is mentioned, there is discussion of a Great Repeal Bill,[128] the aim of which would be to domesticate EU law as the law of the United Kingdom. But even if such a Great Repeal Bill could succeed in binding the United Kingdom to EU law that thus would become UK law, it would not oblige the Member States of the European Union to reciprocate.[129] It would only be a unilateral movement.

As it is noted, the EU treaties will cease to apply to the UK and so will the Recast EIR, because that regulation is based on reciprocity between Member States and they will no longer apply it in their relations with UK after 'Brexit', in the absence of an agreement on this in the exit treaties. Whether the exit treaties will include any special rules on insolvency matters is unknown however it is rather doubtful.[130]

On 13 September 2018, a Guidance was published by the UK Ministry of Justice, Department for Business, Energy & Industrial Strategy, about "Handling civil legal cases that involve EU countries if there's no Brexit deal".

According to this Guidance, after 29 March 2019, if there is no deal, "[t]he majority of the Insolvency Regulation, …, would be repealed in all parts of the UK. We would retain the EU rules that provide for the UK courts to have jurisdiction where a company or individual is based in the UK, and the law will ensure that insolvency proceedings can continue to be opened in those circumstances. But after exit, the EU Insolvency Regulation test would no longer restrict the opening of proceedings, and so it would also be possible to open insolvency proceedings under any of the tests set out in our domestic UK law, regardless of whether (or where) the debtor is based elsewhere in Europe."

Furthermore, it is stated that "EU insolvency proceedings and judgments would no longer be recognizable in the UK under the EU Insolvency Regulation, but may be recognized under the UNCITRAL Model Law on Cross-Border Insolvency, which already forms part of the UK's domestic rules on recognizing foreign insolvencies."

4.8.3 The Influence of EU Regulations on the Global Rules on Conflict-of-Laws Matters in Insolvency Cases Drafted by the American Law Institute and the International Insolvency Institute

The American Law Institute and the International Insolvency Institute published in 2012 a study entitled "Global Rules on Conflict-of-Laws Matters in Insolvency Cases" in which study they proposed rules like those in the European Insolvency Regulation 1346/2000.

---

[128] Parliament, House of Lords, Select Committee on the Constitution, The "Great Repeal Bill" and delegated powers, 9th Report, HL Paper 123 (March 7, 2017), *available at* https://publications.parliament.uk/pa/ld201617/ldselect/ldconst/123/12302.htm.

[129] Block-Lieb (2017), p. 1408.

[130] Carballo Piñeiro (2017), pp. 272–273.

The Global Rules recognize several exceptions to the primacy of the *lex fori concursus*. These exceptions include, among others, those relating to labor and financial contracts, protection of the *in rem* rights of secured creditors under the law of a state other than that of the foreign main proceeding, protection of setoff rights, and defenses to avoidance proceedings, unless the law of the state other than the forum has no substantial relationship to the parties or the transaction, and there is no other reasonable basis for the selection of the law of that state as the law to govern the transaction in question.

The Reporters explained as following the why of so many exceptions; they said that a more limited

> range of exceptions to the dominant role of the *lex concursus* is unlikely to prove commercially convenient or acceptable to the majority of parties engaged in international trade and business, given the present stage of uneven development of national laws governing such sensitive matters as security interests, set-off, and transaction avoidance. We therefore proclaim our allegiance to the alternative approach embodied in articles 4-15 of the EU Regulation (notably in articles 5, 6 and 13) whereby additional exceptions to the application of the *lex concursus* are permitted, under controlled circumstances…[131]

References

Ali FA, Røsæg E (2015–2016) New rules on cross-border insolvencies in Norway. Yearb Priv Int Law 17:385–394

Bailey E (2015) The insolvency of groups of companies in English law. Int Insolv Law Rev:344–363

Bariatti S (2004) Le garanzie finanziarie nell'insolvenza transnazionale: l'attuazione della direttiva 2002/47/CE. Rivista di diritto internazionale privato e processuale:841–876

Barona Vilar S, Esplugues Mota C (2011) International bankruptcy in Spain, pp 73–88. Available at: https://ssrn.com/abstract=1952782

Benedetelli MV (2011) "Centre of Main Interests" of the Debtor under EU Regulation n. 1346/2000 and Insolvency of Cross-Border Groups: a Private International Law Perspective. In: Insolvency and Cross-border Groups (ed) UNCITRAL Recommendations for a European Perspective? Banca d'Italia Eurosistema, vol 69. Quaderni di Ricerca Giuridica della Consulenza Legale, pp 121–134

Block-Lieb S (2017) The UK and EU cross-border insolvency recognition: from Empire to Europe to "Going It Alone". Fordham Int Law J 40:1373–1412

Block-Lieb S (2018) Reaching to restructure across borders (without over-reaching), even after Brexit. Am Bankruptcy Law J 92:1–52

Bork R (2017) The European Insolvency Regulation and the UNCITRAL model law on cross-border insolvency. Int Insolv Rev 26:246–269

Bowen M (2013) An introduction to the fundamental principles governing cross-border insolvency in an English law context. Int Insolv Law Rev:121–131

Brinkmann M (2013) Avoidance claims in the context of the recast EIR. Int Insolv Law Rev:371–383

---

[131] American Law Institute, *Global Rules on Conflict-of-Laws Matters in Insolvency Cases*, *in* Transnational insolvency: global principles for cooperation in international insolvency cases (2012). Available at: http://www.iiiglobal.org/component/jdownloads/finish/557/5932.htm. Professors Bob Wessels and Ian Fletcher were the Reporters.

Carballo Piñeiro L (2014) Towards the reform of the European Insolvency Regulation: codification rather than modification. Nederland International Privaatrecht:207–215
Carballo Piñeiro L (2017) Brexit and international insolvency beyond the realm of mutual trust. Int Insolv Rev 26:270–294
Carruthers JM (2017) Jurisdiction in secondary and territorial proceedings. In: Queirolo I, Dominelli S (eds) European and national perspectives on the application of the European Insolvency Regulation. Aracne editrice, Roma, pp 65–81
Castelló Pastor JJ, Gómez Fonseca F (2017) Scope of application of the regulation (EU) 2015/848 on insolvency proceedings. In: Queirolo I, Dominelli S (eds) European and national perspectives on the application of the European Insolvency Regulation. Aracne editrice, Roma, pp 21–37
Couwenberg O, Lubben SJ (2015) Corporate bankruptcy tourists. Bus Lawyer 70:719–750
Dal Maso E (2013) Ancora sugli effetti dell'apertura di una procedura d'insolvenza transfrontaliera sul sequestro conservativo di nave. Il diritto maritimo:198–204
Daniele L (2002) Legge applicabile e diritto uniforme nel regolamento comunitario relative alle procedure di insolvenza. Rivista di diritto internazionale privato e processuale:33–50
de Boer MB, Wessels B (2008) The dominance of main insolvency proceedings under the European Insolvency Regulation. In: Omar P (ed) International insolvency law. Themes and perspectives. Routledge, London and New York, pp 185–208
De Cesari P (2015) Il regolamento 2015/848. Il Fallimento e le alter procedure concorsuali, pp 1026–1037
De Miguel Asensio PA (2015) La evolución del régimen Europeo sobre procedimientos de insolvencia. La Ley Unión Europea 28:1–8
DeLaughter H (2016) Why two facets of Chapter 15 rulings hinder cross-border insolvency petitions in the United States. Emory Bankruptcy Dev J 32:397–431
Eidenmüller H (2005) Free choice in international company insolvency law in Europe. Eur Bus Organ Law Rev 6:423–447
Eidenmüller H (2009) Abuse of law in the context of European insolvency law. Eur Company Financ Law Rev 6:1–28
Eidenmüller H (2013) A new framework for business restructuring in Europe: the EU commission's proposal for a reform of the European Insolvency Regulation and beyond. Working Paper No 199/2013, ECGI Working Paper Series in Law, March 2013, pp 1–22. Available at: http://ssrn.com/abstract=2230690
Eidenmüller H (2018) What is an insolvency proceeding? Am Bankruptcy Law J 92. Available at: https://ssrn.com/abstract=2712628
Enriques L, Gelter M (2006) Regulatory competition in European company law and creditor protection. Eur Bus Organ Law Rev 7:417–453
Esplugues Mota C (2006) Procedimientos de insolvencia transfronterizos. Revista Sequência 52:9–34
Fabok Z (2017) Grounds for refusal of recognition of (quasi-) annex judgments in the recast European Insolvency Regulation. Int Insolv Rev 26:295–313
Fehrenbach M (2013) Die Rechtsprechung des EuGH zur Europäischen Insolvenzordnung: Der Mittelpunkt der hauptsächlichen Interessen und andere Entwicklungen im Europäischen Insolvenzrecht. Zeitschrift für Europäisches Privatrecht:353–383
Gant JL (2016) Studies in convergence? Post-crisis effects on corporate rescue and the influence of social policy: the EU and the USA. Int Insolv Rev 25:72–96
Ghio E (2017) Case study on cross-border insolvency and rescue law: an analysis of the future of European integration. Irish J Eur Law 20:63–79
Godwin A, Howse T, Ramsay I (2017) The inherent power of common law courts to provide assistance in cross-border insolvencies: from comity to complexity. Int Insolv Rev 26:5–39
Gruber UP (2017) The international jurisdiction for main proceedings: practical difficulties in the application of Art. 3 InsRRecast. In: Queirolo I, Dominelli S (eds) European and national perspectives on the application of the European Insolvency Regulation. Aracne editrice, Roma, pp 39–63

Hermanns R (2013) Consequences of the German equitable life – decision for the use of English schemes of arrangement in cross-border reorganizations. INSOL World 35. Available at: http://www.debrauw.com/wp-content/uploads/2013/09/Insol-World-Consequences-of-the-German-Equitable-Life.pdf
Hoffman L (1995–1996) Cross-border insolvency: a British perspective. Fordham Law Rev 64:2507–2520
Iodice F (2015) *Scheme of arrangement* tra raccomandazione della commissione e riforma del regolamento sulle procedure di insolvenza. Il Fallimento e le altre procedure concorsuali:1093–1105
Johnston S (2007) Why U.S. courts should deny or severely condition recognition to schemes of arrangement for solvent insurance companies. Norton J Bankruptcy Law Pract 16:953–974
Kastrinou A, Jacobs L (2016) Pre-insolvency procedures: a United Kingdom and South African perspective. In: Parry R, Omar PJ (eds) Reimagining rescue. INSOL Europe, Nottingham/Paris, pp 91–108
Keay A (1996) In pursuit of the rationale behind the avoidance of pre-liquidation transactions. Sydn Law Rev 18:56
Keay A (2017) The harmonization of the avoidance rules in European Union insolvencies. Int Comp Law Q 66:79–105
Klerman D (2007) Jurisdictional competition and the evolution of the common law. Univ Chic Law Rev 74:1179
Kortman L, Veder M (2015) The uneasy case for schemes of arrangement under English law in relation to non-UK companies in financial distress: pushing Europe? Nottingham Insolv Bus Law E-J 3:239–261
Kuipers J-J (2012) Schemes of arrangement and voluntary collective redress: a gap in the Brussels I Regulation. J Priv Int Law 8:225–249
Lennarts L (2010) EU corporate insolvency law in the wake of the ECJ's Deko Marty judgment. Eur Company Law 7:106–112
Mangano R (2017) From 'Prisoner's Dilemma' to reluctance to use judicial discretion: the enemies of cooperation in European cross-border cases. Int Insolv Rev 26:314–331
McCormack G (2012) Universalism in insolvency proceedings and the common law. Oxf J Leg Stud:325–347
McCormack G (2014) Reforming the European Insolvency Regulation: a legal and policy perspective. J Priv Int Law:41–67
McCormack G (2016) Something old, something new: recasting the European Insolvency Regulation. Mod Law Rev 79:121–146
McCormack G, Keay A, Brown S, Dahlgreen J (2016) Study on a new approach to business failure and insolvency. Comparative legal analysis of the Member States' relevant provisions and practices. Tender No. JUST/2014/JCOO/PR/CIVI/0075 University of Leeds. Available at: https://ec.europa.eu/info/sites/info/files/insolvency_study_2016_final_en.pdf
Mevorach I (2008) The "home country" of a multinational enterprise group facing insolvency. Int Comp Law Q 57:427–448
Mevorach I (2013) Forum shopping in times of crisis: a directors' duties perspective. Eur Company Financ Law Rev 10:523–553
Mevorach I (2018) The future of cross-border insolvency. Overcoming biases and closing gaps. Oxford University Press
Michalopoulos GN (2013) The pre-bankruptcy procedures of insolvency of the Bankruptcy Code [in Greek]. Nomiki Bibliothiki, Athens
Morton JD (2006) Recognition of cross-border insolvency proceedings: an evaluation of solvent schemes of arrangement and Part VII transfers under U.S. Chapter 15. Fordham Int Law J 29:1312–1363
Moustaira EN (1992) The equality of creditors in international bankruptcy law [in Greek]. Ant.N. Sakkoulas Publishers, Athens/Komotini
Mucciarelli F (2013) Not just efficiency: insolvency law in the EU and its political dimension. Eur Bus Organ Law Rev 14:175–200

Mucciarelli FM (2016) Private international law rules in the insolvency regulation recast: a reform or a restatement of the *Status Quo*? Eur Company Finance Rev:1–30

Nadelmann K (1946) *Solomons v Ross* and international bankruptcy law. Mod Law Rev 9:154–168

Noel J, Lemontey J "Report on the Convention Relating to Bankruptcies, Compositions and Analogous Procedures" (Commission of the European Communities Working Document 16.775/XIV/70-F, 1970)

Omar PJ (2003) Genesis of the European initiative in insolvency law. Int Insolv Rev 12:147–170

Ortega Rueda JD (2016) Insolvencia en la Unión Europea. El principio de la universalidad en los procedimientos concursales transfronterizos. Dottorato di ricerca, Università di Bologna. Available at: http://amsdottorato.unibo.it/7287/1/Ortega_Rueda%2C_José_David_-_tesis.pdf

Payne J (2013) Cross-border schemes of arrangement and forum shopping. Eur Bus Organ Law Rev 14:563–589

Pérez Ragone ÁJ, Martínez Benavides P (2015) Del sobreendeudamiento a la insolvencia: Fase de crisis del deudor desde el derecho comparado europeo. Revista Chilena de Derecho 42:93–121

Pottow JAE (2005) Procedural incrementalism: a model for international bankrutpcy. Va J Int Law 45:935–1015

Renssen S (2017) Corporate restructuring and corporate dissolution of companies in financial distress: ensuring creditor protection. A comparison of the US, UK and Dutch models. Int Insolv Rev 26:204–228

Schürmeyer J (2018) Die Insolvenzgeldvorfinanzierung. Ein Sanierungsinstrument für polnische Insolvenzverfahren? V & R unipress, Universitätsverlag Osnabrück

Strickler P (2017) Die Anerkennung ausländischer Insolvenzverfahren in der Schweiz im Vergleich mit Deutschland, Österreich und der Europäischen Union. Schulthess, Zürich-Basel-Genf

Tirado I (2015) An evolution of COMI in the European Insolvency Regulation: from 'Insolvenzimperialismus' to the recast. Annu Rev Insolv Law:691–722

Torremans P (2008) Coming to terms with the COMI concept in the European Insolvency Regulation. In: Omar P (ed) International insolvency law. Themes and perspectives. Routledge, London and New York, pp 173–184

Tung F (2001) Is international bankruptcy possible? Mich J Int Law 23:31–102

van Calster G (2015) COMIng, and here to stay. The review of the European Insolvency Regulation. Available at: https://ssrn.com/abstract=2637003

van Zwieten K (2016) An introduction to the European Insolvency Regulation, as made and as recast. In: Bork R, van Zwieten K (eds) Commentary on the European Insolvency Regulation. Oxford University Press. Available at: https://ssrn.com/abstract=2775814

Virgós VM, Garcimartín F (2004) The European Insolvency Regulation: law and practice. Kluwer Law International

Virgós M, Schmidt E "Report on the Convention of Insolvency Proceedings", EC Council Document 6500/96, Brussels, 3 May 1996

Warren E (1993) Bankruptcy policymaking in an imperfect world. Mich Law Rev 92:336–387

Weiss M (2015) Bridge over troubled water: the revised insolvency regulation. Int Insolv Rev 24:192–213

Weller M-P, Thomale C, Benz N (2016) Englische Gesellschaften und Unternehmensinsolvenzen in der Post-Brexit-EU. Neue Juristische Wochenschrift:2378–2383

Westbrook JL (2007) Locating the eye of the financial storm. Brooklyn J Int Law 32:1019–1040

Wimmer K, Bornemann A, Lienau MD (2016) Die Neufassung der EuInsVO. Luchterhand Verlag, Köln

Chapter 5
UNCITRAL Model Law 1997

5.1 General Comments

The UNCITRAL Model Law on Cross-Border Insolvency 1997 was developed to address problems and procedural differences between the countries, when handling issues of international insolvency. It was prepared in the frame of, and promulgated by UNCITRAL, "with the goals of enhancing cooperation between the actors in cross-border insolvency, promoting legal certainty in trade and investment, ensuring the fair and efficient administration of cross-border insolvencies, protecting debtors' assets and rescuing businesses."[1]

UNCITRAL's challenge in negotiating the Model Law, it is declared, was to create a text that "could be more inclusive and broader in application"[2] than the texts that other international organizations had proposed the previous years, and that could be accepted by all legal traditions, independently also of the economic development of the aimed countries.[3] It must be pointed out, here, that USA has left a major imprint on this Model Law. As it is stated, it mimics the approach to cross-border insolvencies that United States followed in former Section 304 of the 1978 US Bankruptcy Code and in its elaboration by case law.[4]

Until now, it has been enacted (differently by each country) in 44 countries. Mostly interesting is that, in 2015, the 17 West and Central African States Members of *Organisation pour l' Harmonisation en Afrique de Droit des Affaires* (OHADA), as well as Kenya and Malawi adopted insolvency legislation incorporating the Model Law.

The different way of the Model Law's implementation in different countries as well as the different interpretations given by jurists in the countries that have adopted

[1] Mannan (2016), p. 198.

[2] Clift (2014), p. 25.

[3] Clift (2009), p. 424.

[4] Franken (2014), pp. 115–116.

E. Moustaira, *International Insolvency Law*,
https://doi.org/10.1007/978-3-030-04450-3_5

it, are considered by many as hindrances to the prospect of a harmonization and coordination of international insolvency laws.[5]

The fact that USA and UK have adopted the Model Law has led many to believe that more countries would be encouraged to adopt it, that the incorporation of the Model Law by those two countries, as well as the way they understand and enforce it, would have a precedential value for other countries.[6] Still, there are other opinions, according to which this belief has not been proved right.[7]

The mitigated or modified universalism approach that the Model Law has adopted is rather a very positive evolution.[8]

It is "a pragmatic exercise in the art of the possible", it is stated, and with good reason. It is neutral, thus respecting divergent legal traditions, and makes no attempt at substantive unification of insolvency law. Much is left to local implementation and local rules.

It has no binding force, unless locally enacted and it favors flexibility over certainty, although Article 8 promotes harmonized interpretation of Model Law enactments by the countries,[9] providing that in the interpretation of the Model Law, "regard is to be had to its international origin and to the need to promote uniformity in its application."

The Model Law contains no default reciprocity requirements.[10] It favors unilateral commitments to recognition, relief and cooperation as a first step towards a multilateral framework that would be based on a "critical mass reciprocity", that is, a subset of multilateral reciprocity "sufficient to convince each cooperating state that enough other states have joined in reciprocal relationships to ensure the obtaining of the benefits expected to flow from a particular sort of cooperation."[11]

The probably most effective arm/tool of the institution of bankruptcy/insolvency is that it is a non-piecemeal collective process (whether in the form of liquidation or reorganization), banning the seizures of the debtors' assets by individual creditors that would otherwise jeopardize the hopes for a successful procedure and thus increasing the aggregate value of the pool of assets.[12]

By guaranteeing direct cooperation between the administrators of the insolvency proceedings opened in different countries (Article 26) and by making possible a certain cooperation between the courts that have opened the insolvency proceedings (Article 27), the Model Law extends these advantages of the bankruptcy/insolvency

[5] McCormack (2016), p. 136.

[6] Mevorach (2011), p. 517.

[7] Chandra Mohan (2012), p. 199.

[8] But see Leong (2012), p 110.

[9] Walters (2017).

[10] Yamauchi (2007), p. 145.

[11] Westbrook (1991).

[12] McCormack (2016).

institution,[13] which advantages would be extinguished in case the territorialism reigned.

The Model Law, by providing for the possibility of additional relief and for enhanced cooperation between insolvency representatives in different countries, has also the power to mitigate the 'anti-commons' problem, that is, it can block actions that individual creditors might take with a view to frustrating the wishes of the majority.[14]

This mitigated or modified universalism—or, the "artful compromise between universalism and territorialism"[15]—that the Model Law adopts[16] was very much approved by a US court, in the case *ABC Learning Centres Ltd.*[17] Citing an article written by a defendant of universalism of the insolvency,[18] the court said:

> The Model Law reflects a universalism approach to transnational insolvency. It treats the multinational bankruptcy as a single process in the foreign main proceeding, with other courts assisting in the single proceeding. In contrast, under a territorialism approach a debtor must initiate insolvency actions in each country where its property is found. This approach is the so-called 'grab' rule where each country seizes assets and distributes them according to each country's insolvency proceedings.

Thus, the universalists regard the Model Law as incrementally advancing pure universalism,[19] they regard it as universalism's Trojan horse.[20]

UNCITRAL also issued a *Guide to Enactment of the Model Law* (Original Guide), the same year of its adoption. Its aim was to be really a guide to those countries that will want to adopt the Model Law.

In January 2014, UNCITRAL issued a revised *Guide to Enactment and Interpretation of the Model Law* (Revised Guide) to replace the Original Guide.[21]

5.2 Interpretation of [Enactments of] Model Law

Has Model Law a purposivist nature, as most legal scholars believe? Or should textualism prevail, as it does in most countries' bankruptcy law?[22]

---

[13] Holzer (2011), pp. 1894–1895.

[14] Baird and Rasmussen (2010), p. 67.

[15] Walters (2017).

[16] Dawson (2015), p. 53.

[17] *In re ABC Learning Centres Ltd.* (2013) 728 F3d 301.

[18] Guzman (2000).

[19] Bufford (2013), p. 685.

[20] Walters (2017).

[21] Ho (2014), p. 325.

[22] Dawson (2015), p. 62, mentioning that textualism is the prevailing methodology of interpreting the U.S. Bankruptcy Code.

Some argue that textualism suits better to bankruptcy law because it provides for greater certainty,[23] while others point out that, in practice, textualism does not provide greater certainty than purposivism does, because it is not at all certain that the various judges interpret language in the same manner.

The crucial issue in cross-border insolvency cases, regarding the interpretation of the enactments of the Model Law, is that, while inconsistent interpretations in a national level may not be so far away from each other, since they interpret the same text and share the same legal traditions, differences in the interpretation of the Model Law by courts of different countries may be very significant, since they would be the result of different approaches to statutory interpretation and of different legal traditions.[24]

Local legal methods, in general, should not be ignored. Local legal cultures, local legal traditions are very important, they influence both the creation of laws and their enforcement. Obviously, this is also valid for countries' insolvency systems[25] and their application in the cross-border context.[26]

Different interpretations are not something that can be overcome by legislation, they are a consequence of different legal cultures, different legal mentalities.

5.2.1 Common Law Countries

5.2.1.1 USA

Chapter 15 of title 11 of the United States Code was enacted in 2005, as part of the *Bankruptcy Abuse Prevention and Consumer Protection Act*, replacing Section 304 of the Bankruptcy Code. It is based on the Model Law on Cross-Border Insolvency 1997 of UNCITRAL. It was enacted in "an effort by the United States to harmonize international bankruptcy proceedings for the benefit of American businesses operating abroad".[27]

Chapter 15 replaced Section 304 of the 1978 U.S. Bankruptcy Code according to which, previously, US courts were addressing cross-border insolvencies. However, chapter 15 has many principles in common with its predecessor. It specifically

[23] Rasmussen (1993), p. 565.

[24] Dawson (2015), p. 47.

[25] Sullivan et al. (1994), p. 801.

[26] For example, according to the Greek law 3858/2010 that enacted the UNCITRAL Model Law in Greece, foreign pre-bankruptcy, pre-insolvency proceedings are not covered by the law, while in other countries that also enacted the Model Law, such proceedings are covered. It depends on the way each legal order "translated" the phrase of Model Law' art. 2(a): "the proceeding is pursuant to a law relating to insolvency", see Perakis (2010), p. 429 note 42; Athanassiou (2015), p. 88 and note 38.

[27] Tacon v. Petroquest Res. Inc. (*In re* Condor Ins. Ltd.), 601 F.3d319, 322 (5th Cir. 2010).

mentions that US courts should be guided by principles of comity and cooperation in deciding whether to grant relief to foreign representatives.

Neither Section 304 nor Chapter 15 address issues of choice of law. There is no duty of the American bankruptcy courts to apply foreign insolvency law, including foreign rules of distribution.

"Foreign representative" is "a person or body, including a person or body appointed on an interim basis, authorized in a foreign proceeding to administer the reorganization or liquidation of the debtor's assets or affairs or to act as a representative of such foreign proceeding." 11 U.S.C. § 101(24).

If chapter 15 conflicts with an obligation of the United States arising out of a treaty or other international agreement to which the United States is a party with one or more countries, the requirements of the treaty or the other international agreement will prevail.[28]

Section 1501(a) codified the five principal objectives of Chapter 15. They are: "1) to promote cooperation between the United States courts and parties in interest and the courts and other competent authorities of foreign countries involved in cross-border insolvency cases; 2) to establish greater legal certainty for trade and investment; 3) to provide for the fair and efficient administration of cross-border insolvencies that protects the interests of all creditors and other interested entities, including the debtor; 4) to afford protection and maximization of the value of the debtor's assets; and 5) to facilitate the rescue of financially troubled businesses, thereby protecting investment and preserving employment."

According to 11 U.S.C. §§ 1504, "A case under this chapter is commenced by the filing of a petition for recognition of a foreign proceeding under section 1515." According to 11 U.S.C. § 1515(a) (2012), "A foreign representative applies to the court for recognition of a foreign proceeding in which the foreign representative has been appointed by filing a petition for recognition."

It is pointed out that the recognition stage "reflects a pre-commitment to universalism on a procedural level", while the following stage, the so called cooperation stage hesitates between universalism and territorialism or balances the two principles.[29] It is argued that the universality principle that would seem to reign "is tempered by sections 1506, 1515, 1516, and others, whereby U.S. bankruptcy judges still retain a wide amount of control over the administration of domestic assets and creditors' rights."[30]

One can discern four main characteristics of Chapter 15.

Firstly, American bankruptcy courts decide to recognize a foreign proceeding as a main or non-main insolvency proceeding, "regardless of what a foreign court has held it to be."[31]

---

[28] Gilhuly et al. (2016), p. 58.

[29] Dawson (2015), p. 54.

[30] Adams and Fincke (2009), pp. 80–81.

[31] Franken (2014), p. 127.

Secondly, a U.S. court's decision to grant relief or offer aid to foreign representatives depends a lot on whether American creditors are sufficiently protected.

According to Section 1520(a) [Model Law art. 20(a)], upon recognition of a foreign insolvency proceeding, certain immediate relief is offered, such as the application of the US Bankruptcy Code's automatic stay to property of the debtor within the territorial jurisdiction of the U.S., the provisions on adequate protection of the interests of secured creditors, and the provisions about the use, sale and lease of the debtor's property.

According to Section 1521, the court may grant any appropriate relief to the representatives of a foreign main or non-main proceeding, such as a stay of individual actions, proceedings or execution against the debtor's assets, a suspension of the right to transfer, encumber or otherwise dispose of any of the assets of the debtor, or the entrusting of the administration or realization of all or part of the debtor's assets within the territorial jurisdiction of the U.S. to the foreign representative.

As it is pointed out, the Model Law does not expressly permit the application of foreign insolvency law.[32] There was such a provision during the negotiations that led up to the enactment of the Model Law, but the reactions were heated, so it disappeared from the text.

Section 1521(a)(7) limits the effect of the respective Article 21 of the Model Law that gives authority to a recognizing court to grant various reliefs on a discretionary basis, by expressly excluding from the additional relief the relief available under the transactional avoidance provisions of the U.S. Bankruptcy Court.

According to Section 1522, for a court to grant or deny relief, or modify or terminate relief already granted, it must be satisfied that the interests of the creditors and other interested persons, including the debtor, are sufficiently protected. When it is about the turnover of assets to a foreign bankruptcy proceeding, the court needs to be satisfied that the interests of the creditors in the U.S. are sufficiently protected.[33] It is argued that there is a strong statutory basis for holders of priority claims to seek sufficient protection of their interests before assets are transferred abroad.[34]

Thirdly, Chapter 15 does not make any choice of law therefore distribution of assets located in the U.S. is in principle governed by the US Bankruptcy Code.

Fourthly, in case of a concurrent proceeding in the U.S., Chapter 15 "requires the relief granted under Chapter 15 to foreign proceedings to be molded or terminated so as to be consistent with the relief granted under a full-fledged US bankruptcy proceeding."[35]

In several cases, U.S. courts have interpreted Chapter 15 in ways inconsistent with the Model Law. A first empirical study on Chapter 15 had concluded that U.S. courts recognized foreign proceedings, without putting hurdles in the procedure.[36]

[32] McCormack (2016).

[33] Franken (2014), pp. 127–128.

[34] Gropper (2011), pp. 566, 568.

[35] Franken (2014), p. 129.

[36] Dawson (2009), p. 319.

When interpreting Chapter 15, the statute says that "the court shall consider its international origin, and the need to promote an application of this chapter that is consistent with the application of similar statutes adopted by foreign jurisdictions." 11 U.S.C. § 1508.

While the statutory text of Chapter 15 controls, international sources may be considered to the extent they can be of help to "carry out the congressional purpose of achieving international uniformity in cross-border insolvency proceedings."

5.2.1.1.1 Avoidance Actions: Re Condor Insurance Ltd

On November 16, 2007, Condor Insurance declared bankruptcy in St. Kitts & Nevis and its liquidators filed for Chapter 15 recognition in the U.S. Bankruptcy Court for the District of Mississippi.

On May 18, 2007, the bankruptcy court recognized Condor Insurance as a foreign main proceeding. The foreign liquidator filed an avoidance action under St. Kitts & Nevis law against Condor Guarantee Trust, Condor Insurance's U.S. subsidiary, seeking to invalidate an allegedly fraudulent large transfer of US $313 million that the foreign company has done to its U.S. affiliate.[37]

On July 17, 2008, the U.S. Bankruptcy Court dismissed the avoidance action, stating that Condor Insurance should first file a plenary proceeding under Chapter 7 or Chapter 11 to file for an avoidance action.[38]

According to Section 1523, a foreign representative has the standing to invoke the U.S. avoidance provisions where full bankruptcy proceedings have been commenced in USA under Chapter 7 or Chapter 11 of the U.S. Bankruptcy Code.

However, U.S. and non-U.S. insurance companies may not be debtors under federal bankruptcy law, are precluded from using Chapters 7 and 11, according to Section 109(3) of the U.S. Bankruptcy Code.

Therefore, Condor Insurance (its foreign representative) appealed the U.S. Bankruptcy Court's decision. On February 9, 2009, the U.S. District Court affirmed the Bankruptcy Court's decision.[39]

The foreign representative of Condor Insurance then appealed to the Fifth Circuit. On March 17, 2010, the U.S. Court of Appeals for the Fifth Circuit reversed the two lower court decisions and held that pursuant to Section 1521, U.S. courts may grand avoidance relief via Chapter 15, but only pursuant to a non-U.S. avoidance law applicable in the main insolvency case.[40]

The U.S. Court of Appeals stated that while Section 1521 precludes avoidance under U.S. law, it is silent on avoidance actions under non-U.S. law and interpreted

[37] Schorr (2011), p. 372.

[38] *Fogerty v. Petroquest Res., Inc. (In re Condor Ins. Ltd.)* 2008 WL 2858943 *1 (Bankr. S.D. Miss., July 17, 2008).

[39] *Fogerty v. Petroquest Res., Inc. (In re Condor Ins. Ltd.)* 411 B.R. 314 (S.D. Miss. 2009).

[40] *In re Condor* 601 F.3d 319 (5th Cir. 2010).

that silence as allowing them. The court said that "[t[hough the language does not explicitly address the use of foreign avoidance law, it suggests a broad reading of the powers granted to the district court in order to advance the goals of comity to foreign jurisdictions."[41]

The Court of Appeals referred to the previously valid Section 304[42] and stated that Section 1521 adopts the above rule from *In re Metzeler*,[43] an older case decided by a U.S. district court. In that case, it had been asserted that a non-US insolvency representative may only commence an avoidance action under the non-US law governing the main insolvency case in an ancillary proceeding under Section 304, because the US Bankruptcy Code did not explicitly permit non-US insolvency representatives to invoke US avoiding powers.

The rationale behind this decision was on the one hand to avoid the need for Chapter 7 or Chapter 11 plenary proceedings brought under U.S. law and on the other hand to prevent the country from becoming a haven for fraudulent transfers by insurance companies. As the Court of Appeals stated:

> Congress did not intend to restrict the powers of the U.S. court to apply the law of the country where the main proceeding pends. Refusing to do so would lend a measure of protection to debtors to hide assets in the United States out of the reach of the foreign jurisdiction, forcing foreign representatives to initiate much more expansive proceedings to recover assets fraudulently conveyed, the scenario Chapter 15 was designed to prevent. We are not persuaded that Congress has unwittingly facilitated such tactics – with foreign insurance companies, access to Chapters 7 and 11 is otherwise denied.[44]

So, the Court of Appeals concluded that Condor Insurance's avoidance action could proceed under St. Kitts & Nevis via Section 1521. It also held that the law of a debtor's COMI should govern an avoidance action brought pursuant to Section 1521. It did an excellent and meticulous conflict of law work, pointing out that:

> The application of foreign avoidance law in Chapter 15 ancillary proceeding raises fewer choice of law concerns as the court is not required to create a separate bankruptcy estate. It accepts the helpful marriage of avoidance and distribution whether the proceeding is ancillary applying foreign law or a full proceeding applying domestic law – a marriage that avoids the more difficult depeçage rules of conflict law presented by avoidance and distribution decisions governed by different sources of law.

Commentaries on that decision, rather hostile to the conclusion of the U.S. Court, tried to show that this was not a "correct" decision and that other countries that have enacted the UNCITRAL Model Law, dealt with Article 23 which governs avoidance actions in different ways than USA did. For example, South Africa and Australia, in their versions of the Model Law, provide that foreign insolvency representatives may commence an avoidance action in their respective territories only under South African and Australian law respectively. On the other hand, Japan did not enact

---

[41] *In re Condor* 601 F.3d 319, at 325 (5th Cir. 2010).

[42] Moustaira (1992), pp. 183–191.

[43] 78 B.R. 674, 677 (Bankr. S.D.N.Y. 1987).

[44] *In re Condor* 601 F.3d 319, at 327 (5th Cir. 2010).

Model Law Article 23 however it provides that a non-Japanese insolvency representative may commence an insolvency proceeding in Japan to bring an avoidance action.[45]

The critique focuses on the fact that the Court of Appeals proceeded to statutory interpretation of Sections 1521 and 1523 and to a choice of law determination. It is argued that the two articles "are clear, they do not invite statutory interpretation."[46]

This is only one side of the coin, however. Other commentators point out that the fact that USA does not allow a foreign representative to issue domestic proceeding seeking to overturn previous transactions under their own, non-U.S. law, without issuing domestic proceeding under another chapter of the U.S. Bankruptcy Code is a unique to the USA concept, against the spirit of the Model Law. Furthermore, it is argued, this provision may be seen as an attempt by the U.S. legislature to impose U.S. law on foreign administrations. U.S. courts have circumvented this provision (as the Court of Appeals in *Re Condor* did) by allowing foreign representatives to issue proceedings to recover previous transactions under foreign law.[47]

Would the courts of other countries which have enacted the UNCITRAL Model Law apply foreign law with respect to antecedent transactions as the courts in the USA have done in *Re Condor Insurance Ltd*? It seems that it is still not clear.[48]

5.2.1.1.2 Public Policy Exception

Section 1506 of the Bankruptcy Code provides that a court may refuse to take an action under Chapter 15 if such action "would be manifestly contrary to the public policy of the United States":

> Nothing in this chapter prevents the court from refusing to take an action governed by this chapter if the action would be manifestly contrary to the public policy of the United States.

The exception is read narrowly: legislative history states that "the word 'manifestly' in international usage restricts the public policy exception to *the most fundamental policies of the United States.*"[49]

Thus, according to those in favor of universality, "even the absence of certain procedural or constitutional rights will not itself be a bar under section 1506."

Case law applying Section 1506 is relatively scarce. Most courts have declined to apply the public policy exception.

It has been stated that at least three principles guide courts in their analysis about whether they should apply this exception.[50]

---

[45] Schorr (2011), pp. 365–366.

[46] Schorr (2011), p. 377.

[47] Hannan (2015), p. 130.

[48] It is still undecided whether English courts could do that, according to Ho (2010), pp. 557.

[49] H.R. Rep. No. 109-31, pt.1, at 109 (2005).

[50] Gilhuly et al. (2016), pp. 70–71.

(1) "The mere fact of conflict between foreign law and U.S. law, absent other considerations, is insufficient to support the invocation of the public policy exception."[51]
(2) "the public policy exception applies 'where the procedural fairness of the foreign proceeding is in doubt or cannot be cured by the adoption of additional protections"[52]
(3) (i) a foreign proceeding should not be recognized and an action in a chapter 15 proceeding should not be taken if recognizing such a proceeding or taking such an action "would impinge severely a U.S. constitutional or statutory right" and (ii) an action should not be taken in a chapter 15 proceeding where taking such action would frustrate a U.S. court's ability to administer the chapter 15 proceeding.[53]

However, there are other opinions, of legal scholars, arguing for the broadest interpretation and application of this public policy exception.[54] At the time the chapter 15 was enacted, they warned that Section 1506 would be the battleground for the debate between those following the territorialist approach and those following the universalist approach.[55]

5.2.1.1.3 Treatment of Intellectual Property Licenses in Bankruptcy Proceedings: In re Qimonda AG

Qimonda was a German company, with its headquarters in Munich, major producer of dynamic random access memory (DRAM) chips, claiming to hold about 12,000 patents, including at least 4000 U.S. patents. Between 1995 and 2008, Qimonda entered into joint venture and patent cross-licensing agreements with many corporations, the "Counter-Parties".

In January 2009, insolvency proceeding of Qimonda was opened in Munich and a German insolvency administrator was appointed. The administrator filed a petition, before a U.S. Bankruptcy Court, according to Chapter 15 of the U.S. Bankruptcy Court, asking for recognition of the German insolvency proceeding. In July 2009, the U.S. Bankruptcy Court issued an order recognizing the German proceeding as a "foreign main proceeding" under 11 U.S.C. 1517.

The German administrator sent letters to some of the counter-parties, saying that the patent cross-licensing agreements would be terminated, according to German Insolvency Code § 103. The counter-parties objected, arguing that 11 U.S.C. § 365(n) prohibited this action.

[51] *In re Qimonda AG,* 433 B.R. 547, 568, 570 (E.D. Va. 2010).

[52] *In re ABC Learning Ctrs. Ltd.*, 728 F.3d 301 (3d Cir.2013).

[53] *In re Ashapura Minechem Ltd.*, 480 B.R. 129 (2012).

[54] Chung (2014), p. 95.

[55] Chung (2007), p. 260.

The first Bankruptcy Court decision allowed the German administrator to reject the licenses.[56]

On appeal to the U.S. District Court for the Eastern District of Virginia, the issue was whether the German administrator could terminate the parties' cross-licensing agreements without the counter-parties consent, or whether § 365(n) precludes such an action. The District Court remanded the matter back to the Bankruptcy Court "so that it may, in the first instance, determine whether the relief granted violates fundamental U.S. public policies under § 1506 and principles discussed here."[57]

After remand, the Bankruptcy Court said there were three relevant considerations:

(1) The mere fact that foreign law was different from US law was not enough.
(2) There should be no deference to foreign proceedings when a US court would doubt about the procedural fairness of these proceedings and could not cure it by adopting additional protection.
(3) It was appropriate to have recourse to the public policy exception to prevent actions that would impinge severely on a US constitutional or statutory right.

There was no doubt about the procedural fairness of the German proceedings in this case. The issue at stake, according to the US bankruptcy court, was the fact that German law, if applicable, would permit the cancellation of the US patent licenses. The court acknowledged that this would enhance the value to the debtor's estate but it considered more important the risk to the licensees who had invested substantially in research and manufacturing facilities relying on the freedom provided by the licensing agreements.[58]

Thus, it ruled the following:

> Thus, the court determines that failure to apply § 365(n) under the circumstances of this case and this industry would "severely impinge" an important statutory protection accorded to licensees of U.S. patents and thereby undermine a fundamental U.S. public policy promoting technological innovation. For that reason, the court holds that deferring to German law, to the extent it allows cancellation of the U.S. patent licenses, would be manifestly contrary to U.S. public policy.[59]

11 U.S.C. § 365 governs the treatment of executor contracts in bankruptcy. Section 365(n) applies specifically to executor contracts in the form of intellectual property licenses. It was enacted by the Congress to overturn a decision (*Lubrizol*) by the Fourth Circuit[60] and to promote technological innovation.

High-technology industry groups had considered the *Lubrizol* decision as a big threat to their business and made a successful effort to convince Congress to overturn

---

[56] *In re Quimonda AG*, No. 09-14766-RGM, 2009 WL 4060083.

[57] *In re Qimonda AG,* 433 B.R. 547, 571 (E.D. Va. 2010).

[58] McCormack (2016).

[59] *In re Qimonda AG*, 462 B.R. 165, 185 (Bankr.E.D. Va. 2011).

[60] *Lubrizol Enters., Inc. V. Richmond Metal Finishers, Inc.*, 756 F.2d 1043 (4th Cir. 1985), *cert. denied*, 475 U.S. 1057 (1986).

the Fourth Circuit's decision. The Intellectual Property Protection Act was introduced in Congress in 1987 and enacted in 1988.

According to the archives:

> The purpose of the bill is to amend Section 365 of the Bankruptcy Code to make clear that the rights of an intellectual property licensee to use the licensed property cannot be unilaterally cut off as a result of the rejection of the license pursuant to Section 365 in the event of the licensor's bankruptcy. Certain recent court decisions interpreting Section 365 have imposed a burden on American technological development that was never intended by Congress in enacting Section 365. The adoption of this bill will immediately remove that burden and its attendant threat to the development of American Technology and will further clarify that Congress never intended for Section 365 to be so applied.[61]

There was a further appeal, in *Quimonda* case, directly to the Fourth Circuit.[62] That court ignored the public policy argument, it did not find that Section 365(n) was so fundamental that failure to enforce it would be "manifestly contrary to the public policy of the United States", within the meaning of § 1506.[63]

The Fourth Circuit decided without reference to public policy. It rested its decision on the principle of sufficient protection of creditors. It concluded that:

> the bankruptcy court properly recognized that Jaffé's [the administrator] request for discretionary relief under § 1521(a) required it to consider "the interests of the creditors and other interested entities, including the debtor" under § 1522(a) and that it properly construed § 1522(a) as requiring the application of a balancing test. Moreover, relying on the particular facts of this case and the extensive record developed during the four-day evidentiary hearing, we also conclude that the bankruptcy court reasonably exercised its discretion in balancing the interests of the licenses against the interests of the debtor and finding that application of § 365(n) was necessary to ensure the licensees under Qimonda's U.S. patents were sufficiently protected.[64]

The Fourth Circuit referred to the 4000 U.S. patents at issue, but it was not clear whether the licensees were U.S. or foreign holders of patents, whose scope was limited in the territory of the United States, or U.S. citizens entitled to use the patents worldwide, or U.S. citizens entitled to use the patents only in the United States.

United States government had filed an *amicus* brief in which it had argued that the courts' decisions had improperly restrained the operation of a German statute in Germany.

The Fourth Circuit rejected the position of the U.S. government in a footnote of its decision, stating that the bankruptcy court had properly

> conditioned its grant of power to Jaffé to "administer the assets of Qimonda AG *within the territorial jurisdiction of the United States*," with the limitation that he was taking the company's U.S. patents subject to the preexisting licenses, which he was obliged to treat in a manner consistent with § 365(n). As a result, Jaffé is precluded from rejecting the U.S. patent licenses *as a matter of U.S. law*. Although this limitation may have indirect effects in

---

[61] S. REP. No. 100-505, at 1–2 (1988).

[62] Gropper (2014), pp. 164–169.

[63] *Jaffé v. Samsung Elec. Co., Ltd.*, 737 F.4d 14 (4th Cir. 2013).

[64] *Id.* at 18.

> the German proceeding, it does not represent an impermissible application of U.S. law extraterritorially.[65]

As it is pointed out, "[t]his is about as close as the court came to a conflict of laws analysis."[66]

5.2.1.1.4 COMI: Definition, Description—Chapter 15—EU Regulation

5.2.1.1.4.1 General Comments

Is the description of COMI the same, under the laws that have enacted the UNCITRAL Model Law and the EU Insolvency Regulation that reigns in the laws of the Member States? Is there an interrelationship between them, as was the intention at the beginning of the works and the enactment of those texts?

U.S. Courts have often referred to that interrelationship. The U.S. Bankruptcy Court for the Southern District of New York stated some years ago:

> In the regulation adopting the EU Convention, the COMI concept is elaborated upon as "the place where the debtor conducts the administration of his interests on a regular basis and is therefore ascertainable by third parties." ... This generally equates with the concept of a "principal place of business" in United States law...

It also stated:

> As noted by the European Court of Justice, the COMI presumption may be overcome "particular[ly] in the case of a 'letterbox' company not carrying out any business in the territory of the Member State in which its registered office is situated."[67]

It has been suggested that in cases where a debtor's business was a fraud, the approaches adopted by the two texts may give different results. Under the European Regulation, a public perception that the debtor's business is run from its registered office will be almost determinative of the COMI issue, even if it is a fraud. According to this suggestion, if applying the US approach to COMI under the Model Law, a court should not feel bound by the appearances ("the smoke and mirrors") and should be free to determine the true location of the debtor's COMI.[68]

Not everybody agrees with the above suggestion, though.

The U.S. Bankruptcy Code does not define COMI, so recently it has been held by the U.S. Bankruptcy Court for the Southern District of New York that:

> Because COMI is not statutorily defined, courts are free to develop and consider the particular factors that may be relevant, dependent upon the facts and circumstances present.[69]

---

[65] *Id.* at 25, n. 3.

[66] Gropper (2014), pp. 166–167 note 86.

[67] *Re Bear Stearns High Grade Structured Credit Strategies Master Fund Ltd*, 374 BR 122, 129 (Bankr. S.D.N.Y., 2007).

[68] Ho (2009), p. 549.

[69] *In re Creative Fin., Ltd (In Liquidation)*, 543 B.R. 498, 517 (Bankr. S.D.N.Y, 2016).

Furthermore, there is a disagreement between U.S. Circuit Courts about when it should be the proper time to determine COMI in a cross-border insolvency case: Should it be the petition date or the foreign proceeding's commencement date?[70]

5.2.1.1.4.2 In re Oi Brasil Holdings Coöperatief U.A.

In a recent case[71] before it, the U.S. Bankruptcy Court for the Southern District of New York had to deal with many and very interesting issues that concerned both the Chapter 15 sections and the European Insolvency Regulation rules. The main issue was COMI.

Coop was a Dutch entity, member of a group of Brazilian telecommunications companies (the "Oi Group") that had initiated bankruptcy proceedings in Brazil, in the summer of 2016.

In July 2016, several of these Oi Group companies, including Coop, filed a petition in the U.S. Bankruptcy Court for the Southern District of New York, asking for recognition of the Brazilian bankruptcy proceedings as a foreign main proceeding under Chapter 15 of the U.S. Bankruptcy Code.

The Court granted the recognition, finding Coop's center of main interests (COMI) to be in Brazil, given that Coop was a special purpose financing vehicle for the Oi Group.

At about the same time, some creditors of Coop's took action against Coop in the Netherlands, where also a Dutch bankruptcy proceeding for Coop was commenced. There was much litigation there, but finally the highest national court in the Netherlands upheld the jurisdiction and propriety of Coop's bankruptcy proceedings under Dutch law.

In July 2017, the Dutch Insolvency Trustee filed a petition before the U.S. Bankruptcy Court for the Southern District of New York, seeking on the one hand to have the Court recognize Coop's Dutch bankruptcy proceedings as a foreign main proceeding under Chapter 15 and on the other, and consequently, to overturn the prior recognition by the U.S. Court of Coop's Brazilian bankruptcy.

The Dutch petition was supported by some creditors who made up the International Bondholder Committee (the "IBC") and opposed by the debtors joined by a separate group of creditors (the "Steering Committee").

After a trial and extensive submissions by the parties, the U.S. Court denied the Dutch petition, on December 4, 2017.[72]

---

[70] DeLaughter (2016), pp. 412–430.

[71] Three cases, jointly administered.

[72] As it is mentioned at a note of the decision, certain information relevant to the Court's determination in this case was sensitive commercial information or subject to confidentiality restrictions under Dutch law. Such confidential information has been redacted from this decision; reductions have been kept to minimum, though, because of the interest of transparency in these proceedings.

In the Dutch petition before the U.S. Bankruptcy Court, the movants also used an estoppel argument[73] seeking to bar Coop from asserting a position on COMI under Chapter 15 based upon (1) the jurisdictional statements made by Coop in its Dutch petition and (2) Coop's failure to legally contest or appeal any of the Dutch courts' findings regarding Coop's COMI.

The U.S. Court declared that the estoppel argument that the Movants used, failed because the COMI finding under the EU Regulation in the Dutch proceeding is not the same as a COMI finding under Chapter 15 of the Bankruptcy Code.

It admitted that "Chapter 15's use of the COMI concept stems indirectly from the EU Regulation" and that "[a]s a result of their related histories, Chapter 15 and the EU Regulation share many significant traits, especially with respect to the concept of COMI."

However, it refused that the EU Regulation and the Chapter 15 are identical. On the contrary, it pointed out several conceptual and procedural differences, according to its findings, that "have evolved under separate lines of case law written by judges operating with different purposes and concerns." Among the differences that it stated, were the following:

The timeframe is different: the EU Regulation looks to the date of the filing of the foreign insolvency proceeding, whereas U.S. courts' inquiry centers on the date of the Chapter 15 recognition petition.

Both regimes include a registered office presumption, however divergent case law has led to different application of that presumption under the EU Regulation than under Chapter 15. EU courts rather uphold the presumption unless it is demonstrated that a debtor's management and assets are located in a different country and that such facts are ascertainable by third parties. In the USA, the registered office presumption is applied merely "[f]or speed and convenience in instances in which the COMI is obvious and undisputed."[74] However, the presumption "does not shift the risk of non-persuasion, i.e., the burden of proof, away from the foreign representative seeking recognition as a main proceeding."[75]

5.2.1.1.5 USA—UK: Similarities & Differences in the Enactment and Enforcement by Them of the Model Law Provisions

The understanding and enforcement of the Model Law by these two countries is not identical. In fact, there are several differences that usually appear at the moment of the enforcement of the relevant provisions by the courts of each country.

One of those differences in wording—a rather significant one—is the following: The Model Law provides for the recognition of foreign insolvency proceedings.

[73] The doctrine of judicial estoppel prevents a party from asserting a factual position in one legal proceeding that is contrary to a position that is successfully advanced in another proceeding.

[74] *In re Creative Fin., Ltd (In Liquidation)*, 543 B.R. 498, 514–515 (Bankr. S.D.N.Y, 2016).

[75] *In Re Bear Stearns High Grade Structured Credit Strategies Master Fund Ltd*, 374 BR 122, 129 (Bankr. S.D.N.Y., 2007).

Under Section 101(23) of the US Bankruptcy Code, foreign proceeding covers proceedings in a foreign country 'under a law relating to insolvency or adjustment of debt'. The respective rule in UK, that is, the Cross-Border Insolvency Regulations 2006, Sch 1, reg 2(i), does not specifically define foreign proceedings to include proceedings for the adjustment of debts.

A case that provoked much distaste or disappointment in USA was *In re Rubin*.[76] It was about the recognition in United Kingdom of a judgment obtained in an American bankruptcy case against various defendants. Among those parties was Eurofinance, a company that had not appeared in the U.S. proceeding.

The U.S. court had found that it had "long-arm" jurisdiction[77] over Eurofinance, under U.S. law, with the justification that Eurofinance was sufficiently active in the United States. Therefore, the court entered judgment against it along with other defendants that were found to have participated in a large fraud on thousands of United States consumers.[78]

The United Kingdom Supreme Court found that the United States court did not have personal jurisdiction over Eurofinance according to the common law rules about enforcement of foreign judgments.

The US main Chapter 11 case had been recognized in the United Kingdom under the provisions of the Cross-Border Insolvency Regulations 2006 (that had incorporated the rules of the UNCITRAL Model Law). The Article 25 of these Regulations states that a United Kingdom court may cooperate with foreign courts. It was brought as an argument before the United Kingdom Supreme Court, by the applicants for the enforcement of the U.S. judgment against Eurofinance, but the UK Supreme Court overruled the case, refusing to agree that judgments in international insolvency cases might be subject to a more liberal rule.

What the UK Supreme Court did in that case was that it reaffirmed what it considered to be a fundamental principle of private international law: that a foreign judgment would be enforceable only if the defendant was either present within the jurisdiction, or had, in some other way, submitted to the jurisdiction of the foreign court.[79]

This case was not a case in which enforcement of a reorganization plan was sought nor was it a case where property was sought to be transferred. Nevertheless, United States jurists were feeling a certain anxiety that the English courts might not enforce reorganization judgments from the United States against parties that would try to avoid personal jurisdiction. They were (and are) thinking that such an attitude of the English courts would jeopardize reorganization's success.

The negative critiques also focused on something that Lord Collins, judge of the UK Supreme Court, said. He said that '[t]ypically today the introduction of new rules for enforcement of judgments depends on a degree of reciprocity'. However,

---

[76] *Rubin v. Eurofinance SA* [2012] UKSC 46; [2013] 1 AC 236.

[77] Moustaira (1995), pp. 27–28.

[78] Westbrook (2015), p. 567.

[79] McCormack and Hargovan (2015), p. 389.

the UK had declined to make reciprocity a condition for recognizing and granting assistance under the Model Law.[80]

On the other side, what Lord Collins also said, was that if a radical departure from substantially settled law were to be made, it should rather be made by legislation than by the courts.[81]

5.2.1.2 Australia

Australia enacted the Model Law by annexing it as Schedule 1 to the *Cross-Border Insolvency Act 2008*.[82]

The above provisions do not amend the existing statutory provisions allowing the courts to assist foreign courts, nor change the common law in relation to the recognition and assistance to be granted to foreign proceedings.[83]

The existing statutory provisions (Sections 580 and 581 of the *Corporations Act*) require the Australian courts to assist the courts of certain prescribed countries; they also give the Australian courts discretion as to whether to assist the courts of other, non-prescribed countries.[84] These statutory provisions continue to apply, to the extent they are consistent with the provisions of the Model Law[85]; in case they are not, the provisions of the Model Law prevail.[86]

Foreign corporations that are registered or recognized under the *Corporations Act 2001*, including the corporations that are registered as foreign corporations, can be wound up under the provisions of the *Corporations Act*, either voluntarily or by the courts. The Australian courts also have the power to wind up other body corporates that have a principal place of business in Australia.[87]

---

[80] Kirshner (2013), p. 27.

[81] See also Zhihe Ji (2017), who points out that "[t]he lesson from this may be that changes which the common law might make under its own steam are not to be tailored or nuanced so as to do damage to those who held legitimate expectations, and that legislation may provide the best available answer."

[82] On these, implementing the UNCITRAL Model Kaw rules, see Mason (2012), p. 105; Hargovan (2008), p. 188.

[83] Hannan (2015).

[84] Mason (2006), p. 145.

[85] According to McCormack and Hargovan (2015), p. 389, the above provisions may be criticized on various grounds, among which for the fact that the prescribed/non-prescribed distinction and the discretion to refuse assistance to non-prescribed countries are not really in the spirit of the Model Law regime. The authors point out that there are some similarities between Sections 580 and 581 with Section 426 of the UK Insolvency Act 1986, but that there are also differences. A very significant difference is that Section 426 of the UK Insolvency Act authorizes the application of foreign insolvency law, while the Australian provisions only permit the application of local law.

[86] Hannan (2015), p. 37.

[87] According to *Corporations Act 2001* (Cth) s 583(a), "Principal place of business is the place of the corporate body's registered office.

Australian courts can wind up foreign corporations that have only assets such as real estate in Australia, but that do not carry on business or have a principal place of business in the country, if Australia is an 'appropriate forum'.

The common law principle of comity also applies in Australia. That means that foreign representatives/administrators may be recognized using this common law principle.

The *Cross-Border Insolvency Act 2008* was promoted because it was believed that in that way there would be developed a uniform, internationally recognized framework for administering cross-border insolvencies.[88]

5.2.1.3 New Zealand

New Zealand also enacted the UNCITRAL Model Law, as Schedule 1 to the *Insolvency (Cross-border) Act* 2006.

Prior to its enactment and because of the lack of rules regarding the cross-border insolvencies, New Zealand courts relied heavily on the principle of comity to recognize a foreign insolvency decision—and consequently, a foreign administrator.[89]

The 2006 Act on the one hand enacts the Model Law and on the other deals with cross-border insolvency generally, making special provisions in relation to the High Court of the country acting in aid of overseas courts.

An originality of this enactment is that it gives power to the High Court of New Zealand, while interpreting the Model Law, to refer to:

> any document that relates to the Model Law on Cross-Border Insolvency that originates from the United Nations Commission on International Trade Law, or its working group for the preparation of the Model Law on Cross-Border Insolvency.[90]

It is argued that through this provision the court cannot only refer to the versions of those documents that existed at the date of enactment of the Model Law in the country, but it can also consider updates to these documents, including the UNCITRAL Guide.[91]

The enactment of the Model Law did not change New Zealand's inclination to rely on the principle of comity. Section 8 of the 2006 Act provides that if a court of another country in an insolvency proceeding makes an order requesting the aid of the High Court in respect of a person to whom Article 1 of the Model Law applied, the High Court may, if it thinks fit, act in aid of and be auxiliary to that court in insolvency proceedings.

Generally, the New Zealand High Court's position is that "a Universalist approach to international insolvency should be adopted."[92]

---

[88] McCormack and Hargovan (2015), p. 389.

[89] Godwin et al. (2017), p. 9.

[90] *Insolvency (Cross-border) Act 2006* s 5(1)(b).

[91] Hannan (2015), p. 32.

[92] Hannan (2015), pp. 42–44.

5.2.1.4 Canada

Canada implemented the Model Law via Chapter 47 of the Statutes of Canada, 2005,[93] which introduced new provisions into the Bankruptcy and Insolvency Act (BIA) and Companies' Creditors Arrangement Act (CCAA).[94]

As it is pointed out, Canada's development of provisions on cross-border insolvency is shaped by the economic, social and political forces of Canadian society.[95]

Chapter 47 introduced a modified version of the Model Law; it adopted many of its fundamental objectives, but departed on particular aspects. Some characteristics of this version—and, consequently, of Canada's international insolvency law—, are the following:

Where an insolvency proceeding has been opened in respect of a debtor company in a foreign country, a certified copy of the opening the proceeding order is, in the absence of evidence to the contrary, proof that the debtor company is insolvent and also proof of the appointment of the foreign representative made by that order.

The above presumption is very important especially for the recognition of such orders issued by courts of countries where access to reorganization/restructuring proceedings/mechanisms does not require insolvency, while Canadian law does. A country's legislation that does not require insolvency for the opening of reorganizing proceedings is U.S. Bankruptcy Code Chapter 11. Obviously, such a provision in Canadian legislation is very useful since many international insolvency cases concern both Canada and USA.

The foreign representative/administrator, when recognized, can have direct access to the Canadian courts. It is mentioned that a notable difference between the U.S. and Canadian versions of the Model Law is that Chapter 15 states that, when recognized, the foreign representative may sue or be sued in U.S. courts, subject to

---

[93] Generally, about the implementation by Canada of the UNCITRAL Model Law, see Sarra (2007), p. 19.

[94] Let it be mentioned here, that Section 91(21) of the Canada's Constitution Act, 1867 vests in the federal government exclusive legislative authority to enact laws in relation to "Bankruptcy and Insolvency". In 1919, the first Canadian bankruptcy statute was enacted. When there is a conflict between a federal and a provincial statute, the provincial statute is rendered inoperative by a court, pursuant to the principle of federal paramountcy. As it is explained, the paramountcy principle contains two branches that identify two different types of conflict. The first branch refers to an operational conflict which occurs when it is impossible to comply with both the federal and the provincial statutes. The second involves frustration of purpose which occurs when the operation of the provincial statute frustrates the purpose of the federal statute. In both cases, courts should try to adopt a harmonious interpretation of federal and provincial statutes that would not result in conflict. If such a harmonious co-existence of two statutes would not be possible, the paramountcy principle comes into play and the federal statute must take precedence, see Wood (2016), pp. 28–31.

[95] See Sarra (2007), p. 39, where she originally and interestingly parallels Canada's development of cross-border provisions with "*aurora borealis*", that is, Northern Lights. She states that (phrase copied from Wikipedia): "Each curtain of the *aurora borealis* consists of many parallel rays, each lined up with the local direction of the magnetic field lines, suggesting that aurora is shaped by the Earth's magnetic field; auroral electrons spiraling around magnetic field lines while moving earthwards."

any consistent with Chapter's 15 policy limitations that the U.S. court may impose.[96] The Canadian Chapter 47 does not contain such a provision and, in any case, under BIA, insolvency officers are protected from such suits in most circumstances.[97]

Contrary to what has done the U.S. legislator, the Canadian provisions do not contain the public policy exception of the Article 6 of the Model Law. This has not prevented Canadian courts, though, from referring to public policy concerns. Furthermore, there are provisions in Chapter 47 that state clearly that a Canadian court does not have to make any order that is not in compliance with the laws of Canada or to enforce any such order made by a foreign court.[98]

According to Section 284 of the BIA, nothing in that Act prevents a court, upon application of any foreign representative or other interested party, from applying under the legal and equitable rules governing recognition of foreign insolvency orders and to provide aid to foreign representatives which are not inconsistent with the Act.

It is interesting, that even when an order for recognition of a foreign insolvency decision is sought, under the provisions of the CCAA that enacted part of the Model Law, insolvency proceedings may be commenced under the BIA or the *Winding-up and Restructuring Act*. This is one of the key differences between the Model Law and the Canadian Chapter 47. The Model Law states in Article 28, that after the recognition of a foreign main insolvency proceeding, another insolvency proceeding may be commenced under the law of the recognizing country; the effects of the latter shall be restricted to the assets of the debtor that are located there and, if necessary, for the sake of cooperation and coordination of proceedings, also to other assets of the debtor that, under the law of the recognizing country, should be administered in that proceeding. From the wording of the article it seems that it precludes commencement of concurrent main proceedings. The Canadian law, though, seems to allow concurrent main proceedings. It is not at all sure that there might not be conflicts, not really easy to resolve.

Prior to the introduction of the Model Law, comity was very important in the bankruptcy context.[99] The Supreme Court of Canada, in its decision on *Beals v Saldanha*, had confirmed that it might apply the principle of international comity and recognize a foreign judgment but there had to be a real and substantial connection with Canada.[100] The Supreme Court also determined that traditional jurisdictional bases, such as residence, presence in the foreign jurisdiction serve to strengthen the real and substantive connection. Comity is still very important in Canada. As it is pointed out, anyway, the Chapter 47 provisions were the codification of many practices of Canadian courts.[101]

[96] Section 1509(b)(1) of Chapter 15, U.S. Bankruptcy Code.

[97] Sarra (2007), p. 41.

[98] Sections 61(2), 284(2), Chapter 47. See Sarra (2007) Northern Lights, … p. 44.

[99] Godwin et al. (2017), p. 9.

[100] *Beals v Saldanha*, [2003] 3 SCR 416, 437.

[101] Sarra (2007), p. 57.

It is an easily discernible fact that, although the initial influence on Canada's insolvency law was English common law, during the last two decades many significant amendments have been made, influenced by U.S. law and practices.[102] There is a kind of tradition that has been created regarding the cooperation of the two countries' courts, and this diminishes the problems that arise in cross-border insolvencies. Things are more difficult to resolve when the countries "involved" in a cross-border insolvency have not many common elements.[103]

5.2.1.5 Singapore

On 23 May 2017, as part of certain amendments to the Companies Act (CAP 50, 2006 Rev. Ed.), Singapore adopted the Model Law (Sections 354A, 354B, 354C and the XIV Schedule of the Companies Act). A certain aim of the country was and is to become a hub for international insolvencies[104]; that is also why a Committee to Strengthen Singapore as an International Centre for Debt Restructuring had been created.

Before the adoption of the Model Law, the courts were hesitant about whether to adopt universalism or territorialism, as far as the administration of international insolvency proceedings opened in more than one country was concerned.

In the case *TPC Korea*,[105] a company that had been incorporated in the Republic of Korea and that was doing business in the shipping, trading and other related to those, sectors, filed an application before a Korean court, asking to be rehabilitated under proceedings analogous to the Chapter 11 of the U.S. Bankruptcy Code.

Furthermore, the company managed to obtain preservation orders from the Korean courts, according to which, any already opened proceedings against any ship owned by the company which was under the rehabilitation regime, would automatically be stayed and any attempt to open new proceedings would be prohibited.

The only "presence" of the company in Singapore were the interests that the company had in five vessels which regularly were in the ports of Singapore. The company applied for an order of the Singapore High Court, asking it to convene a meeting of the company's creditors in Singapore, with the purpose of considering and approving the Korean Rehabilitation plan, pursuant to Section 210(10) of the Singapore Companies Act; pending the proceedings about the approval of the Korean Rehabilitation plan, all actions against the company's assets, the five vessels included, were to be restrained.

---

[102] Morawetz (2012), p. 5.

[103] See Sarra (2007), p. 61: "Moreover, for Canada's cross-border cases with jurisdictions other than the U.S., these problems may manifest themselves differently, given that the jurisdictions will not have had the history of comity and co-operation in insolvency proceedings that Canada has had with its neighbor to the south."

[104] Ajinderpal and Ng (2018), p. 7.

[105] *Re TPC Korea* [2010] 2 SLR 617.

The Judicial Commissioner rejected the application, saying that he had no jurisdiction to grant the asked order. He noted that the Singapore High Court had no jurisdiction to enforce the scheme of arrangement provisions on a foreign corporation that neither had assets in Singapore nor had a sufficient nexus or connection with the country.

Another very interesting decision, issued before the Singapore's adoption of the Model Law, was the very recent *Pacific Andes Resources Development Ltd.*[106]

Pacific Andes Resource Development Ltd is the Bermudian parent company of China Fishery Group. Its shares were listed in the Singapore stock exchange and it also had issued SGD 200 million dollars' worth of bonds in Singapore, in 2014.

On 30 June 2016, the China Fishery Group started restructuring proceedings in Peru and filed for Chapter 11 before the U.S. Bankruptcy Courts. On 1 July 2016, Pacific Andes Resource Development Ltd and some of its subsidiaries started restructuring proceedings in Singapore. The latter, afterwards, filed for a moratorium on proceedings against them, in Singapore and overseas, under Section 210(10) & (11) of the Companies Act. They read as follows:

Section 210(10): "*Where no order has been made or resolution passed for the winding up of a company and any such compromise or arrangement has been proposed between the company and its creditors or any class of such creditors, the Court may, in addition to any of its powers, on the application in a summary way of the company or of any member, creditor or holder of units of shares of the company restrain further proceedings in any action or proceeding against the company except by leave of the Court and subject to such terms as the Court imposes.*

Section 210(11): *"In this section –*

"arrangement" includes a reorganization of the share capital of a company by the consolidation of shares of different classes or by the division of shares into shares of different classes or by both these methods;

"company" means any corporation liable to be wound up under this Act;

"holder of units of shares" does not include a person who holds units of shares only beneficially."

Main aim of the application for moratorium on proceedings was for the applicants—Pacific Andes Resources Development Ltd and some of its subsidiaries—to stall so that they could enact a group-wide restructuring plan that would encompass both the Peruvian proceedings and the U.S. Chapter 11 proceedings.

The Singapore High Court did grant a moratorium but only on proceedings against Pacific Andes Resources. It refused to grant a moratorium in respect of proceedings against its subsidiaries and of proceedings against both the Pacific Andes Resources and its subsidiaries outside of Singapore.

The court held that it had no jurisdiction to restrain the creditors of the parent company and its subsidiaries from commencing proceedings in other countries, because of the territorial effect of the Section 210. Furthermore, the court held that

---

[106] *Pacific Andes Resources Development Ltd.* [2016] SGHC 219.

the subsidiaries—applicants for moratorium had no sufficient connection to Singapore, to seek relief under Section 210(10) of the Singapore Companies Act.

The decision was issued on 27 September 2016. Right afterwards, creditors of the Pacific Andes Resources and its subsidiaries filed for winding up proceedings against them, in Bermuda and the British Virgin Islands. Pacific Andes Resources and its subsidiaries withdrew the Singapore scheme and filed for Chapter 11 proceedings, before a U.S. court, also asking for a worldwide stay of proceedings.[107] Obviously, whether such a stay of proceedings will be enforced worldwide, depends on whether the courts of the other countries will recognize and enforce the U.S. order/decision.

After the adoption of the UNCITRAL Model Law and most recently (24.1.2018), its rules were applied by the Singapore High Court in its decision on *Re Zetta Pte Ltd and others*.[108]

5.2.2 *Latin America*

5.2.2.1 Mexico

One of the first countries that implemented UNCITRAL Model Law 1997 in its own legislation was Mexico. On May 12, 2000, Mexican Federal Congress passed a new insolvency law, *Ley de Concursos Mercantiles* (LCM)[109] which, among other issues, regulates cross-border insolvency issues.[110]

Several Latin American countries amended their insolvency laws at about that time, beginning of the twenty-first century, pursuant to the recommendations of UNCITRAL's Model Law.[111] The main reason was the financial and economic conditions of the Latin American countries and the consequent increasing number of corporations under distress, especially during the 1990s. Another reason was the trend of the recent decades, to restructure companies in distress rather than liquidate them.

According to LCM (Articles 278–285, 292–303), foreign insolvency proceedings are recognized in Mexico, as are foreign representatives too. Foreign creditors (Articles 286–291) may participate in insolvency proceedings that are opened in Mexico and have the same rights with Mexican creditors, there is no discrimination. International cooperation of the courts and the administrators is foreseen (Articles 304–305). There are also detailed rules about the case of parallel insolvency proceedings, in Mexico and other country or countries (Articles 306–310). It is stated that, especially regarding the latter chapter (parallel proceedings), the LCM is based

[107] Ajinderpal and Ng (2018), p. 9.

[108] *Re Zetta Pte Ltd and others* [2018] SGHC 16.

[109] Martinez (2001), p. 75.

[110] Graham-Canedo (2007), pp. 19–20.

[111] Olivares-Caminal (2010).

on principles and models that have been universally accepted and that permit LCM to be characterized as a vanguard document.[112]

5.2.2.1.1 Mexico—USA: Cooperation in Cross-Border Insolvency Cases?

All the above means that Mexico is open to a kind of judicial cooperation in insolvency matters that involve Mexico and other countries. An example of this cooperation capability is the case *Satélites Mexicanos (Satmex)* restructuring proceedings, in which a Mexican Federal Court and a U.S. Bankruptcy Court for the Southern District of New York[113] cooperated very well, in spite of their differences in substantive issues of their respective insolvency laws.[114]

Often, unfortunately, jurists of countries with different legal culture, different legal mentality, tend to criticize rather superficially the legal systems that they do not really know, tend to have a rather condescending opinion on those systems, using old clichés that sometimes are far from reality. Further, even when these clichés are still valid, one must have a deep knowledge of the other than one's own legal systems, before expressing one's opinion about them. Comparing laws does not really mean evaluating them as "good" or "bad", as "better" or as "worse" than others.

Thus, stating that "[j]udges in civil law systems do not interpret, but rather apply the laws as written, collected, and codified by the system's legislative body"[115] is a rather simplistic opinion that furthermore ignores that not all civil law systems are the same, as not all common law systems are the same. The taxonomy in families of laws is rather considered obsolete by contemporary comparative law scholars. Thus, stating also that Mexico is a civil law country,[116] obviously considering the initial influences of its law by European laws during the nineteenth century, is not exact.

5.2.2.1.2 Compañia Mexicana de Aviación

Another case that concerned both Mexican and U.S. courts was that of the Mexican air company, Mexicana de Aviación.

The company had been created in Mexico City, in 1921, under the name Compañia Mexicana de Transportación Aérea.[117] In 1924, the company had new U.S. owners and was renamed as Compañia Mexicana de Aviación S.A. In 1929,

---

[112] Quintana Adriano (2007), p. 904.

[113] *In re Satélites Mexicanos, S.A., de C.V.*, No. 05-13862 (Bankr. S.D.N.Y. filed May 2005).

[114] Beavers (2003), p. 988.

[115] Springer (2012), p. 84.

[116] Ferreres Comella (2011), p. 1967.

[117] See Forero-Niño (2011), p. 362, who mentions that Americans piloted Mexicana's first flights for passengers.

after Pan American Airways purchased stock in Mexicana, the company began to service international routes. Charles Lindbergh piloted Mexicana flights and participated in the restructuring of the company.

Although for many years the company had been very popular, in 1967 it was near bankruptcy because of the harsh competition in airline industry but was finally saved. In 1982, because of economic turmoil in Mexico, the stockholders sold the company and the Mexican government purchased 54% of Mexicana's stock. During the following years, ownership changed hands several times, at several percentages; however, the Mexican government continued to maintain a percentage of its shares, until 2005, when the government sold Mexicana for $165.5 million to Grupo Posadas, a Mexican hotel company.

In 2010, after having received numerous awards all the previous years and having been distinguished as the "leading carrier in Mexico and Central America", Mexicana reported two consecutive years of economic losses and asked the Mexican government for assistance but the latter refused to bail out the company.

On August 2, 2010, Mexicana, immersed in a profound financial crisis, suspended its payments[118] and filed for bankruptcy protection in Mexico and in the United States and on August 28, suspended flights for its three airlines until further notice.[119] According to many commentators, the crisis' origin was the entrepreneurial irresponsibility together with the wrong movements of the Mexican government. The company itself stated that the causes for its financial problems were mainly the non-competitive labor costs.

Thus, Mexicana filed a petition for an insolvency proceeding in a Mexico City District Court on August 2, 2010, which petition was admitted by the bankruptcy judge on August 4, 2010 and the company was granted temporary injunctive relief "to prevent creditors from exercising their rights over [the company's] outstanding debt obligations".

On the same day, Mexicana (its Mexican representative) filed a petition in a New York Bankruptcy Court, asking it to recognize Mexicana's insolvency proceeding just commenced in Mexico as a "foreign 'main' proceeding" under Chapter 15 and to provide the protections and benefits identified in the U.S. Bankruptcy Code.[120]

The petition was granted and the Mexican Insolvency proceeding was recognized. During the following years, the revival of Mexicana was sought, but in vain. In April 2014, a Mexican judge ordered an end to efforts to revive the company, saying that no credible new investor had expressed interest in the carrier. An administrator was appointed to start selling off the company's assets to repay the airlines obligations. Eight years after the opening of the insolvency proceeding, it seems that the end of the repayment has not been written yet.

---

[118] Montarcé (2016), p. 202.

[119] Forero-Niño (2011), pp. 362–364.

[120] Forero-Niño (2011), pp. 369–372.

5.2.2.1.3 Vitro

Vitro, one of the largest glass manufacturers in the world, had been created under Mexican law in 1909. It operated through a chain of subsidiaries. It had distribution centers in 11 countries in the Americas and Europe. About 85% of the 17,000 workers were living in Mexico.[121]

Between February 2003 and February 2007, Vitro borrowed approximately $1.2 billion, mainly from U.S. investors.

The global financial crisis of 2008 had negative repercussions on Vitro's sales and affected demand for its key industries. The consequence was that Vitro was unable to meet all its financial obligations. After its counter-parties filed lawsuits in the Supreme Court of New York demanding payment of $240.3 million plus interest, in February 2009,[122] Vitro announced plans to restructure its debts.

Vitro began soliciting creditors' consent in November 2010 for a prepackaged voluntary *concurso* filing. To file for it, Mexican insolvency law required that 40% of the unsecured creditors supported the plan. Vitro filed the petition in the Mexican court on December 13, 2010, although almost all its unsecured creditors had rejected the plan. Vitro claimed that its substantially intercompany debts were unsecured creditors and included these claims in the 40%.

Even before Vitro filed the petition in the Mexican court, unsecured creditors objected to its movements and had sought to secure their rights to Vitro's subsidiaries' assets in the USA. One group of unsecured creditors commenced an involuntary bankruptcy proceeding under Chapter 11 of the U.S. Bankruptcy Code against 15 Vitro subsidiaries in the Bankruptcy Court of the Northern District of Texas. Other groups of creditors filed for similar proceedings in the Bankruptcy Court of the Southern District of New York. A day after filing its petition in the Mexican court, Vitro filed a petition in the Bankruptcy Court of the Southern District of New York, seeking cross-border insolvency protection under Chapter 15 of the U.S. Bankruptcy Code[123]—among other measures the automatic stay of the commencement or continuation of judicial proceedings against a debtor within the territorial jurisdiction of the USA.[124]

On January 7, 2011, the Fourth District Court for Civil and Labor Matters in the Mexican State of Nuevo León denied confirmation of the voluntary *concurso* plan that Vitro had submitted. Following that decision, Vitro withdrew its Chapter 15 petition in the U.S. Court and at the same time appealed the Mexican trial court's ruling.

---

[121] Springer (2012), p. 86.

[122] E.g., Complaint at 2, Barclays Bank PLC v. Vitro Envases Norte America S.A. de C.V. (No. 600521), 2009 WL 6045772 (N.Y. Sup. Ct. Feb. 18, 2009); Complaint at 5, Deutsche Bank A.G. v. Vitro Envases Norte America, S.A. de C.V. (No. 600612-09), 2009 WL 7233058 (N.Y. Sup. Ct. Feb. 26, 2009).

[123] Springer (2012), p. 88.

[124] 11 U.S.C. § 1520(a)(1) (2006), applying § 362(1).

After 3 months, on April 11, 2011, the appellate Mexican Second Unitary Court of the Fourth Circuit, in Monterrey, reversed the trial court's ruling and reinstated the prepackaged plan. Vitro filed then a new petition in the Bankruptcy Court for the Southern District of New York for Chapter 15 protection. In response to all that, the creditors who had initiated the above-mentioned proceedings filed motions asking that the Chapter 11 and Chapter 15 cases be administered together and that the consolidated case be transferred to be judged by the Bankruptcy Court of the Northern District of Texas.[125]

On August 15, 2011, the Mexican Fourth District Court for Civil and Labor Matters affirmed the appellate court's ruling, announcing the ranking of claims in the Mexican insolvency proceedings. According to that ranking, Vitro's intercompany claims were considered equal to other unsecured creditors, with the result that Vitro had the right to participate in negotiations on the submitted insolvency plan.

On February 3, 2012, the reorganization plan was approved by the Mexican Fourth District Court for Civil and Labor Matters and on March 2, 2012, Vitro's foreign representative filed a motion with the U.S. Bankruptcy Court for the Northern District of Texas, in which Vitro sought the recognition and enforcement of the reorganization plan (Enforcement Motion). The U.S. Court concluded that a part of the Mexican Court's decision could not be recognized nor enforced in USA.[126]

The issues before the U.S. Bankruptcy Court were a) whether the plan's nonconsensual third-party releases could be extended to creditors in the USA through Section 1521 or 1507 consistent with the principles of comity; and b) if so, whether the exception in Section 1506, that limits the reach of comity where it would be "manifestly contrary" to U.S. public policy, prevented the enforcement of the Mexican court's order approving the Concurso Plan.

The Bankruptcy Court held, among others, that the Concurso Plan did not provide for the distribution of proceeds of the debtor's property substantially in accordance with U.S. bankruptcy law, but instead provided "drastically different treatment in that the noteholders receive a fraction of the amounts owed under the indentures from Vitro and their rights against the other obligors are cut off."[127]

Answering to the second issue, the U.S. Bankruptcy Court stated that it could not conclude that the Mexican proceeding was unfair to the objecting parties. However, it held that the protection of third-party claims in a bankruptcy case is a fundamental policy of the USA, and that the Concurso plan that sought to extinguish such claims, was manifestly contrary to such policy of the United States and could not be enforced in the case before it.

---

[125] *Vitro, S.A.B. de C.V. v. ACP Master, Ltd. (Vitro)*, 455 B.R. 571 (Bankr. N.D. Tex. 2011).

[126] Ochoa Torres (2013).

[127] *Vitro, S.A.B. de C.V. v. ACP Master, Ltd. (In re Vitro, S.A.B. de C.V.)*, 473 B.R. 117 (Bankr. N.D. Tex. 2012).

The denial of the Enforcement Motion by the U.S. Bankruptcy Court was appealed directly to the Court of Appeal for the Fifth Circuit. On appeal, the enforcement issues were narrowed[128] and presented as follows:

> Whether the Bankruptcy Court erred as a matter of law when, after it concluded that the *Concurso* Approval Order was the product of a process that was not corrupt or unfair to the Appellees, it refused to enforce the *Concurso* Approval Order solely because the *Concurso* plan novated guarantee obligations of non-debtor parties and replaced them with new obligations of substantially the same parties.

In addressing this issue, the Fifth Circuit stressed the importance of comity in cross-border insolvency proceedings. However, because under U.S. Bankruptcy Law (§ 1507) non-consensual third-party releases were not available and the Mexican court process had led to the approval of the non-consensual third-party releases, the Fifth Circuit found them inappropriate. It upheld the Bankruptcy Court's decision refusing to enforce the releases.[129]

It is rightly pointed out that this result is at odds with the aims of comity and that the practical implications could be that "[i]f a debtor in a foreign proceeding has assets or operations within the United States, that debtor (or applicable court officer) would have the shadow of U.S. bankruptcy law looming over every order entered by a foreign court."[130]

On March 4, 2013, Vitro announced that it had reached a settlement with its creditors (holders of the Original Notes). Among other things, they agreed to mutual releases and to drop all legal disputes arising out of, concerning, or otherwise relating to the *Concurso* and the Original Notes.

5.2.2.2 Chile

On January 9, 2014, Chile approved the Law 20.720: "Ley de Reorganización y Liquidación de Activos de Empresas y Personas". The Law entered into force in October of the same year. It was the first major reform of Chile's insolvency laws since 1982 and its aim is to encourage current and potential investors in the country from other countries of the world "by creating a more transparent and predictable domestic insolvency regime and by easing the access of insolvency administrators to assets of foreign debtors and their affiliates in Chile."[131]

One of the main aims of this law was to offer as a viable option to the bankruptcy, the procedure of restructuring the companies, and, thus, attract foreign investments.

---

128 Ramsey and Napier (2013), p. 61.

129 *Ad Hoc Group of Vitro Noteholders v. Vitro, S.A.B. de C.V. (In re Vitro, S.A.B. de C.V.)*, No. 12-10542, 2012 WL 5935630 (5th Cir. Nov. 28, 2012).

130 Ramsey and Napier (2013), p. 63.

131 Mears and Reveco (2015), pp. 18–19.

Thus, the new insolvency law focuses on reorganization. As it is stated, it has as its primary goal to change the previous approach to insolvency, from that of strong disapproval and hence liquidation of those entities that were considered responsible for their insolvency to a more lenient treatment that facilitates their reorganization seeks to maximize the value of the debtor's assets.[132] Nevertheless, liquidation is always possible if the reorganization plan is not approved by the required majorities of creditors. There is also the possibility of conversion between the different types of proceedings in appropriate circumstances, provision that adopted the solution envisioned by the UNCITRAL Legislative Guide.[133]

Chile is considered as one of the most solid economies of Latin America and has signed bilateral treaties of free trade with more than 80 countries. Between 1996 and 2014, Chile entered into 16 such free trade agreements with foreign countries such as Mexico (1998), the USA (2004), the Republic of Korea (2004), China (2006), Japan (2007), as well as with countries' unions such as MERCOSUR (1996) and the European Union (2002). The aim was to enhance Chile's international trade regime.[134]

Bankruptcy Law (*Ley de Quiebras*) of Chile constitutes the 4th book of Commercial Code. It was established in 1982 and, subsequently, was reformed. In 2002, in one of the reforms of the bankruptcy laws, an administrative agency charged to supervise the bankruptcy proceedings, was created: Superintendencia de Quiebra.

In 2005, new procedures that would be the alternative to the liquidation/bankruptcy were for the first time introduced. According to those, a debtor could reach an agreement with his/her creditors and that agreement should be approved by a court.

The Law of 2005 had no rules on international insolvency. The New Law, of 2014, is the first law that has such rules.

Articles of the New Law establish the approval by Chile of the UNCITRAL Model Law of 1997. Title 3 (Articles 314–323) is about the recognition of a foreign proceeding and the measures that may be adopted.

Article 314 establishes the procedure necessary to ask for the recognition of an insolvency procedure opened in another country.

The New Law protects equally all the creditors, local and foreign. According to the Article 312:

> Acceso de los acreedores extranjeros a un procedimiento seguido con arreglo a esta ley.
>
> Los acreedores extranjeros gozarán de los mismos derechos que los acreedores nacionales respecto del inicio de un Procedimiento Concursal y de la participación en él con arreglo a esta ley.
>
> Los acreedores extranjeros se sujetarán al orden de prelación de los créditos contenido en el Título XLI del Libro IV del Código Civil y en las demás leyes especiales aplicables, en todos los Procedimientos Concursales iniciados con arreglo a la presente ley.

---

[132] Mears and Reveco (2015), pp. 26–27.

[133] About the UNCITRAL Legislative Guide, see *infra*, Sect. 5.3.

[134] Mears and Reveco (2015), p. 18.

5.2.2.3 Colombia

Colombia was one of the first Latin American countries that enacted in its legislation the UNCITRAL Model Law. The Law 1116 of 2006, or *Nuevo Régimen de Insolvencia Empresarial Colombiano*[135] included the rules of the Model Law almost in their integrity (except of some small modifications) in its Title III (five chapters, Articles 85–116).[136]

The articles, among other things, concretize the types of cross-border insolvency that may appear (Article 86) and state that foreign creditors may participate in an insolvency proceeding opened in Colombia and will have the same rights with the national/local creditors (Article 98).

The fact that the Model Law does not have rules for everything that concerns an international insolvency, has led some authors to state—and with good reason—that even if it constitutes a very important progress since, by adopting it, Colombia was incorporated in the spectrum of the international commercial law,[137] it is not a panacea when dealing with cross-border insolvencies, as some commentators argue. On the contrary, it is stated, European Union has progressed much more, with its Regulations, the first and the Recast.[138]

It is also noted that there have not arisen many cases in Colombian courts where they could apply the rules of the law 1116/2006 on cross-border insolvency.[139]

5.3 UNCITRAL Legislative Guide on Insolvency Law

UNCITRAL has also created the Legislative Guide on Insolvency Law "to be used as a reference by national authorities and legislative bodies when preparing new laws and regulations or reviewing the adequacy of existing laws and regulations."[140]

It contains both legislative recommendations and a commentary.

The commentary refers to identifying an issue and elaborating on its importance, to describing the various solutions that the issue would have under national laws, to discussing the pros and contras of those national solutions and it concludes with a preferred option.

[135] Wilches Durán (2008), pp. 197–218.

[136] Wilches Durán (2009), p. 165.

[137] See Rodríguez Espitia (2007), who points out that the introduction of the UNCITRAL Model Law rules in the country, through this Law, was a necessity that the Colombian bankruptcy legislation was demanding since years, especially because of the augmenting economic alliances that Colombian enterprises are establishing with foreign markets day by day.

[138] Wilches Durán (2009), p. 190.

[139] Vásquez Valencia and Ángel Posada (2011), p. 162.

[140] U.N. COMMISSION ON INTERNATIONAL TRADE LAW, LEGISLATIVE GUIDE ON INSOLVENCY LAW, intro. para. 1, U.N. Sales No. E.05.V.10 (2005), *available at* http://www.uncitral.org/pdf/english/texts/insolven/05-80722_Ebook.pdf.

The recommendations focus on harmonizing substantive law,[141] though they do not refer exhaustively to all the issues mentioned in the commentary. This fact shows the difficulty of achieving consensus.[142]

Although the Model Law does not contain any choice of law rules, the Legislative Guide does and it does it by deciding in favor of the *lex fori concursus*, with two exceptions.[143]

It declares that "[t]he insolvency law of the State in which insolvency proceedings are commenced (*lex fori concursus*) should apply to all aspects of the commencement, conduct, administration and conclusion" of an insolvency proceeding.[144]

It acknowledges two exceptions that may be subject to another law: "the effects of insolvency proceedings on the rights and obligations of the participants in a payment or settlement system or in a regulated financial market"[145] and "the effects of insolvency proceedings on rejection, continuation and modification of labour contracts."[146]

The reason for these two exceptions is that the rights of the participants in a regulated market and of the local employees are often subject to special protections in insolvency proceedings.[147]

The Legislative Guide's solutions differ from those of the European Insolvency Regulation (the only binding international text that deals with choice of law) in that the second acknowledges several exceptions to the primacy of the *lex fori concursus*.

References

Adams ES, Fincke J (2009) Coordinating cross-border bankruptcy: how territorialism saves universalism. Columbia J Eur Law 15:43–85

Ajinderpal S, Ng GX (2018) Cross-border Insolvency in Singapore: the effectiveness of the judicial insolvency network and the JIN guidelines on the administration of cross-border insolvency matters. INSOL International. Technical Series Issue No. 40

Athanassiou LI (2015) Maritime cross-border insolvency [in Greek]. Nomiki Bibliothiki, Athens

Baird DG, Rasmussen RK (2010) Anti-bankruptcy. Yale Law J 119:648–699

Beavers E (2003) Bankruptcy law harmonization in the NAFTA countries: the case of the United States and Mexico. Columbia Bus Law Rev:965–1006

Block-Lieb S, Halliday T (2007) Harmonization and modernization in UNCITRAL's legislative guide on insolvency law. Tex Int Law J 42:475–514

[141] Block-Lieb and Halliday (2007), p. 475.

[142] Clift (2014), p. 37.

[143] Gropper (2014), p. 160.

[144] *Id.* recital 31.

[145] *Id.* recital 32.

[146] *Id.* recital 33.

[147] Gropper (2014), pp. 160–161.

Bufford SL (2013) Coordination of insolvency cases for international enterprise groups: a proposal. Penn State Law Research Paper No. 1-2014. Available at: https://ssrn.com/abstract=2382123
Chandra Mohan S (2012) Cross-border insolvency problems: is the UNCITRAL model law the answer? Int Insolv Rev 21:199–223
Chung JJ (2007) The retrogressive flaw of Chapter 15 of the Bankruptcy Code: a lesson from maritime law. Duke J Comp Int Law 17:253–304
Chung JJ (2014) *In Re Qimonda AG*: the conflict between comity and the public policy exception in Chapter 15 of the Bankruptcy Code. Boston Univ Int Law J 32:91–121
Clift J (2009) International insolvency law: the UNCITRAL experience with harmonization and modernization techniques. Yearb Priv Int Law 11:405–424
Clift J (2014) Choice of law and the UNCITRAL harmonization process. Brooklyn J Corp Financ Commer Law 9:20–47
Dawson AB (2009) Offshore bankruptcies. Nebraska Law Rev 88:317–340
Dawson AB (2015) The problem of local methods in cross-border insolvencies. Berkeley Bus Law J 12:45–80
DeLaughter H (2016) Why two facets of Chapter 15 rulings hinder cross-border insolvency petitions in the United States. Emory Bankruptcy Dev J 32:397–431
Ferreres Comella V (2011) Courts in Latin America and the constraints of the civil law tradition. Tex Law Rev 89:1967–1975
Forero-Niño L (2011) Mexicana airlines, one of the world's oldest airlines, files for bankruptcy protection in Mexico and the United States and suspends flights until further notice. Law Bus Rev Am 17:361–374
Franken SM (2014) Cross-border insolvency law: a comparative institutional analysis. Oxf J Leg Stud 34:97–131
Gilhuly PM, Posin KA, Malatesta AE (2016) Bankruptcy without borders: a comprehensive guide to the first decade of Chapter 15. Am Bankruptcy Inst Law Rev 24:47–132
Godwin A, Howse T, Ramsay I (2017) The inherent power of common law courts to provide assistance in cross-border insolvencies: from comity to complexity. Int Insolv Rev 26:5–39
Graham-Canedo J (2007) Comparative analysis of bankruptcy legal provisions from Mexico and the United States: which legal system is more attractive? DePaul Bus Commer Law J 6:19–28
Gropper AL (2011) The payment of priority claims in cross-border insolvency cases. Tex Int Law J 46:559–577
Gropper AL (2014) The curious disappearance of choice of law as an issue in Chapter 15 cases. Brooklyn J Corp Financ Commer Law 9:152–179
Guzman A (2000) International bankruptcy: in defense of universalism. Mich Law Rev 98:2177–2215
Hannan NF (2015) Do words matter?: a comparative analysis of the UNCITRAL model law on cross-border insolvency in Australia, Canada, New Zealand, United Kingdom and the United States of America. Doctoral thesis. University of Western Australia School of Law. Available at https://api.research-repository.uwa.edu.au/portalfiles/portal/5338528/Hannan_Neil_2015.pdf
Hargovan A (2008) The cross-border insolvency act 2008 (Cth) – issues and implications. Aust J Corp Law 22:188–197
Ho LC (2009) Cross-border fraud and cross-border insolvency: proving COMI and seeking recognition under the UK model law. J Int Bank Financ Law 29:537–542
Ho LC (2010) Applying foreign law – realising the model law's potential. J Int Bank Law Regul. Available at: https://ssrn.com/abstract=1675487
Ho LC (2014) The revised UNCITRAL model law enactment guide – a welcome product? J Int Bank Law Regul:325–340
Holzer J (2011) Die Empfehlungen der UNCITRAL zum nationalen und internationalen Konzerninsolvenzrecht. Zeitschrift für Wirtschaftsrecht 40:1894–1900
Kirshner JA (2013) The (false) conflict between due process rights and universalism in cross-border insolvency. Camb Law J 72:27–31

Leong J (2012) Is Chapter 15 universalist or territorialist? Empirical evidence from United States Bankruptcy Court Cases. Wisconsin Int Law J 29:110–137

Mannan M (2016) Are Bangladesh, India and Pakistan ready to adopt the UNCITRAL model law on cross-border insolvency? Int Insolv Rev 25:195–224

Martinez E (2001) The new environment of insolvency in Mexico. Conn J Int Law 17:75–78

Mason R (2006) Local proceedings in a multi-state liquidation: issues of jurisdiction. Melb Univ Law Rev 30:145–190

Mason R (2012) Cross-border insolvency and legal transnationalisation. Int Insolv Rev 21:105–126

McCormack G (2016) US exceptionalism and US localism? Cross-border insolvency law in comparative perspective. Leg Stud 36:136–162

McCormack G, Hargovan A (2015) Australia and the international insolvency paradigm. Sydn Law Rev 37:389–416

Mears P, Reveco R (2015) Chile's new bankruptcy legislation to attract more foreign direct investment and international trade. Int Insolv Law Rev:18–30

Mevorach I (2011) On the road to universalism: a comparative and empirical study of the UNCITRAL model law on cross-border insolvency. Eur Bus Organ Law Rev 12:517–557

Montarcé I (2016) La quiebra de Compañia Mexicana de Aviación: Análisis del conflicto jurídico-político y sus consecuencias en los trabajadores. Alegatos 92:201–226

Morawetz G (2012) Acceptance remarks of the honourable Geoffrey Morawetz. Emory Bankruptcy Dev J 29:5–13

Moustaira EN (1992) The equality of creditors in international bankruptcy law [in Greek]. Ant. N. Sakkoulas Publishers, Athens/Komotini

Moustaira EN (1995) Forum non conveniens. Equity in the frame of legality [in Greek]. Ant. N. Sakkoulas Publishers, Athens/Komotini

Ochoa Torres E (2013) La cooperación internacional en la legislación Mexicana en materia de concurso mercantil. Tesis realizada para obtener el grado de Doctor en Derecho. Universidad Autónoma de Nuevo León, Facultad de Derecho y Criminologia, Subdirección de Posgrado. Available at: https://cd.dgb.uanl.mx/bitstream/handle/201504211/16567/21074.pdf?sequence=1&isAllowed=y

Olivares-Caminal R (2010) Expedited debt restructuring in Latin America. Warwick School of Law Research Paper Series. Available at: https://ssrn.com/abstract=1548438

Perakis EE (2010) Bankruptcy law [in Greek]. Nomiki Bibliothiki, Athens

Quintana Adriano EA (2007) El impacto de la quiebra transfronteriza en las legislaciones internas. Boletín Mexicano de Derecho Comparado, pp 881–906

Ramsey T, Napier J (2013) Enforcing orders of foreign courts under Chapter 15: *In Re Vitro S.A.B. de C.V.* Advocate, pp 60–64

Rasmussen RK (1993) A study of the costs and benefits of textualism: the Supreme Court's bankruptcy's cases. Wash Univ Law Q 71:535–598

Rodríguez Espitia JJ (2007) Aproximación al derecho concursal colombiano. REVIST@e – Mercatoria 6(2)

Sarra J (2007) Northern lights, Canada's version of the UNCITRAL model law on cross-border insolvency. Int Insolv Rev 16:19–61

Schorr S (2011) Avoidance actions under Chapter 15: was condor correct? Fordham Int Law J 35:350–384

Springer TS (2012) Paved with good intentions: creditors face a new roadblock to recovery in Mexican Bankruptcies. Law Bus Rev Am 18:83–93

Sullivan TA, Warren E, Westbrook JL (1994) The persistence of local legal culture: twenty years of evidence from the Federal Bankruptcy Courts. Harv J Law Public Policy 17:801–865

Vásquez Valencia MV, Ángel Posada AF (2011) La insolvencia transfronteriza: generalidades de un fenómeno económico con impacto jurídico. Criterio Jurídico 11:145–164

Walters A (2017) Modified universalisms & the role of local legal culture in the making of cross-border insolvency law. Available at: https://ssrn.com/abstract=3084117

Westbrook JL (1991) Theory and pragmatism in global insolvencies: choice of law and choice of forum. Am Bankruptcy Law J 65:457–490

Westbrook J (2015) Ian Fletcher and the internationalist principle. Nottingham Insolv Bus Law e-J 3:565–572

Wilches Durán RE (2008) Vacíos e inconsistencias estructurales del nuevo régimen de insolvencia empresarial colombiano. Identificación y propuestas de solución. Revista Universitas 117:197–218

Wilches Durán RE (2009) La insolvencia transfronteriza en el derecho colombiano. Revista de Derecho, Universidad del Norte 32:162–198

Wood RJ (2016) The paramountcy principle in bankruptcy and insolvency law: the latest word. Can Bus Law J 58:27–56

Yamauchi KD (2007) Should reciprocity be a part of the UNCITRAL model cross-border insolvency law? Int Insolv Rev 16:145–179

Zhihe Ji J (2017) Cross-border rehabilitation: an impediment to ship arrest in Singapore? CML Working Paper Series No 17/04. March 2017 http://law.nus.edu.sg/cml/wps.html

Chapter 6
Protocols

6.1 General Comments

Another theory about dealing with international insolvencies—implemented already, in specific cases—that has been proposed is the contractualist theory. According to that, parties may choose the regime that will govern an international insolvency.

"Contractualist" solutions may be supportive to the achievement of universalism of international insolvencies, it is suggested.

According to the contrary opinion, though, these solutions cannot "appreciate the multiparty nature of insolvency regimes and the divergence in the nature of claimants",[1] that is why it has gained little support.[2]

An intermediate way that might have some good results and contribute to an effective implementation of universalist solutions in international insolvencies could be an ad hoc contractualism, that would be achieved during the international insolvency proceedings, by way of "cross-border agreements" or "protocols" that may be concluded between the parties about the way to coordinate the international insolvency process[3] and that are then endorsed by the court.[4]

Thus, protocols are considered by many "a means to achieve the efficient universalist goal absent laws." [5] The arguments in favor of this approach are several, the most crucial of which is that protocols are flexible tools[6] and that they ensure predictability and cooperation.[7]

---

[1] Mevorach (2014), p. 226,

[2] Warren and Westbrook (2005), pp. 1201, 1248–1254.

[3] Mevorach (2010), p. 405.

[4] Sarra (2008), p. 84.

[5] Wouters and Raykin (2013), p. 418.

[6] Which might be used in cases of a group of companies' insolvency too, see *infra*, 7.

[7] Not a very strong argument, though, for those who believe that the State should always control such—sensitive, for many reasons—cases.

E. Moustaira, *International Insolvency Law*,
https://doi.org/10.1007/978-3-030-04450-3_6

There are voices that doubt the correctness—and efficiency—of this approach, though. They also point out that the praxis has shown that they cannot really be considered a panacea for the difficulties that arise in cross-border insolvencies. Furthermore, there is always this difference between common law and civil law systems, which is also mirrored in the proposed solution of protocols, where what is won in flexibility and adjustment to the concrete situation is lost in certainty of law and foreseeability of success.[8]

The European Insolvency Recast Regulation, in its recital 48, last period, states that

> [w]hen cooperating, insolvency practitioners and courts should take into account best practices for cooperation in cross-border insolvency cases, as set out in principles and guidelines on communication and cooperation adopted by European and international organisations active in the area of insolvency law, and in particular the relevant guidelines prepared by the United Nations Commission on International Trade Law (Uncitral).

However, it is rightly noted that best practices are not easily collectable[9] and that the data collected regarding continental Member States show that practitioners and courts are not particularly used to cross-border cooperation.[10] It is different where common law countries are involved. Therefore, the most "best practices" collected refer to common law approaches and solutions.

Their contents may vary; however, they have a common element: they try to harmonize procedural issues rather than substantive laws' aspects.[11]

Many of these protocols have followed the model of the *IBA Cross-Border Insolvency Concordat*, adopted in 1995 by International Bar Association (IBA).

6.2 Private International Law Issues

The juridical qualification of these protocols/contracts is necessary to decide about their regulation. When these contracts aim at the cooperation of insolvency proceedings that are restricted in a country's territory, they are considered public law procedural contracts.

In case these contracts are international, aiming at the cooperation of insolvency proceedings in more countries, which is the applicable law to them? Could they be considered public international law contracts? Neither the judges of the insolvency proceedings nor the administrators are subjects of public international law, hence this option is excluded.[12]

---

[8] Veneziano (2004), pp. 60–63.

[9] Queirolo and Dominelli (2017), pp. 132–133.

[10] Specifically about drawing up protocols in accordance with German law, see Busch et al. (2010), p. 417.

[11] Miguens (2018), p. 56.

[12] Moustaira (2002), p. 1578.

The admissibility and the consequences of procedural contracts are governed by *lex fori*, that is, the law of the country the courts of which examine these contracts.[13] Nevertheless, whether such a contract has been validly concluded, seems more reasonable to be decided according to the applicable law to a contract.

Contracting parties of such a contract, either national or international, are the judges and the administrators involved. It is not an easy situation, especially for civil law countries—or other, non-common law, countries—the fact that such a contract/protocol of cooperation tries to "cover" the lack of a public international law contract/convention with an *ad hoc* private agreement. Furthermore, given the fact that judicial cooperation is necessary in these cases, such a protocol almost invalidates the constitutional obligation of the judge to be bound by the law.[14]

One potential problem would arise in case of parallel proceedings on the property of the same debtor: the fact that the administrators would conclude such a contract that would create rights and obligations for the debtor, could be considered as a non-permitted "insider trading" and in this case other juridical constructions should be found for such a contract to be considered valid.

Lastly, let it be said that, whether and under which conditions there is an obligation of concluding such a contract, will be governed by the *lex fori*. Suggesting that comity would be the basis of this obligation is not convincing, since the relations between courts and administrators of different countries are not public international law relations.

6.3 History: The First Cross-Border Insolvency Protocol

Probably the first cross-border insolvency protocol between insolvency administrations was concluded at the beginning of the twentieth century. Involuntary liquidation proceedings had been commenced in India (Madras) and in England (London), regarding an Anglo-Indian merchant and banking partnership, following the death of one of the partners.[15]

The administrators in London and in Madras had to collect, realize, and distribute assets to the English and the Indian creditors respectively. To have the best results, they came to an agreement on admitted claims and promised that if there were surplus sums, they would be remitted toe the other proceedings, so that all creditors could be satisfied. The agreement was confirmed by both the English and the Indian courts. An English creditor sought to challenge the agreement but the English court stated that it was "clearly a proper and common-sense business arrangement" and that it was "manifestly for the benefit of all parties interested."[16]

---

[13] Eidenmüller (2001), p. 30.

[14] Paulus (1998), p. 981.

[15] Mannan (2016), p. 205.

[16] *In re P. Macfadyen & Co. Ex parte Vizianagaram Co., Ltd.* [1908] 1 K.B. 675.

It has been commented that, "[s]adly, such a spirit of cross-border civil cooperation does not continue to prevail in India or its neighbouring states" and that now "a rudimentary framework for dealing with cross-border insolvency cases exists in all three countries [India, Pakistan & Bangladesh] which broadly reflect a territorial approach."[17]

However, the situation is not so simple, not so black and white. At that time, India was still a colony and its law was very much "English style".[18] Cooperation is not so difficult when legal regimes are similar or look very much alike—of course these similarities had been "achieved" then by force, explicit or implicit. Now, that the former colonies are independent countries, even when their laws still keep their common law influences,[19] there are more or other interests at stake. Further, as it has been above mentioned, territoriality is the principle considered to respect state sovereignty.

Cooperation via protocols was and is a proposition inspired by common law countries. Their insolvency laws may present various—and many, at times—differences, nevertheless they share a common mentality which can help in these situations. The question is whether the protocol approach can be adopted by other countries' laws and, most importantly, whether it can be successfully applied.

6.4 Recent Cases

6.4.1 Maxwell Communications

The most famous case until some years ago was *Maxwell Communications*.[20] Insolvency proceedings had commenced both in New York, USA (Chapter 11) and in London, England. A U.S. *examiner* was appointed as mediator between the two

[17] Mannan (2016), p. 205.

[18] At the beginning of the twentieth century, courts in British India (composed of the three actual countries: India, Pakistan, Bangladesh) could evidently cooperate easily with courts in London, since their laws were very much influenced by English law at the time they were Great Britain's colonies. Today, all three countries adopt a rather territorial approach towards cross-border insolvency cases. None of those treats differently domestic and foreign creditors in their company law regarding preferential payments. There is, though, one exception: according to Bangladesh's bankruptcy law, local banks and financial institutions may, on certain conditions, be prioritized before foreign secured creditors in case a corporation is declared bankrupt, see Mannan (2016) p. 205.

[19] See Shaaban Masoud (2014), p. 196, who states: "Notably, the existing regimes in most of the SSA [Sub-Saharan Africa] countries are traceable from the historical colonial legacy. As such, a fair assessment of the regimes must take that fact into account and consider the corresponding legal families in which they are situated. The application of the common law to Anglophone SSA countries is the best example of the continuing influence of the colonial legacy. This legacy also applies to cross-border insolvency aspects of the common law jurisdictions in SSA."

[20] *In re Maxwell Comm'n Corp.*, 170 B.R. 800 (Bankr. S.D.N.Y. 1994), *aff'd*, 186 B.R. 807 (S.D.N.Y. 1995), 93 F.3d 1036 (2d Cir. 1996).

proceedings and he managed to enter into a protocol with the UK administrator. The case involved $2 billion in assets and over $4 billion in liabilities.[21]

The protocol provided that all the assets would be pooled together and not carved out for each court.[22] Creditors in either country could submit their claims to their respective court.

The cooperation between the U.S. examiner and the U.K. administrator went amazingly well, without material conflicts. The court described the case as a "remarkable" orderly liquidation.[23]

It has also been talked about the "Myth of Maxwell", though. It has been underlined that in reality the positive solution was very much owed to the facts of the case: It was about the bankruptcy of a holding company, there were no U.S. creditors, there was not one English creditor who could have the power to nominate a private *receiver*, and notwithstanding the fact that the initial proceedings had as their aim the restructuring of the company, the agreement consecrated the liquidation of the holding; therefore, the protocol was not in reality an instrument for the global recuperation of the Maxwell business.[24]

6.4.2 *Lehman's Collapse*

Lehman Brothers Holdings Inc. (LBHI) filed for Chapter 11 procedure in the U.S. Bankruptcy Court on September 15, 2008. It was the largest ever bankruptcy in the world, involving assets of US $691 billion.[25]

Before it filed for bankruptcy protection, LBHI[26] was the fourth largest investment bank in the USA, with approximately US $700 billion in assets, and corresponding liabilities on capital of approximately $25 billion. The assets were predominantly long-term, while the liabilities were largely short-term.[27] It had a $35 trillion derivative portfolio, representing about 5% of the worldwide derivatives market. The immediate cause of its failure was the repo market, and "Lehman's growing inability to access funding for its operations.[28]

[21] Wouters and Raykin (2013), p. 420.

[22] Westbrook (1996), p. 2535.

[23] Flaschen and Silverman (1998), p. 592.

[24] Homan (2001), pp. 250–252.

[25] Lee (2013), p. 284.

[26] The "ultimate parent company" of all the Lehman entities, see McDermott and Turetsky (2011), p. 416.

[27] Report of Anton R. Valukas, Examiner at 3, *In re Lehman Bros. Holdings*, No 08-13555 (Bankr. S.D.N.Y.Mar.11, 2010), ECF No. 7531. Available at: www.lehmansecuritieslitigation.com/pdf/BK%20[Dkt.%207531]%20Report%20Anton%20Valukas,%20Examiner%20(Vols.%201%20-%205).pdf.

[28] Lubben 2017.

It had over 900 legal entities in more than 40 countries, of which entities more than 650 were in other than USA countries.[29]

As the finally effectuated Cross-Border Insolvency Protocol for the Lehman Brothers Group of Companies ("Lehman Protocol") stated:

> For more than 150 years, Lehman was a leader in the global financial markets by serving the financial needs of corporations, governmental agencies, institutional clients and individual investors located worldwide. Its headquarters in New York and regional headquarters in London and Tokyo were complemented by a network of offices in North America, Europe, the Middle East, Latin America and the Asia Pacific region.[30]

Could the collapse be avoided? Could LBHI be saved and why was it not, when the tendency is to save large institutions that are too big to fail,[31] since otherwise too many businesses, too many people may be destroyed?

Myriad are the stories that can be told about Lehman Brothers' collapse[32]; simplifying are the stories,[33] mystifying, though, the reasons. Most truthful appears the growing loss of confidence in Lehman among clients and counterparties,[34] their loss of faith that Lehman could survive.[35]

Chain reactions followed in all levels, private and public. As it has been stated, "[t]he process replicated throughout the Western world, leading to much observation on the growth of interconnectedness in the global financial system."[36]

Lehman's bankruptcy filings all over the world had as result more than 75 separate insolvency proceedings[37] in 9 countries (USA, The Netherlands, Germany, Switzerland, Japan, France, Hong Kong,[38] Singapore, Australia), with more than 16 administrators.

6.4.2.1 Lehman's Legal Structure: Lehman's Protocol

As it was above mentioned, Lehman had hundreds of legal entities worldwide. Moreover, many of its entities, to obtain the lowest cost of capital available to Lehman, operated unincorporated branches in other countries. For example, Lehman's primary London-based subsidiary (LBIE) operated branches in Holland,

[29] Lee (2013), p. 289.

[30] 'Background' in Lehman Protocol. Available at: http://www.ekvandoorne.com/files/CrossBorderProtocol.pdf.

[31] Davidoff and Zaring (2009), p. 474.

[32] Lubben and Pei Woo (2014), p. 296.

[33] Levitin (2009), p. 1007.

[34] Hashmall (2010), p. 839.

[35] Okamoto (2009), pp. 196–198.

[36] Lubben and Pei Woo (2014), p. 297.

[37] More than one hundred separate bankruptcy proceedings, according to Kirshner (2018), p. 2.

[38] In Hong Kong, there were opened insolvency proceedings for eight subsidiaries of Lehman Brothers, see Ali and Wang Kwok (2011), p. 153.

Germany, Switzerland, France, Italy, Dubai, Qatar, Spain, Korea, Sweden, and Israel.[39]

In New York, Lehman operated two primary entities: Lehman Holdings (LBHI) and Lehman Brothers Inc. (LBI). Both Lehman Holdings and LBI had unincorporated branches in London. LBI was Lehman's entity for conducting trades on domestic U.S. stock exchanges.

Lehman's broker-dealer in London was Lehman Brothers International (Europe) (LBIE). Leman Holdings and LBIE were the two central entities in Lehman business.

During the decade before its collapse, Lehman's growth was tremendous.[40] Its total assets, in millions, grew from $312,061 in 2003, to $503,545 in 2006, and to $691,063 in 2007.[41]

The many insolvency proceedings in the various countries were creating a chaos. Furthermore, there were irreconcilable judgments by different national courts.[42]

After many efforts to find a solution, some of Lehman's entities decided to have resort to a protocol. Nothing could guarantee the end of such a chaos and it seems that neither this solution was a real success, since 10 years after the Lehman collapse its repercussions are still felt.

The Lehman Protocol was released on May 12, 2009. Its aim was to establish a framework for the cooperation and coordination of the various insolvency proceedings against LBHI that had commenced or were expected to commence in various countries/jurisdictions[43] and, consequently, facilitate the orderly management of the various LBHI insolvency estates.[44] As it is stated, "the protocol took seven months

---

[39] Lubben and Pei Woo (2014), p. 302 and note 37.

[40] Lubben and Pei Woo (2014), p. 305 note 56.

[41] LEHMAN BROS. HOLDINGS INC., FORM 10-K 29 (2008), *available at* http://www.sec.gov/Archives/edgar/data/806085/000110465908005476/a08-3530_110k.htm.

[42] Sexton (2012), p. 833.

[43] Among other proceedings, there was one proceeding before English courts, about a proposed scheme of arrangement between the administrators of Lehman Brothers International (Europe) [LBIE] and creditors of the company—account holders that had potential claims on the assets held by LBIE. The scheme creditors were required to release all claims against LBIE, as well as those against the scheme supervisors, the administrators and other scheme creditors in exchange for the right to have such a part of the asset held in trust as was available for distribution under the scheme. The subject of the dispute was the legality of the arrangement as a scheme of arrangement under Part 26 of the Companies Act. The administrators argued that the main objective of the scheme was not to vary or extinguish the property rights of the company's clients, but to vary their contractual relationships with LBIE as creditors and debtor. The Companies Court judge disagreed with the administrators, stating that the scheme was mostly about eliminating LBIE's obligations towards its clients and, consequently fell outside the jurisdiction of Part 26. The Court of Appeal concurred with the Companies Court judge, pointing out that "an arrangement between a company and its creditors must mean an arrangement, which deals with their rights *inter se* as debtor and creditor", see Nana (2012), pp. 4–7.

[44] Lee (2013), p. 289.

to complete, could not be enforced in court, and did not bind the entities whose representatives did not sign it."[45]

On March 2010, Lehman filed a Joint Chapter 11 Plan of Reorganization. On April 14, 2010, it filed a Joint Chapter 11 Plan of Reorganization and Disclosure Statement. On December 6, 2011, the U.S. Bankruptcy Court confirmed Lehman's Third Amended Joint Chapter 11 Plan.

As it was above mentioned 10 years after the Lehman collapse the damage done worldwide has not really been extinguished.[46]

6.4.2.2 Should Banking and Bankruptcy Be Divided?

Should financial institutions' cross-border insolvency be dealt on in the same way as the "real-economy debtors"?[47] Or should it be acknowledged that financial institutions are unique creatures?[48] According to that opinion, if in times of distress operations are separated from finance, legal entities whose existence is merely a result of financing decisions and which are not really needed to operate the business, must be cleared away to facilitate the insolvency/restructuring process. Further, if one was concentrating on the core entities in the financial institution, the number of countries that would need to be parties to such an agreement/protocol would be reduced. Thus, in the Lehman case, such an agreement could only have involved the United States of America and the United Kingdom and not the myriad other jurisdictions dealing with Lehman insolvency cases.[49]

Banking and bankruptcy should be divided? Historically it had been accepted in many countries' laws that banks and insurance companies were different from other companies and that they should be excluded from the normal bankruptcy process.[50]

In USA, most big business was excluded from the first permanent American Bankruptcy Law in 1898, so the exclusion of banks and insurance companies was

---

[45] Kirshner (2018), p. 6.

[46] In 2010, just two years after Lehman Brothers Holdings Inc. (LBHI) filed for Chapter 11 procedure in the U.S. Bankruptcy Court, no one could foresee what would be the repercussions of the whole situation and how long they would be felt. Jurists too were anxious to see how the insolvency laws of the countries involved would deal with this tremendously dangerous situation. Thus, for example, Wattermoli (2010), p. 161, was declaring: "Por otra parte, la dimensión mundial de la crisis parece representar una ocasión propicia para verificar, en un contexto más general, el estado de evolución del procedimiento de *Reorganización*, analizando desde la óptica de la tutela de los intereses de los acreedores; esto permitirá en un momento posterior formular algunas hipótesis sobre el contenido del plan de reorganización de Lehman Brothers Holdings Inc. y, por lo tanto, el impacto que tal desequilibrio puede tener respecto a los sujetos que están implicados."

[47] Westbrook (2006), p. 337.

[48] Ayotte and Skeel (2010), p. 469.

[49] Lubben and Pei Woo (2014), pp. 299–300.

[50] See Lubben (2011), p. 1263, speaking about American Bankruptcy Law.

consistent with the general tendency of specialized law for the large enterprises.[51] Until recently, large financial institutions in USA would be subjected to Chapter 11 of the U.S. Bankruptcy Code plus one specialized regime when they failed. This exclusion from the other rules of the U.S. Bankruptcy Code was not considered positively by all jurists.[52]

On the other hand, it is pointed out that the Bank Holding Company Act, which does have regulatory powers over SIFI's holding companies, does not contain insolvency provisions, therefore there is not really a dual banking system[53]—or, at least, there was not, before the Dodd-Frank Act.

Lehman's bankruptcy was a shock worldwide and it prompted—if not obliged—the national laws to bring into force new rules that would protect investors in the event of a financial institution.

Such rules, in UK, are the Banking Act 2009 which came into effect on February 8, 2011. It was supplemented by the Investment Bank Special Administration (England and Wales) Rules 2011 ("SAR Rules") and the Client Asset Sourcebook ("CASS"), existing guidelines set down by the Financial Services Authority (the "FSA").[54]

In USA, the *Dodd-Frank Wall Street Reform and Consumer Protection Act ("Dodd-Frank Act")* was signed into law on July 21, 2010. Among other things, this law expands the government's authority to protect consumers of financial services.[55] To implement and enforce the new consumer protection rules, the U.S. Congress created the Bureau of Consumer Financial Protection within the Federal Reserve System. Dodd-Frank Act also created a new "orderly liquidation authority" (OLA) to handle the big cases of large financial institutions "in financial distress".[56]

Following Dodd-Frank, a distressed bank holding company and its bank subsidiary will be addressed in a single forum.[57]

---

[51] Lubben (2004), p. 1420.

[52] McAlister (2008), p. 129.

[53] Butler and Macey (1997), p. 698.

[54] Certain UK cases, related to the Lehman collapse, and referring to CASS were tried by the Court of Appeal, the decision of which was affirmed by the UK Supreme Court, on 29 February 2012. As it is mentioned, "[e]ssentially, the Supreme Court decision prevented the clients from becoming unsecured creditors and therefore rendering their money in the company's client account to be subject to the *pari passu* rule for bankruptcy distribution.", see Lee (2013), p. 298.

[55] See Lubben (2011), p. 1268: "The new law partially supersedes chapter 11 as applied to financial companies, granting the Treasury Secretary the authority to appoint the FDIC as receiver of a systematically important financial company, with certain important limitations …".

[56] Lubben (2018), p. 1377, says it is incredibly difficult to actually use OLA.

[57] Maybe, says Lubben (2011), p. 1270.

References

Ali S, Wang Kwok JK (2011) After Lehman: international response to financial disputes – a focus on Hong Kong. Richmond J Glob Law Bus 10:151–177

Ayotte K, Skeel DA Jr (2010) Bankruptcy or Bailouts? J Corp Law 35:469–498

Busch P, Remmert A, Rüntz S, Vallender H (2010) Kommunikation zwischen Gerichten in grenzüberschreitenden Insolvenzen – Was geht und was nicht geht. Neue Zeitschrift für Insolvenz und Sanierungsrecht, pp 417–430

Butler HN, Macey JR (1997) The myth of competition in the dual banking system. Cornell Law Rev 73:677–718

Davidoff SM, Zaring D (2009) Regulation by deal: the government's response to the financial crisis. Adm Law Rev 61:463–541

Eidenmüller H (2001) Der nationale und der internationale Insolvenzverwaltungsvertrag. Zeitschrift für Zivilprozessrecht, pp 3–36

Flaschen ED, Silverman RJ (1998) Cross-border insolvency cooperation protocols. Tex Int Law J 33:587

Hashmall AM (2010) After the fall: a new framework to regulate "Too Big to Fail" non-bank financial institutions. N Y Univ Law Rev 85:829–866

Homan M (2001) An insolvency practitioner's perspective. In: Bridge M, Stevens R (eds) Cross-border security and insolvency. Oxford University Press, pp 243–255

Kirshner J (2018) International bankruptcy. The challenge of insolvency in a global economy. University of Chicago Press, Chicago

Lee E (2013) Investor protection in Lehman Brothers' insolvency litigation. J Comp Law 7:284–306

Levitin A (2009) The crisis without a face: emerging narratives of the financial crisis. Miami Law Rev 63:999–1010

Lubben SJ (2004) Railroad receiverships and modern bankruptcy theory. Cornell Law Rev 89:1420–1475

Lubben SJ (2011) Financial institutions in bankruptcy. Seattle Univ Law Rev 34:1259–1278

Lubben SJ (2017) Lehman's derivative portfolio. In: Faber D, Vermunt N (eds) Bank failure: lessons from Lehman Brothers. Oxford University Press. Available at: https://ssrn.com/abstract=22698234

Lubben SJ (2018) A functional analysis of SIFI insolvency. Tex Law Rev 96:1377–1402

Lubben SJ, Pei Woo S (2014) Reconceptualizing Lehman. Tex Int Law J 49:295–325

Mannan M (2016) Are Bangladesh, India and Pakistan ready to adopt the UNCITRAL model law on cross-border insolvency? Int Insolv Rev 25:195–224

McAlister LS (2008) The inefficiencies of exclusion: the importance of including insurance companies in the Bankruptcy Code. Emory Bankruptcy Dev J 24:129–158

McDermott MA, Turetsky DM (2011) Restructuring large, systemically-important, financial companies: an analysis of the orderly liquidation authority, Title II of the Dodd-Frank wall street reform and consumer protection act. Am Bankruptcy Inst Law Rev 19:401–451

Mevorach I (2010) Towards a consensus on the treatment of enterprise groups in insolvency. Cardozo J Int Comp Law 18:359–423

Mevorach I (2014) Cross-border insolvency of enterprise groups: the choice of law challenge. Brooklyn J Corp Financ Commer Law 9:226–249

Miguens HJ (2018) El derecho internacional privado de la insolvencia en Argentina. Propuestas de reforma "de lege lata" y "de lege ferenda" para Argentina y el MERCOSUR. Editorial Acadèmica Española, Mauritius

Moustaira EN (2002) Insolvency proceedings in the European Union Member States [in Greek]. Elliniki Dikaiosyni 43:1569–1578

Nana CN (2012) In Re Lehman Brothers international (Europe): positivism or the Rigour of Pedantry? Int Insolv Rev 21:1–16

Okamoto KS (2009) After the bailout: regulating systemic moral hazard. UCLA Law Rev 57:183–236

Paulus CG (1998) Protokolle – ein anderer Zugang zur Abwicklung grenzüberschreitender Insolvenzen. Zeitschrift für Wirtschaftsrecht, pp 977–982

Queirolo I, Dominelli S (2017) Cooperation between authorities and insolvency office holders. In: Queirolo I, Dominelli S (eds) European and national perspectives on the application of the European insolvency regulation. Aracne editrice, Roma, pp 117–185

Sarra J (2008) Maidum's challenge, legal and governance issues in dealing with cross-border business enterprise group insolvencies. Int Insolv Rev 17:73–122

Sexton A (2012) Current problems and trends in the administration of transnational insolvencies involving enterprise groups: the mixed record of protocols, the UNCITRAL model insolvency law and the EU insolvency regulation. Chicago J Int Law 12:811–840

Shaaban Masoud B (2014) The context for cross-border insolvency law reform in Sub-Saharan Africa. Int Insolv Rev 23:181–200

Veneziano A (2004) Il risanamento dell'impresa in crisi. Problemi e soluzioni nell'ottica dell'insolvenza transfrontaliera, Aracne, Roma

Warren E, Westbrook JL (2005) Contracting out of bankruptcy: an empirical intervention. Harv Law Rev 118:1197–1254

Wattermoli D (2010) Chapter 11 y tutela de ls acreedores (Anotaciones al caso Lehman Brothers). ADCo 19:159–185

Westbrook JL (1996) The lessons of Maxwell communication. Fordham Law Rev 64:2531–2541

Westbrook JL (2006) Multinational financial distress: the last hurrah of territorialism. Tex Int Law J 41:321–337

Wouters N, Raykin A (2013) Corporate group cross-border insolvencies between the United States & European Union: legal & economic developments. Emory Bankruptcy Dev J 29:387–423

Chapter 7
Groups of Companies

7.1 General Comments

A multinational corporate group is an enterprise that operates in more than one country through more entities—a parent company and few or many subsidiary companies—which have separate legal personality.

Should all companies of a multinational corporate group (or multinational enterprise group, or "multinational" company[1] or enterprise group[2]) be included in the same insolvency proceeding, wherever it may be opened, even when the companies of the group are in different countries, in different jurisdictions? Or, better, should insolvent subsidiaries belonging to the same multinational corporate group be able to have their insolvency proceedings opened by the same court?[3] And even further, should a procedural consolidation, if achieved, lead to a substantive consolidation?

The ensuing issues are really difficult to handle. Corporate distress is already complicated, since it is subject to both insolvency law and corporate law.[4] The *"labyrinthus creditorum"* becomes even more difficult to tread on, when it comes to the insolvency of all or several companies of a group.[5] Cultural differences, among other issues, contribute to the difficulties in dealing with such insolvencies.[6]

Many are those who argue in favor of a territorialist approach to the serious issue of group of companies' insolvency, being anxious that the opposite approach would lead to a "lifting of the corporate veil", something that the parent company tried to avoid, anyway, when it created or bought the other companies of the group.

---

[1] Almaskari (2016), pp. 2–3.

[2] Gropper (2015), p. 364.

[3] Mevorach (2007), p. 179.

[4] Schmidt (2015), p. 125.

[5] About the interaction of corporate law and corporate bankruptcy, scholars had already discussed years ago, see Skeel (2015), p. 1021.

[6] Wouters and Raykin (2013), p. 387.

E. Moustaira, *International Insolvency Law*,
https://doi.org/10.1007/978-3-030-04450-3_7

According to them, countries may not like the possibility that their own insolvency laws and policies would be subordinated to the laws and policies of other countries.[7] Furthermore, the different treatment of creditors' claims and the priorities foreseen by each national insolvency law do not really contribute to the idea of consolidating the insolvency proceedings of the members of an enterprise group.[8]

However, there are those too who fervently support a universalist approach to this issue, "whereby a single jurisdiction governs the proceeding and applies its laws (the laws of the forum) regarding the insolvency matters, subject to limited exceptions."[9]

Thus, it is argued that universalism applied to an international group of companies would often be the best approach,[10] since many such groups operate a single global business and a group-wide insolvency solution would be the most appropriate one.[11] It is stated that fears that such a solution would interfere with the corporate form are unjustified, since the choice of law determination does not necessarily lead to a "lifting of the corporate veil". In the contrary case, eventual multiple insolvency proceedings opened by courts in different countries[12] would have resulted expensive and probably inefficient processes and, unavoidably, uncertainty of the whole situation.[13]

It is generally admitted though that there is no unique ideal solution and that more universalist solutions would be needed that would be adaptable to each, different, case. According to this approach, it is not the substantive consolidation that is aimed[14]—that is, the pooling of assets and debts of the different group entities together in the course of insolvency—something that would really lead to veil lifting. What is sought for is a private international law solution that would be appropriate for each case. Modified universalism is ideal for that, it is said. "Through cooperation and centralization of group proceedings as appropriate for the group at hand", it is argued, "modified universalism facilitates group-wide solutions …".[15]

On the other hand, there are those who believe that a substantive consolidation should also take place. They point out that asset and claims allocation is an expensive and uncertain process: It is not simply about allocation of proceeds to the respective entities that "owned" the assets. It is also about the "assignment of claims to entities, a resolution of relative priority of claims (…), and a reconciliation of

---

[7] Avi-Yonah (2003), pp. 8–9.

[8] See about that, specifically regarding the European Union Member States' insolvency laws, Merlini (2016), pp. 120–121.

[9] Mevorach (2014), p. 227.

[10] Mevorach (2010).

[11] See Mevorach (2018), p. 10: "Only where the insolvency process imitates the commercial reality of integration and allows the group or its relevant parts to be kept together is it possible to restructure the group as a whole or apply other group-wide solutions that can maximize value."

[12] Gopalan and Guihot (2015), p. 1225.

[13] Sarra (2009), p. 547.

[14] As Pottow (2015), p. 348, points out: "universalism is agnostic to substantive consolidation".

[15] Mevorach (2018), p. 227.

inter-company claims (…).” It is also about possible “wrongful transactions among entities, or on behalf of entities, that would need to be recovered in order to assure a full and fair distribution to all creditors.”[16]

To reduce such a massive cost for the above process, maybe substantive consolidation would be a good solution, especially in the context of an international insolvency, where choice of law intervenes.

A very interesting approach is that one which uses the internalization theory to explain the way of operation inside the network of subsidiaries.[17] As it is stated, internalization of certain activities inside the multinational corporate groups reduces transaction costs.

Multinational corporate groups use control to connect members together. The relationships among group member companies in such a group may be of great value. It is argued that “the value of these relationships may consist of a large part of ‘group going concern value’.[18] One could easily say the opposite too: that the value of these relationships may constitute a large part of ‘group going concern value’.

Going concern value only exists when a company is kept intact and running, that is, when it is not broken up.[19] One can say the same, by analogy, for the group going concern value: it only exists when the relationships among group member companies are kept intact.

7.2 National and International Regulations

In USA, chapter 15 does not provide for a central bankruptcy proceeding of an enterprise group that has separate legal entities in different countries.[20] “[C]reditor rights are determined on an entity-by-entity basis”, as it is pointed out,[21] and insolvency cases of separate debtors-companies of an enterprise group are not necessarily consolidated, even if the group was integrated, because it is presumed that creditors rely on the separate form of the company to which they extended credit. Some commentators have suggested modifications of chapter 15 so that the alternative would be offered to integrated multinational corporations to file in one venue[22] for a consolidated insolvency proceeding,[23] but their suggestions have received no answer so far.

---

[16] Clark (2014), pp. 113–114.

[17] Zhang (2017), pp. 339–341.

[18] Zhang (2017), p. 340.

[19] Baird and Rasmussen (2002), p. 758.

[20] LoPucki (2005), p. 152.

[21] Gropper (2015), p. 364.

[22] Bufford (2005), p. 105.

[23] Miller (2012), p. 185.

Nevertheless, under the U.S. Law, all members of an enterprise group that have place of incorporation, place of business or property in the USA may file in the same court,[24] thereby permitting a single proceeding for all group members. Foreign subsidiaries of a group with a U.S. parent company, do not file in the same U.S. court, even if they have property or a place of business in the USA, where U.S. debtors wish to preserve them out of formal U.S. proceedings.[25]

Most European Union Member States do not have special provisions for insolvent groups of companies. Therefore, according to the insolvency laws of most Member States, a separate insolvency proceeding must be opened on each insolvent company of a group.[26] In some countries, though, there are certain particularities. In any case, there is no specific provision about the possibility of opening joint insolvency proceedings of domestic and foreign companies too, members of the same group.

In English insolvency law, there are no express provisions in the legislation governing the insolvency of enterprise groups, either in legislation or in the judge made law. It is pointed out that "[t]he 'English approach' to group insolvency is pragmatic and flexible".[27] It is possible, for example, to have resort to schemes of arrangement[28] or company voluntary arrangements for a group of companies.

On the other hand, it is pointed out that the English courts were the first to promote a global treatment of enterprise groups' insolvency proceedings. The way they used to achieve that, was to determine the COMI based upon the concept of "head-office-functions". This approach is also known as "mind of management theory".[29] The point was to localize the country in which the most strategic decisions regarding the administration, the finance planning and the marketing of the enterprise group were taken. That way, the English courts were able to proceed to a consolidation of the different entities' insolvency proceedings, most of the times procedural but some other times also substantive.[30]

Italy was one of the first countries in Europe that introduced, in 1979 (law 957/1979), a regulation of the group insolvency, for the specific procedure "*Amministrazione straordinaria delle grandi imprese in crisi*", with the so-called legge Prodi. It was substantially revised in 1999 (Legislative Decree 270/1999, the so-called legge Prodi bis) and in 2003 (Law Decree 343/2003, converted into law 39/2004) and 2008 (Law Decree 80/2008 converted into law 111/2008).[31]

---

[24] 11 U.S.C. § 109(a) requires that a business entity that files a bankruptcy petition have a domicile (place of incorporation or formation), a place of business or property in the United States. 28 U.S.C. § 1408 sets forth the venue provisions.

[25] Gropper (2012), p. 212.

[26] Wessels et al. (2017), p. 344.

[27] Bailey (2015), p. 344.

[28] See *supra*, Sect. 4.8.2.1.

[29] García Gutiérrez (2015), pp. 215–217 and note 57.

[30] García Gutiérrez (2015), p. 216.

[31] Bianco and Marcucci (2011), pp. 90–91.

It is argued that, generally, this law's provisions are considered as a rational and advanced model for coordination of insolvency proceedings within an enterprise group. It is pointed out, though, that one can discern certain weaknesses: (1) this special regime may only be applied to very large enterprises; (2) there is a certain legal uncertainty, because of all its revisions which were the result of efforts to save each time a specific large company; (3) the administrative authority has central role, while creditors' role is quite limited; and (4) because there are different versions of this procedure, the legal framework is "highly fragmented".[32]

It took much time for Italy to extend these rules so to cover the ordinary bankruptcy procedures of commercial corporations too.[33]

In France, the Article L. 621-2 of the *Code de Commerce* provides that "… One or more other persons may be joined to opened proceedings where their property is intermixed with that of the debtor or where the legal entity is a sham. The court that has opened the initial proceedings shall remain competent for this purpose."[34]

The CJEU, which so far has not really favored a global treatment of an enterprise group's insolvency, in its judgment on the case *Rastelli Davide e C. Snc v Jean-Charles Hidoux, liquidator of Médiasucre International*, scrutinized the above French provision and limited the meaning of it:

> … the possibility that a court designated under that provision as having jurisdiction, with regard to a debtor, to join another legal entity to insolvency proceedings on the sole ground that their property has been intermixed, without considering where the centre of that entity's main interests is situated, would constitute a circumvention of the system established by the Member States, which the Regulation specifically intended to prevent in order to ensure uniform treatment of insolvency proceedings within the European Union.[35]

In Germany, according to one opinion, since the first decade of the twenty-first century "the search for the practical design of a group related insolvency law has replaced the question for its need", since "the advantages are evident in cases of a group's reorganization" and all that would be in favor of German insolvency law's primary goal, that is "the maximization of the estate and, thus, an increase of the creditor's satisfaction."[36]

Not all German scholars are of the same opinion, though.

When draft legislation was made available in Germany on the facilitation of Managing Corporate Group Insolvency Proceedings (*Entwurf eines Gesetzes zur*

---

[32] See Bianco and Marcucci (2011), pp. 92–93, who mention that the Parmalat crisis led to the Marzano law and the Alitalia crisis led to the enactment of a different version of the Marzano law.

[33] Panzani (2016), p. 1154.

[34] Wessels et al. (2017), p. 345.

[35] CJEU 15 December 2011, C-191/10 ECLI:EU:C:2011:838.

[36] Paulus (2011), pp. 36–37.

Erleichterung der Bewältigung von Konzerninsolvenzen)[37] there were jurists who were still asking: "Do we need "this" new corporate group insolvency law?"[38]

Now that it is already law, comments are still harsh. The German legislator decided for a cautious regulation of group of companies' insolvency.[39] It was decided that neither a procedural nor a substantive consolidation of the insolvency proceedings was advisable,[40] each separate legal entity is subject to its own insolvency proceeding.

In §§ 269 d-i InsO, only a coordination of group's members' insolvency proceeding is foreseen. It can be lodged by the insolvent debtor, an administrator and a creditors' committee. A coordination administrator is appointed, who can suggest a coordination plan. This plan, to be enforced, must be approved by the court and by the group creditors' committee, if formed.

In Spain, there is no systematic regulation of the groups of companies, in general. The Spanish law lacks a concept of group [of companies].[41]

The current law (*Ley Concursal*, LC) 22/2003 addresses issues—mainly procedural—of a group of companies, in various articles.[42]

According to Article 25 of the *Ley Concursal*, debtors belonging to the same enterprise group can request the joint commencement of their insolvency proceedings. Also, a creditor holding claims against companies belonging to the same enterprise group may request the joint commencement of insolvency proceedings of those companies. Furthermore, the court that has jurisdiction to open the insolvency proceedings of the parent company or of the company with the highest amount of liabilities, will have jurisdiction to commence insolvency proceedings on all the remaining companies of the group.[43]

7.3 European Recast Regulation

The EIR 1346/2000 does not have any rules on the insolvency of an enterprise group. Of course, groups are not excluded from its scope, but there is no specific regime for them. Most probably it was a choice made then by the European legislator. The group insolvency issues were and are very complicated and probably it was

[37] Deutscher Bundestag Drucksache 18/407 of 30 January 2014. As conceptual approach, it was the main influence for Chapter V of the European Recast Insolvency Regulation (2015), see Wessels et al. (2017), p. 346 note 1152.

[38] Hermann (2015), p. 394.

[39] See Madaus (2018), p. 4: "Der Gesetzgeber entschied sich – in Berlin wie in Brüssel – für eine behutsame Regelung der Konzerninsolvenz."

[40] See Madaus (2018), p. 5: "Es ist eine Berliner Schöpfung, die als solche auch auf der europäischen Ebene eingeführt und schließlich in den Art. 61 bis 77 EuInsVO verankert wurde."

[41] García Gutiérrez (2015), p. 206.

[42] Sánchez-Calero and Fuentes Naharro (2011), pp. 51–52.

[43] Wessels et al. (2017), p. 346.

thought that any institutionalized solution would present gaps and further complications, and that pragmatic solutions would be found when such cases would arise. In any case, the focus was rather on the individual company and not on its possible status as a member of a group of companies.[44]

The Court of Justice was also reluctant to proceed in a procedural consolidation of insolvency proceedings. As it is pointed out, in the *Rastelli* case,[45] the Court "rejected the proposition that a single COMI could automatically be inferred from the intermixing of the property of two related companies."[46]

Things changed a lot during the recent years. The absence of explicit rules for groups of companies created many complications and, in general, uncertainty.[47] Many were those that pressured for a certain regulation of this matter.[48]

European Regulation 848/2015 contains rules for the group of companies' insolvency in its Chapter V (Articles 56–77) on 'group coordination proceedings'.[49] It allows procedural consolidation, however it speaks about procedural coordination.[50] According to commentators, the European legislator anticipated the national legislators, providing for a uniform discipline of group of companies' insolvency proceedings, while there is no such provision in the national legal orders.[51]

In its Article 2(13), the Recast Regulation gives the definition of a group of companies: It is

> a parent undertaking and all its subsidiary undertakings.

A "parent undertaking" is defined as

> an undertaking which controls, either directly or indirectly, one or more subsidiary undertakings. An undertaking which prepares consolidated financial statements in accordance with Directive 2013/34/EU of the European Parliament and of the Council shall be deemed to be a parent undertaking.

It is a very careful step—"a small step forward, but a small step indeed"[52]—that was taken.[53] There is a possibility of opening coordination proceedings, but the

---

[44] McCormack (2016), p. 113.

[45] CJEU Judgment of 15.12.2011—C-191/10.

[46] McCormack (2016), p. 113.

[47] See Siemon and Frind (2013a), p. 1: "Das Konzerninsolvenzrecht im nationalen und im europäischen Bereich befindet sich in einer Sackgasse".

[48] de Vette (2011), p. 216.

[49] Reumers (2013), p. 554.

[50] Reumers (2016), p. 225.

[51] Bertini (2016).

[52] Van Galen (2016), p. 67.

[53] But see Wimmer et al. (2016), pp. 175–176: "Einen an der Konzernleitungsmacht oder *head office functions* orientierten "**Konzern-COMI**" wird die Verordnung auch in ihrer Neufassung nicht kennen. Auch bzw. erst recht hat der Verordnungsgeber davon abgesehen, **Einheitsverfahren** zu schaffen, in deren Rahmen in Überwindung der im *Rastelli*-Urteil entwickelten Grundsätze die Insolvenzabwicklung von konzernangehörigen Unternehmen zusammengefasst werden könnte, die ihre Interessenmittelpunkten in unterschiedlichen Mitgliedstaaten haben."

possibility of multiple decentralized proceedings is also maintained. The decisions of the coordinating forum are not binding and decentralized cases remain autonomous.[54] It was considered that institutionalizing a centralized decision-making would be "politically unfeasible".[55]

Those who were and are in favor of setting rules about the group of companies' insolvency, were arguing that the uncoordinated approach of such an insolvency makes it difficult to save single companies, while a group approach could avoid the insolvency of a still viable economic entity.[56]

Interesting—and perhaps, "dangerous"?—is the Article 66 of the EIR Recast, that introduces something completely new in the area of European and national rules on international insolvency[57]: a certain party autonomy in the selection of jurisdiction by way of written agreements that can be concluded by two thirds of all insolvency holders up until the insolvency procedure is opened. It seems that the only formal requirement is that such an agreement must be written.[58]

In any case, regulating a group of companies' insolvency is not an easy issue. When the subsidiaries' COMIs are in the same place as their parent's COMI and they are ascertainable to third parties, things are easier, insolvency proceedings of subsidiaries could be opened in that place[59] without real hurdles. Even when there is a lack of respective regulation, this lack could be filled—as it sometimes happens—"on a voluntary basis through the creation of policies between practitioners, creditors, shareholders, and, occasionally the courts."[60]

Things are much more complicated when the subsidiaries' COMIs are in different countries. Would courts conduct an in depth COMI analysis for the subsidiaries which are registered in different countries than the one of their parent companies?[61] There would (or will) be a harsh battle between managers and creditors, about who would bring before the court the most convincing evidence.

Voices are heard, about solidifying the presumption of the registered place and making it difficult to be rebutted.[62] Furthermore, it is argued that only in the case of multinational corporate groups in which the parent company has the absolute control is it possible to apply the head office function and admit that all the subsidiaries have their COMIs in the same country in which the parent company has its own COMI.[63]

---

[54] Mevorach (2018), p. 234.

[55] Madaus (2015), p. 232.

[56] Siemon and Frind (2013b), p. 61; Siemon and Frind (2013a), p. 1.

[57] Thole and Dueñas (2015), p. 216.

[58] Queirolo and Dominelli (2017), p. 178.

[59] Paulus (2007), pp. 819–820.

[60] Merlini (2016), p. 128.

[61] Winkler (2008), p. 369.

[62] Latella (2014), p. 479.

[63] Zhang (2017), p. 344.

On the other hand, moving the subsidiaries' COMIs to one country with the aim of procedural consolidation may be dangerous. Foreign subsidiaries may have been created there exactly because they wanted to get advantages that those countries may were giving. Movement of their COMIs would result to the loss of these advantages.[64]

What could also be very dangerous would be the cost that such a movement would cause to junior creditors. Such an example was the *Wind Hellas* case, where six companies of the group transferred their COMIs to the UK to use the prepack administration and schemes of arrangement that UK law allows.[65] The result for the unsecured creditors was disastrous: they were left with 1.5 billion euros unpaid.[66]

7.4 UNCITRAL Model Law 1997

Neither UNCITRAL Model Law 1997 contains any specific provisions for groups of companies' insolvencies. However, as it is pointed out, the Model Law does not exclude groups of companies from its scope.[67] Thus, often in group of companies' cases, insolvency proceedings on companies of a group have been centralized in a single forum and recognition was granted to that forum's decision, based on the rules of the Model Law.[68] This has been achieved primarily because the headquarters of a group's companies are often at a single country.[69]

As it was above mentioned, the situation is far more difficult when a group of companies is structure with greater decentralization.

In 2010, UNCITRAL issued part three of the Legislative Guide on Insolvency Law, which part focuses on the treatment of enterprise groups in insolvency.[70] It adopted a set of recommendations that were added to the Legislative Guide.

Now, the Legislative Guide includes recommendations on procedural coordination, substantive consolidation, intra-group post-commencement finance, voidable

[64] Interesting is the comment of Smaliukas (2015), p. 381, that the rebuttable presumption about COMI of the subsidiary [of a group of companies] shall often be rebutted before the Lithuanian court with the result that this court will refuse to open in Lithuania the main insolvency proceeding, therefore, he argues, it is the new rules on the secondary proceedings that will become even more important to effectively deal with the insolvency of a Lithuanian subsidiary. If we consider this argument well grounded, we can imagine that the situation will be the same in other countries too, where similar politico-economic conditions reign and whose law, including insolvency law, was transplanted from other laws.

[65] Zhang (2017), p. 345.

[66] Rutstein and Bloomberg (2010), p. 156.

[67] Mevorach (2015), p. 216.

[68] Mevorach (2011a), pp. 537–543.

[69] Mevorach (2008), pp. 440–445.

[70] United Nations Commission on International Trade Law, *Legislative Guide on Insolvency Law, Part three: Treatment of enterprise groups in insolvency* (6 December 2010).

intra-group transactions, joint reorganization plans.[71] It is argued that these recommendations, these proposals "represent a breakthrough in the area of group insolvency as almost for the first time they suggest ways to treat international groups in default."[72]

Since substantive consolidation has been proven difficult—or even impossible—to achieve, especially when the companies members of the enterprise group are in different countries, different jurisdictions, works have focused on procedural consolidation of the insolvency proceedings that has been achieved in some cases—mostly, if not only, in courts of common law countries.[73]

When the companies members of an enterprise group are in the same country, the Legislative Guide proposes: the possibility for the companies to file jointly for the opening of insolvency proceedings; the formation of a unique creditors' committee; the appointment of a representative who would assume the duty to coordinate the administrators of the various insolvency proceedings or the appointment of a unique insolvency administrator for all the companies members of the group. Furthermore, it is proposed that all the companies elaborate the same reorganization plan or more reorganization plans that would be coordinated between them.

When the companies members of an enterprise group are in different countries, the only recommendation is to appoint only one representative/insolvency administrator for all the insolvency proceedings. In case conflicts of interests arise and there is a danger that the administrator loses his independence or neutrality, it is proposed that the courts have the possibility to intervene.

The other proposed measures are measures of procedural cooperation, such as: direct communication between the courts, coordinated audiences and adoption of protocols.

UNCITRAL's Working Group V[74] had reflected, previously, on whether a concept of an enterprise group COMI could be inserted in the Guide, but had rejected it. However, the Working Group had the intention to look at this issue again—it still has that intention.

The diverse nature of enterprise groups and the varying degree of control that is centralized makes it rather impossible to create a uniform set of rules for dealing with them.[75]

Furthermore, the Working Group had to deal with several very difficult issues that arise in enterprise groups with members in more than one country. Some of them are: (1) in case of restructuring of an enterprise group, it would be difficult, for public policy reasons, to convince the countries in which the subsidiaries are domiciled, to relieve the subsidiaries' officers of their personal liabilities; (2) whether domestic creditors should be bound by a foreign insolvency proceeding, where

[71] Mevorach (2015), p. 217.

[72] Mevorach (2011b), p. 105.

[73] Ziegel (2002), p. 376.

[74] The UNCITRAL's Working Group that works on Insolvency issues.

[75] Hannan (2015), p. 237.

there had never been any relation between these creditors and that foreign entity; (3) whether solvent members of an enterprise group should be included within restructuring proceedings that commence because of the insolvency or decision or other members of the group.[76]

It is rightly suggested, that "[a]ny law seeking to deal with enterprise groups should be supported by common rules of accounting which would assist in the identification of assets and liabilities between States, as well as standardised laws in respect of some procedural matters such as priority payments in an attempt to overcome an individual State's political priorities."[77] It would be very difficult to achieve something like that, though.

Following the Lehman Brothers group collapse in 2008, the urgent need for a specific regime was felt. In 2013, the UNCITRAL Working Group V stated that it had to continue its work on this topic. Therefore, since 2014, in parallel to the work on model provisions regarding enforcement of judgments, it resumed work on the insolvency of groups of companies, linked to previous work that had been concluded in 2010.

7.5 Jurisprudence of Various Countries

7.5.1 Babcock & Wilcox Canada Ltd.

A very interesting case that was brought before a Canadian court was the case *Babcock & Wilcox Canada Ltd.*[78]

The applicant, Babcock & Wilcox Canada Ltd., a solvent Canadian company, applied for recognition of U.S. Chapter 11 restructuring proceedings that had been commenced before a U.S. Bankruptcy Court by its parent and several of its subsidiaries and for relief with respect to these proceedings.[79]

The Canadian company was not a party to the Chapter 11 proceedings nor had been commenced any insolvency proceedings, involving it, in Canada. The parent company and its subsidiaries had commenced the restructuring proceedings in U.S. to protect themselves against mass asbestos claims that could have as consequence the insolvency of these companies. They were afraid that similar claims could be advanced against the Canadian subsidiary. Since the funds of that subsidiary too were needed for the U.S. restructuring proceedings to succeed, what was required was a stay of individual actions by creditors against the Canadian subsidiary.

The U.S. Bankruptcy Court, in the frame of Chapter 11 proceedings, issued an order restraining the plaintiffs in the mass asbestos actions from commencing claims

[76] Hannan (2015), p. 238.

[77] Hannan (2015), p. 239.

[78] *Babcock & Wilcox Canada Ltd, Re* (2000), 5 BLR (3d) 75, 18 CBR (4th) 157 (Ont SC).

[79] Ouatu (2014), p. 101.

against "non-debtors affiliates" and requested the Canadian courts to assist in the carrying out of the order.[80] Thus, the Canadian subsidiary filed before a Canadian court, asking for recognition of the U.S. Chapter 11 proceedings and for a stay of proceedings that creditors having asbestos claims could bring against it (the Canadian subsidiary) in Canada.

The Canadian court, examining whether it should grant recognition and relief, had to consider whether the U.S. Chapter 11 proceedings within the definition of foreign proceeding mentioned in Section 18.6 paragraph (1) of the CCAA (now abrogated). For a debtor to ask for a U.S. Chapter 11 proceeding, he/she has not to be insolvent. On the contrary, for a debtor company to commence a CCAA restructuring proceeding, insolvency had to be proved.

Therefore, the Canadian court had to decide whether, to recognize the foreign proceeding based on Section 18.6 paragraph (1), the debtor in that foreign proceeding should be insolvent.

The court answered negatively the above question, arguing that the definition was intended to have a broad scope:

> … the 1997 Amendments contemplated that it would be inappropriate to pigeonhole or otherwise constrain the interpretation of s. 18.6 since it would be not only impractical but also impossible to contemplate the myriad of circumstances arising under a wide variety of foreign legislation which deal generally and essentially with bankruptcy and insolvency but not exclusively so.

7.5.2 *Cross-Border Fraud and Cross-Border Insolvency:* In re Stanford International Bank Ltd Case

A very complicated case, in which many issues of international insolvencies were brought up, was the *Stanford case.*[81]

U.S. fraudsters had set up a bank in Antigua as part of a pyramid, that is, a Ponzi scheme, in U.S. terminology, which defrauded investors worldwide. The bank, Stanford International Bank Ltd (SIB), was incorporated in Antigua and maintained there its registered office.

On February 16, 2009, the United States Security Exchange Commission (SEC) filed a complaint against Mr. (Sir, then) Stanford, his associates, SIB, Stanford Group Company and Stanford Capital Management, LLC, alleging securities fraud—among other causes of action. On the same day, the U.S. court issued an order by which it appointed a receiver over the worldwide assets of Mr. Stanford, his associates, SIB, Stanford Group Company and Stanford Capital Management, LLC as well as of other legal entities owned and controlled by any of them.

---

[80] Obviously this could never happen in case the court was of a civil law country. This sort of direct cooperation between courts is not allowed.

[81] Ouatu (2014), pp. 106–109.

On February 19, 2009, the Financial Services Regulatory Commission (FSRC) of Antigua and Barbuda appointed receiver/managers for SIB. A week later, on February 26, the Antiguan court appointed the receiver/managers as Antiguan receivers of the SIB. On March 24, 2009, the Financial Services Regulatory Commission of Antigua and Barbuda filed a petition before the Antiguan court, asking that it orders the winding up of SIB and appoints the Antiguan receivers as liquidators. On April 15, 2009, the Antiguan court granted the order for the winding up of the SIB and appointed the Antiguan receivers as liquidators.[82]

So, a [insolvency] liquidation proceeding was opened in Antigua and a receivership in the United States.[83]

The Antiguan liquidators and the U.S. receiver were trying to recover the assets that were in other countries and especially in England and in Canada, so they filed for recognition of the respective [insolvency] proceedings before the courts of those two countries.

The [insolvency] proceedings that had been opened against Allen Stanford's banks in Antigua and in USA had as a further consequence—among others—, conflicting rulings from Canadian and English courts.

The Quebec Superior Court issued two rulings—later upheld by the Quebec Court of Appeals—in which it found the U.S. receivership to be the proper foreign main proceeding.

The most heated "battle" took place before the English courts. As it is pointed out, "this case provided the English court with the first major contested case on the enactment of the Model Law, the Cross-Border Insolvency Regulations 2006".[84]

The UK High Court held that the U.S. receivership was not a foreign proceeding for the purpose of CBIR, while the Antiguan liquidation was such a proceeding.[85]

The court did not assess whether the foreign proceedings were foreign proceedings as defined by the Model Law by reference to the local insolvency laws, but it did so by reference to the criteria set by the relevant definition, which specified that the proceeding should be:

a) a collective judicial or administrative proceeding;
b) based on a law relating to insolvency;
c) a proceeding in which the assets and affairs of the debtor are subject to control or supervision by a foreign court; and
d) for the purposes of reorganization or liquidation.[86]

The English court held that to be a collective proceeding, the foreign proceeding had to be for the benefit of all the creditors and to guarantee a *pari passu* distribution to all of them. The U.S. receivership did not comply with this criterion, since it had

---

[82] Ho (2011), p. 395.

[83] Morris et al. (2018), p. 134.

[84] Ho (2011), p. 395.

[85] *Re Stanford International Bank* [2009] EWHC 1441 (Ch); [2009] BPIR 1157.

[86] Ouatu (2014), p. 108.

as its purpose to collect and preserve the debtor's assets for the benefit only of the investors and it did not preclude creditors from commencing individual proceedings against the debtor, under certain circumstances.

Interpreting the second criterion, the UK High Court adopted a non-restrictive approach and suggested that the provisions under which the foreign proceeding had been commenced did not have to deal exclusively with insolvency; what was required was for the proceeding to have been commenced under those provisions, on the ground that the debtor was insolvent.

The U.S. receivership did not comply with the above criterion either. The U.S. court order pursuant to which this proceeding had been commenced was not based in the insolvency of the debtor, but on the need to prevent the dissipation of the debtor's assets because of its involvement in securities fraud.

On the contrary, the UK High Court found that the Antiguan liquidation had been commenced pursuant to a law relating to insolvency, even if the order opening it had been made based on an act concerned with the winding up of companies and pursuant to a provision that allowed such a winding up to be commenced on just and equitable grounds—and the insolvency of a debtor was such a ground.

Both the Antiguan liquidator and the U.S. receiver were claiming that the COMI of SIB was in their respective countries.

The SIB had its registered office in Antigua, so the English court said that Antigua was presumed, absent proof to the contrary, to be the SIB's COMI. It summarized the facts that it considered as leading to the conclusion that the presumption could not be rebutted.

The public face of the SIB had been created, the court said, by the company's place of incorporation, the place of its physical headquarters, the place where the company's employees worked, the place where the operations departments were conducted, the information included in the disclosure statement provided to potential depositors, which information included the identity of its creditors, the law that governed the contracts that SIB entered into and the disputes that would have arisen from these contracts, the SIB's principal operating bank account, the location of SIB's assets, the place where the meetings of the Board of directors were held, and the place where the accounts of the SIB were audited.[87]

The court, next, tried to identify the facts that revealed the SIB's connections with the Stanford group, and, finally, considered the facts that, in its view, were related to the fraud that the Stanford group was involved in, for example, the location of the persons who were taking the strategic decisions with respect to the group.

The court concluded that the COMI of SIB was in Antigua.[88] It based its decision on the reasoning of the European Court of Justice in the *Re Eurofood IFSC Ltd* case.[89] It held that the formulation and the context in which COMI was used in both international instruments—the Regulation and the Model Law—were similar. It

[87] Ouatu (2014), p. 119.

[88] Not happy about it, Ho (2009), pp. 537–542.

[89] *Eurofood IFSC Ltd*, C-341/04, [2006] ECR I-3854.

also stated that the drafters of the Model Law intended to provide a "complementary regime" to that created by the Regulation.[90]

The U.S. liquidators/receiver filed an appeal. The UK Court of Appeal approved the judgment and recognized the liquidation in Antigua as a foreign main proceeding.[91]

In the meantime, the administrators of both insolvency proceedings were also trying to recover assets in other countries, such as Switzerland. Also, beginning of 2010, the Antiguan liquidators applied for recognition in the United States and creditors in the U.S. receivership asked for permission to file involuntary bankruptcy proceedings in USA against Allen Stanford entities.

In late January 2010, the U.S. District Court Judge presiding over the Securities and Exchange Commission (SEC) receivership and the petition for recognition in the United States agreed to cancel various matters pending settlement discussions between the U.S. receiver and the Antiguan liquidators.

As of February 2010, the U.S. receiver had collected about $145 million and spent 40% of that recovery (almost $58 million) in fees and costs for operating expenses, receivership costs, and fees.[92]

The problems were huge. There was no sign of an eventual cooperation. On July 30, 2012, a federal district court in Texas denied recognition to the Antiguan proceeding as a foreign main proceeding; it recognized it as a non-main proceeding. It pierced the corporate veils of the Stanford Entities and held that the presumption that SIB's COMI was in Antigua because it was registered there was rebutted by many other factors that, according to its opinion, located the COMI in the USA.

On November 11, 2015, the Joint Liquidators of Stanford International Bank (in Liquidation), submitted their 7th Report before the Eastern Caribbean Supreme Court. It seems that the insolvent estate was holding $39 million on hand, funds that have been allocated for costs and fee payments.

Sadly, Stanford case is one of those never-ending international insolvency cases.

7.5.3 Nortel: "The Cross-Border Insolvency Case of the Century"

Nortel Networks Group of Companies case became the "cross-border insolvency case of the century".[93] It was also a case that concerned U.S. and Canadian courts,[94] among others.

[90] Ouatu (2014), p. 120.

[91] *Re Stanford International Bank* [2010] EWCA Civ 137; [2011] Ch 33.

[92] Clark and Goldstein (2011), p. 521.

[93] Westbrook (2015), p. 498.

[94] *Re Nortel Networks Corp.* [2015] ONSC 2987 (Can. Ont. Sup. Ct); *Re Nortel Networks Inc., et al., Debtors* 532 B.R. 494 (2015).

Nortel case, a unique case, it seems, "should be seen as a triumph", it is argued, "for the universalist school of transnational insolvency."[95]

The Nortel enterprise was an enormous telecommunications group of companies. It had its headquarters in Canada but it also had significant operations in the U.S., Europe, the Middle East, and in African—130 subsidiaries in 100 countries.

The Great Recession, as it is called, of 2008 resulted to an enormous losses for the group's companies. Following the failure of a reorganization attempt, bankruptcy was unavoidable.

On January 2009, Nortel Networks, Inc. and certain of its U.S.-based affiliates filed voluntary petitions in the U.S. Bankruptcy Court for the District of Delaware for relief under chapter 11 of the U.S. Bankruptcy Code.[96]

On the same day, certain of the Nortel Networks, Inc. Canada-based affiliates initiated insolvency proceedings in the Ontario Superior Court of Justice under Canada's Companies' Creditors Arrangement Act (CCAA). At the outset of the Canadian Proceedings, the Canadian Court appointed a Monitor[97] and furthermore it appointed a Canadian law firm to represent the interests of approximately 20,000 former employees of the Canadian Debtors.

Also, on the same day, certain of the U.S. Debtors' affiliates that were based in Europe, in the Middle East, and in Africa, initiated insolvency proceedings in the United Kingdom, in Israel and in France.[98]

On August 9, the U.S. Bankruptcy Court entered an order establishing September 30, 2009, as the claims bar date in the U.S. insolvency proceedings.

On August 14, 2009, the Canadian Court entered an order pursuant to Section 18.6 of the CCAA, recognizing the above U.S. Court's order.

What is very interesting is that the companies of the group did not file for bankruptcy protection in the way that international instruments anticipate. They filed for "equal", parallel proceedings in Canada and in USA, there was not a "main" proceeding, nor were "ancillary" proceedings. The proceedings in Canada and in USA were coordinated and simultaneous.[99]

The major creditors of the Nortel Group and the various Nortel debtors agreed (by entering into a protocol) to liquidate the group assets as a going concern on a consolidated basis and not sell them piece by piece. From 2009 to 2011, the Nortel Debtors executed a series of sales which both the U.S. Court and the Canadian Court approved in joint hearings. By the end of June 2011, the sale of the main lines of business as well as Nortel Group's significant intellectual property portfolio

---

[95] Pottow (2015), p. 333.

[96] 11 U.S.C. § 101 *et seq.*

[97] The Monitor acts as a fiduciary to the Canadian estate. Among other duties, the Monitor is responsible for communicating with creditors regarding the claims process.

[98] As Pottow (2015), p. 334, points out, Nortel was global in reach, but if anyone tried to assess the COMI of the corporate group, it would likely have been Canada.

[99] Pottow (2015), p. 335.

produced about US$ 7.3 billion,[100] amount which would be available for distribution among the creditors.

Unfortunately, despite a provision of the protocol counseling mediation over the division of proceeds amongst the three bankruptcy estates (Canada, U.S., and collectively, Europe, Middle East, and Africa) consensual allocation had no success ("Allocation Dispute"), so they had to ask for judicial determination, last refuge under the protocol.

On April 13, 2013, both the U.S. Bankruptcy Court for the District of Delaware and the Ontario Superior Court of Justice decided to have a coordinated cross-border trial, with joint hearing between the two courts, to resolve the competing claims to the same property.[101]

After several months' work, on May 12, 2015—"[t]wo years after these groundbreaking decisions and one year after commencement of the first coordinated, cross-border trial"[102]—the Canadian Court and the U.S. Court issued their rulings on the Allocation Dispute, both adopting a pro rata methodology.[103]

As it is mentioned, the *Nortel* courts avoided disaster by invoking the procedures of the Model Law that facilitate cooperation. The trial on how to allocate the proceeds was run in two different courts, in two different countries, Ontario, Canada and Delaware, USA, simultaneously, with the judges communicating frequently between themselves. Nevertheless, the courts had clarified that each would decide independently about how the allocation of the proceeds would have to be done.[104]

It was not an easy task for the courts, especially given the fact that each group of creditors was trying to persuade the courts to divide the proceeds in a manner that would accord its members the largest share.

Certain parties in the USA and Canada appealed those decisions, but the appeals were withdrawn as a condition of the global settlement agreement which was confirmed by the courts and became legally effective on 8 May 2017.[105]

---

[100] The business and intellectual property sales had raised approximately $9.0 billion, of which approximately $7.3 remained in the "lockbox", to be distributed among the creditors, see Peacock (2015), p. 544.

[101] *In re Nortel Networks, Inc.*, No. 09-10138, 2013 WL 1385271 (Bankr. D. Del. Apr. 3, 2013), *aff'd* 737 F.3d 265 (3d Cir. 2013); *Nortel Networks Corp. (Re)*, 09-CL-7950, 2013 ONSC 1757 (Can. Ont. Sup. Ct. J. Apr. 3, 2013).

[102] Peacock (2015), pp. 544–545. As it is stated, this first cross-border insolvency trial commenced on May 12, 2014 and continued for 6 weeks. The two courts "simultaneously heard testimony of tens of witnesses and admitted into evidence over 2,000 exhibits and designations from numerous depositions." The parties submitted post-trial briefs of more than 1000 pages and two full days of closing arguments were made in September 2014.

[103] *In re Nortel Networks, Inc.*, No. 09-10138, 2015 WL 2374351 (Bankr. D. Del. May 12, 2015); *Nortel Networks Corp. (Re)*, 09-CL-7950, 2015 ONSC 2987 (Can. Ont. Sup. Ct. J. May 12, 2015).

[104] Pottow (2015), p. 340.

[105] Interestingly, it is stated in the Plan that "[t]he Plan recognizes the corporate integrity of each Debtor and, therefore, Allowed Claims against a particular Debtor will be satisfied only from the assets of that Debtor's bankruptcy estate (with the exception of Allowed Claims against NNCC, which will be satisfied out of the estate of the Consolidated Debtors in accordance with the

It has been stated that this case, having lasted around 2930 days, is the sixth-longest U.S. Chapter 11 corporate bankruptcy.[106] The fees for lawyers and advisors, globally, is said to have reached nearly $1.9 billion—"so over-lawyered" a case, it was commented.

It is argued that this case is an example of the efficacy of the UNCITRAL Model Law and its procedural framework, which "allows" the cooperation and coordination between courts of different countries.[107]

On the other hand, courts of common law countries, and especially those of Canada and U.S., had always the procedural opportunity to cooperate between each other, if they wanted to.

7.6 Virtual Territoriality

7.6.1 Virtual Contractual/Synthetic Secondary Proceedings

An original way that courts of some European countries have found, to vest control of the subsidiaries in the administrator in the main case and to avoid the opening of secondary proceedings, is that of the so called virtual contractual secondary proceedings[108]—an application of the "virtual territoriality".

The courts treat the creditors of the subsidiaries the same way as these would be treated in local insolvency cases, even if this treatment is better than the treatment the creditors would receive in the jurisdiction of the main proceedings.[109]

It is a [legal] practice followed in some countries to overcome the different ranking of claims that different national insolvency laws have. Courts treat foreign (from other Member States of the EU) creditors "as if" a secondary insolvency proceeding had been opened in their respective jurisdictions.[110] Thus, proceedings are simplified through consolidation of local priorities and assets are distributed according to a hypothetical territorial distribution.

---

substantive consolidation of NNI and NNCC pursuant to *Section 6.2* (*Substantive Consolidation of NNI and NNCC*) of the Plan)". See for the U.S. Court, *In re Nortel Networks Inc., et al.,* Case no. 09-10138 (KG), U.S. Bankruptcy Court for the District of Delaware, Doc. 17502, Dec. 1, 2016. NNCC is Nortel Networks Capital Corporation, a Delaware corporation; NNI is Nortel Networks Inc., a Delaware corporation.

[106] According to a database maintained by UCLA Law School Prof. Lynn M. LoPucki, see Hals (2017).

[107] Ajinderpal and Ng (2018), p. 6.

[108] Menjucq and Dammann (2008), pp. 145–158.

[109] Gropper (2011), p. 576.

[110] Wessels (2014), p. 76.

It is a form of procedural consolidation: it allows for different insolvency procedures but unites them in a single forum. It is a step toward a unified group insolvency.[111]

These "synthetic secondary proceedings" (or "synthetic secondaries")[112] are promoted and welcomed by certain "universalists", who stress the fact that these proceedings reduce transaction costs of local proceedings. They say that "synthetic secondaries are a territorialist step backward for a universalist leap forward".[113]

There is no doubt that this is an opposite discrimination of creditors, but it is done on purpose, believing that this solution is better than letting creditors file for secondary proceedings in other countries, thus much reducing the hopes for a successful outcome of the whole insolvency situation.

There has also been proposed another—rather complicated—approach, an alternative that according to the author would have analogous results with that of the "virtual territoriality". This approach is called "virtual universalism" and, under it, the court in a non-main proceeding would apply the applicable law of the COMI. It is argued that this approach too would reduce incentives to commence a secondary proceeding.[114]

7.6.2 Collins & Aitkins Case

Notable example of the above way of handling insolvencies of groups of companies is the *Collins & Aitkins case*.[115]

The enterprise, an automobile parts maker, had its headquarters in the United States and had 23,000 employees in 17 countries, among which there were 24 companies in 10 EU Member States employing 4500 people.

It filed insolvency proceedings in the United States (Chapter 11 proceedings), Canada, and the United Kingdom. It contended that the center of main interests of its European operations was in London[116] and for that reason filed for insolvency administration of all its European subsidiaries before the English court.

Creditors in Spain and Germany threatened to open local cases in the respective countries, on the ground that they would receive better treatment in secondary proceedings there. The administrators appointed by the U.K. court, to avoid the costs and the complications of separate proceedings, promised those creditors better treatment that the one they would receive under English law. Obviously, this was

[111] Hirte (2008), p. 218.

[112] Pottow (2011), p. 584.

[113] Pottow (2014), p. 206.

[114] Mooney (2014), pp. 121–122.

[115] *Re Collins & Aitkins Corp. Group*, [2005] EWCH 1754 (Ch).

[116] Janger (2014), pp. 180–201 (183)

opposite to Article 4 of the EC Regulation 1346/2000 that requires the application of the lex fori concursus, that is, in that case the English law.

However, the administrators were able to convince the English court to authorize a distribution violating English priorities. They presented three grounds for that and the judge accepted them. These grounds were:

1) The express powers of the English legislation;
2) The inherent jurisdiction of the English court over the joint administrators; and
3) The principle "based on morality" that "if and officer of the court is under an obligation of conscience, then the Court will direct the officer to fulfill that obligation."[117]

The morality principle was based on the fact that the administrators had made a promise to the Spanish and German creditors which they should fulfill.[118]

Furthermore, the court stated that the administrator had the power to make different payments, based on Section 66 Schedule B1 of the Insolvency Act 1986.[119] It stated in so many words: "The administrator of a company may make a payment otherwise than in accordance with paragraph 65 or paragraph 13 of the Schedule 1 if he thinks that it is likely to assist the achievement of the purpose of the administration."[120]

References

Ajinderpal S, Ng GX (2018) Cross-border insolvency in Singapore: the effectiveness of the judicial insolvency network and the JIN guidelines on the administration of cross-border insolvency matters. INSOL International. Technical Series Issue No. 40

Almaskari BJ (2016) Towards legal certainty: European cross-border insolvency law and Multinational Corporate Groups. Thesis submitted for the degree of Doctor of Philosophy at the University of Leicester School of Law. Available at https://lra.le.ac.uk/bitstream/2381/39163/1/2016AlmaskariBJPhD.pdf

Avi-Yonah RS (2003) National regulation of multinational enterprises: an essay on comity, extraterritoriality, and harmonization. Columbia J Transnatl Law 42:5–34

Bailey E (2015) The insolvency of groups of companies in English law. Int Insolv Law Rev:344–363

Baird D, Rasmussen R (2002) The end of bankruptcy. Stanford Law Rev 55:751–789

Bertini R (2016) L'insolvenza del gruppo alla luce del Regolamento (UE) N. 848/2015. Cammino Diritto. Rivista di informazione giuridica. https://www.camminodiritto.it/public/pdfarticoli/1637_9-2016.pdf

Bianco M, Marcucci M (2011) Groups and groups' bankruptcy discipline in Italy. In: Insolvency and Cross-border Groups (ed) UNCITRAL Recommendations for a European Perspective? Banca d'Italia Eurosistema. Quaderni di Ricerca Giuridica della Consulenza Legale, 69, pp 81–102

[117] *Re Collins & Aikman Corp. Group*, [2006] EWHC 1343 (Ch) at [15].

[118] Gropper (2011), p. 576.

[119] Madaus (2017), pp. 223–241.

[120] *Re Collins & Aikman Corp. Group*, [2006] EWHC 1343 (Ch) at [31].

Bufford SL (2005) Global venue controls are coming: a reply to Professor LoPucki. Am Bankruptcy Law J 79:105–141
Clark LM (2014) Managing distribution to claimants in cross-border enterprise group insolvency. Brooklyn J Corp Financ Commer Law 9:111–119
Clark LM, Goldstein K (2011) Sacred cows: how to care for secured creditors' rights in cross-border bankruptcies. Texas Int Law J 46:513–558
de Vette EMF (2011) Multinational enterprise groups in insolvency: how should the European Union act? Utrecht Law Rev 7:216–228
García Gutiérrez L (2015) Reflexiones aceca de la regulación de la insolvencia de los grupos internacionales de sociedades en la Unión Europea. Revista Jurídica de la Universidad Autonoma de Madrid 31:205–226
Gopalan S, Guihot M (2015) Recognition and enforcement in cross-border insolvency law: a proposal for judicial gap-filling. Vanderbilt J Transnatl Law 48:1225–1284
Gropper AL (2011) The payment of priority claims in cross-border insolvency cases. Texas Int Law J 46:559–577
Gropper AL (2012) The arbitration of cross-border insolvencies. Am Bankruptcy Law J 86:201–242
Gropper AL (2015) United States approaches to the insolvency of enterprise groups. Int Insolv Law Rev:364–378
Hals T (2017) Nortel cleared to end bankruptcy, distribute $7 billion to creditors. Available at: https://www.reuters.com/article/us-nortelworks-bankruptcy/nortel-cleared-to-end-bankruptcy-distribute-7-billion-to-creditors-idUSKBN1582TO
Hannan NF (2015) Do words matter?: a comparative analysis of the UNCITRAL model law on cross-border insolvency in Australia, Canada, New Zealand, United Kingdom and the United States of America. Doctoral thesis. University of Western Australia School of Law. Available at https://api.research-repository.uwa.edu.au/portalfiles/portal/5338528/Hannan_Neil_2015.pdf
Hermann O (2015) The corporate group in insolvency – today and tomorrow, chances and risks. Int Insolv Law Rev:383–395
Hirte H (2008) Towards a framework for the regulation of corporate groups' insolvencies. Eur Company Financ Law Rev 5(2):213–236
Ho LC (2009) Cross-border fraud and cross-border insolvency: proving COMI and seeking recognition under the UK Model Law. J Int Bank Finance Law 9:537–542
Ho LC (2011) Misunderstanding the model law: *Re Stanford International Bank*. Butterworths J Int Bank Financ Law:395–404
Janger EJ (2014) Silos: establishing the distributional baseline in cross-border bankruptcies. Brooklyn J Corp Finan Commer Law 9(183):180–201
Latella D (2014) The "COMI" concept in the revision of the European insolvency regulation. Eur Company Financ Law Rev 11:479–494
LoPucki LM (2005) Universalism unravels. Am Bankruptcy Law J 79:143–167
Madaus S (2015) Insolvency proceedings for corporate groups under the new insolvency regulation. Int Insolv Law Rev 6:232–247
Madaus S (2017) Die Zusicherung nach Art. 36 EuInsVO – Das Ende virtueller Sekundärinsolvenzverfahren? In: Festschrift fur Klaus Pannen, Munchen, pp 223–241
Madaus S (2018) Das Konzerninsolvenzrecht – die Ziele des Gesetzgebers. Neue Zeitschrift für Insolvenzrecht-Beilage:4–6
McCormack G (2016) Groups of companies and the "recast" European insolvency regulation. In: Parry R, Omar PJ (eds) Reimagining rescue. INSOL Europe, Nottingham, pp 109–117
Menjucq M, Dammann R (2008) Regulation No. 1346/2000 on insolvency proceedings: facing the companies group phenomenon. Bus Law Int 9:145–158
Merlini A (2016) Reorganisation and liquidation of groups of companies: creditors' protection vs. going concern maximisation, the European dilemma, or simply a misunderstanding in light of the new EU Insolvency Regulation No 2015/848. Int Insolv Law Rev:119–135

Mevorach I (2007) Appropriate treatment of corporate groups in insolvency: a universal view. Eur Bus Organ Law Rev 8:179–194

Mevorach I (2008) The "Home Country" of a multinational enterprise group facing insolvency. Int Comp Law Q 57:427–448

Mevorach I (2010) Towards a consensus on the treatment of enterprise groups in insolvency. Cardozo J Int Comp Law 18:359–423

Mevorach I (2011a) On the road to universalism: a comparative and empirical study of the UNCITRAL model law on cross-border insolvency. Eur Bus Organ Law Rev 12:517–557

Mevorach I (2011b) Multinational enterprise groups in insolvency: a comment on UNCITRAL's proposals and future prospects within the EU. In: Insolvency and Cross-border Groups (ed) UNCITRAL recommendations for a European perspective? Banca d'Italia Eurosistema. Quaderni di Ricerca Giuridica della Consulenza Legale, 69, pp 103–108

Mevorach I (2014) Cross-border insolvency of enterprise groups: the choice of law challenge. Brooklyn J Corp Financ Commer Law 9:226–249

Mevorach I (2015) Beyond the search for certainty: addressing the cross-border resolution gap. Brooklyn J Corp Financ Commer Law 10:183–223

Mevorach I (2018) The future of cross-border insolvency. Overcoming biases and closing gaps. Oxford University Press, Oxford

Miller RW (2012) Economic integration: an American solution to the multinational enterprise group conundrum. Richmond J Global Law Bus 11:185–237

Mooney CW Jr (2014) Harmonizing choice-of-law rules for international insolvency cases: virtual territoriality, virtual universalism, and the problem of local interests. Brooklyn J Corp Financ Commer Law 9:120–151

Morris HP, Moss G, Mucciarelli FM, Paulus CG (2018) Cross-border insolvencies after Brexit: views from the United Kingdom and Continental Europe. In: Fitzgerald OE, Lein E (eds) Complexity's embrace – the international law implications of Brexit. Centre for International Governance & Innovation Press, Waterloo, pp 127–153

Ouatu M (2014) Modified universalism for cross-border insolvencies: does it work in practice? A thesis submitted in partial fulfillment of the requirements for the degree of Master of Laws in the Faculty of Graduate & Postdoctoral Studies. The University of British Columbia. Available at https://open.library.ubc.ca/collections/ubctheses/24/items/1.0103613

Panzani L (2016) La disciplina della crisi di gruppo tra proposte di riforma e modelli internazionali. Il Fallimento 10:1153–1162

Paulus C (2007) Group insolvencies – some thoughts about new approaches. Texas Int Law J 42:819–830

Paulus CG (2011) Ways towards a group insolvency law. In: Insolvency and Cross-border Groups (ed) UNCITRAL recommendations for a European perspective? Banca d'Italia Eurosistema. Quaderni di Ricerca Giuridica della Consulenza Legale, 69, pp 29–46

Peacock LL (2015) A tale of two courts: the novel cross-border bankruptcy trial. Am Bankruptcy Inst Law Rev 23:543–570

Pottow JAE (2011) A new role for secondary proceedings in international bankruptcies. Texas Int Law J 46:579–599

Pottow JAE (2014) Beyond carve-outs and toward reliance: a normative framework for cross-border insolvency choice of law. Brooklyn J Corp Financ Commer Law 9:202–225

Pottow JAE (2015) Two cheers for universalism: *Nortel*'s Nifty Novelty. Annu Rev Insolv Law:333–366

Queirolo I, Dominelli S (2017) Cooperation between authorities and insolvency office holders. In: Queirolo I, Dominelli S (eds) European and national perspectives on the application of the European insolvency regulation. Aracne editrice, Roma, pp 117–185

Reumers M (2013) Cooperation between liquidators and courts in insolvency proceedings of related companies under the proposed revised EIR. Eur Company Financ Law Rev 10:554–593

Reumers M (2016) What is in a name? Group coordination or consolidation plan – what is allowed under the EIR recast? Int Insolv Rev 25:225–240

Rutstein M, Bloomberg L (2010) A wind blows through an English Brothel. Corp Rescue Insolv 4:156

Sánchez-Calero J, Fuentes Naharro M (2011) Grupos y concurso: las recomendaciones de UNCITRAL y el Derecho español. In: Insolvency and Cross-border Groups (ed) UNCITRAL Recommendations for a European Perspective? Banca d'Italia Eurosistema. Quaderni di Ricerca Giuridica della Consulenza Legale, 69, pp 47–80

Sarra J (2009) Oversight and financing of cross-border business enterprise group insolvency proceedings. Texas Int Law J 44:547–576

Schmidt K (2015) Interaction of corporate law and insolvency law: German experience and international background. In: Parry R, Omar PJ (eds) International insolvency law: future perspectives. INSOL Europe, Nottingham, pp 125–147

Siemon K, Frind F (2013a) Der Konzern in der Insolvenz - Zur Überwindung des Dominoeffekts in der (internationalen) Konzerninsolvenz. Neue Zeitschrift für Insolvenzrecht:1–11

Siemon K, Frind F (2013b) Groups of companies in insolvency: a German perspective overcoming the domino effect in an (international) group insolvency. Int Insolv Rev 22:61–84

Skeel D (2015) Rediscovering corporate governance in bankruptcy. Temple Law Rev 87:1021–1034

Smaliukas A (2015) Insolvency of group of companies in the scope of the new EIR: Lithuanian perspective. Int Insolv Law Rev:379–382

Thole C, Dueñas M (2015) Some observations on the new group coordination procedure of the reformed European insolvency regulation. Int Insolv Rev 24:214–227

Van Galen R (2016) The recast insolvency regulation and groups of companies. In: Parry R, Omar PJ (eds) Reimagining rescue. INSOL Europe, Nottingham, pp 53–67

Wessels B (2014) Contracting out of secondary insolvency proceedings: the main liquidator's undertaking in the meaning of Article 18 in the proposal to amend the EU insolvency regulation. Brooklyn J Corp Financ Commer Law 9:63–110

Wessels B, Madaus S, Boon GI (2017) Rescue of business in insolvency law. Instrument of the European Law Institute. Available at: https://www.iiiglobal.org/sites/default/files/Rescue%20of%20Business%20in%20Insolvency%20Law.PDF

Westbrook JL (2015) Nortel: the cross-border insolvency case of the century. Buttersworth J Int Bank Financ Law 30:498

Wimmer K, Bornemann A, Lienau MD (2016) Die Neufassung der EuInsVO. Luchterhand Verlag, Köln

Winkler M (2008) From whipped cream to multibillion Euro financial collapse: the European regulation on transnational insolvency in action. Berkeley J Int Law 26:352–371

Wouters N, Raykin A (2013) Corporate group cross-border insolvencies between the United States and European Union: legal & economic developments. Emory Bankruptcy Dev J 29:387–423

Zhang D (2017) Reconsidering procedural consolidation for multinational corporate groups in the context of the recast European insovency regulation. Int Insolv Rev 26:332–347

Ziegel J (2002) Corporate groups and cross-border insolvencies: a Canada – United States perspective. Fordham J Corp Financ Law 7:367–393

Chapter 8
Restructuring

8.1 Proposed EU Directive on Preventative Restructuring Frameworks

Restructuring is the tendency of the national laws during the last years, when countries try to handle corporate economic crises. Obvious is the influence that U.S. law and UK law have on other laws which move towards these models, especially towards Chapter 11 of the U.S. Bankruptcy Code.[1]

In 2014, the European Commission emitted a Recommendation on a new approach to business failure and insolvency.[2] That non-binding EC Recommendation encouraged the Member States to implement efficient reorganization procedures based on the proposed common features.[3]

The Member States were invited to implement these principles by March 14, 2015.[4] The evaluation report that the European Commission published 6 months later, concluded that the EC Recommendation 2014 had been implemented differently in the Member States. Thus, the EC Recommendation 2014 was not considered as successful.

On November 22, 2016, EU proposed a Restructuring Directive[5]: Directive 2016/723, of the European Parliament and of the Council on Preventive Restructuring Frameworks, Second Chance and Measures to Increase the Efficiency of Restructuring, Insolvency and Discharge Procedures and Amending Directive 2012/30/EU.[6]

---

[1] Pulgar Ezquerra (2016), p. 119.

[2] Commission Recommendation of 12 March 2014 on a new approach to business failure and insolvency, 2014/135/EU (OJ 2014, L74/65).

[3] Madaus (2014), p. 81.

[4] Vanmeenen (2016), pp. 161–162.

[5] Eidenmüller (2017), p. 273; Eidenmüller and van Zwieten (2015), p. 625.

[6] 2016 O.J. L 141/19.

E. Moustaira, *International Insolvency Law*,
https://doi.org/10.1007/978-3-030-04450-3_8

It is undoubtedly intended to prompt Member States to adopt national legislation authorizing such restructuring.[7] Its aim is to strengthen the rescue culture with a hopefully positive impulse for the economy in the European Union.[8]

In its Article 4(1) it requires Member States:

> [To] ensure that, where there is likelihood of insolvency, debtors[9] in financial difficulty have access to an effective preventive restructuring framework that enables them to restructure their debts or business, restore their viability and avoid insolvency.

It is obviously—and once more—an influence by UK and U.S. laws (especially U.S. law) which favor a rescue culture.[10]

The purpose of the preventive restructuring procedures is to enable enterprises to restructure at an early stage and thus avoid insolvency. The directive contains provisions of substantive insolvency law that are subdivided into three main themes:

i) preventive restructuring procedures;
ii) discharge for entrepreneurs; and
iii) measures to be taken to increase the efficiency of insolvency procedures in general.[11]

The cross-border effectiveness of the preventive restructuring procedures adopted by a Member State of European Union is ensured by the EIR Recast specifically regarding those national restructuring proceedings that are included in Annex A of the Regulation.[12] As regards the effectiveness of these procedures in third countries, the answer will depend on the private international rules of those countries.

Comments on this Proposed Directive have been many and conflicting between each other. Is this like a lightning in a sky full of black clouds? Will that cause an unlawful competition of regimes? Or is it an enrichment of the toolbox of the national insolvency laws of the Member States?[13]

Or should we first put the question: Is every proceeding that has as its aim to avoid insolvency, insolvency proceeding? This is the legal mentality of the U.S. insolvency law, where the debtor can at whatever time and even without being insol-

---

[7] Block-Lieb (2017), p. 1406.

[8] Vallender (2017), p. 538.

[9] Only debtors may have the initiative for such a preventive restructuring procedure, see Ganter (2017), p. 205.

[10] Thery (2016), p. 139, argues that the Recast EIR is faced with two very different models that are difficult to reconcile: (1) the English model, in which restructuring is almost only possible as a pre-insolvency procedure and (2) the German model, within whose formal insolvency proceedings both liquidation and financial and operational restructuring are possible—the last model, having similarities with the U.S. model that expressly provides for a cram-down. Between these two models there are the other national systems, also differing from each other.

[11] Tollenaar (2017), p. 65.

[12] Garcimartín (2016), p. 90.

[13] Dammann (2017), p. 163.

vent, start an insolvency proceeding, so that he/she, by consensus of his/her biggest creditors, may make a reorganization plan.

Those in favor of copying such a solution in their own laws too, argue that in contemporary [law] society all collective proceedings must be considered as insolvency proceedings, if and when they wish to resolve a common pool-problem—even a potential problem of this kind.[14] The proposed EU Directive is of this mentality.

However, there are also jurists who oppose to the inclusion of the restructuring procedures in the general frame of insolvency proceedings. They believe that insolvency proceedings must be functionally distinguished from the restructuring proceedings[15]; that insolvency principles as liquidation principles can only in classic insolvency proceedings be applied, while restructuring or reorganization proceedings follow their own principles that must be derived from the general civil law and more specifically from the law on contracts.

U.S. legal system is much more based on private ordering, on private bargain than civil law systems or other legal systems are. It is literally stated that chapter 11 of the U.S. Bankruptcy Code is distinguished characteristic of a market economy where it is assumed that "successful reorganizations are neither primarily the product of the judicial process nor basically adversarial in nature, but instead reflect the persuasive power of 'private ordering'".[16] Negotiation is a key feature of the U.S. corporate reorganization regime.[17] This is a crucial difference of the US (and of the other common law countries too) from the countries where the private bargain either has no status at all or has an inferior power than that of the judicial body.

In any case, one can hardly predict the length of the negotiation and drafting process. If there will be an agreement, Member States will have 2 years to implement the text of the Directive in their national legislations.

8.2 Par conditio creditorum: Pari passu

Equality of creditors, equal treatment of creditors, el *alfa* y el *omega* del derecho de insolvencia,[18] die "*Magna Carta* des Insolvenzrechts"[19]: Is it a principle that always reigns in insolvency cases? Is it a principle that must reign in international insolvencies too?[20]

[14] Eidenmüller (2016), p. 150.

[15] Madaus (2017), p. 446.

[16] Johnston (1991), p. 216.

[17] Baird and Picker (1991), p. 312.

[18] Goldenber Serrano (2010), p. 73.

[19] Landfermann (2017), p. 430.

[20] Moustaira (1992). It was my PhD.

The answer to the first question is not clear. The existence of preferences, privileges of creditors undermines its hypothetical sovereignty.[21] As it is very accurately stated,[22] if all creditors must suffer a loss—since the debtor's property does not suffice to satisfy them in full—*par conditio creditorum* appears as the best principle, while that of priorities/privileges as the worst one.

For example, in the case *Swissair*, the English High Court said that nothing prevented an English court from ordering remittal of assets to a foreign liquidator if the local law of that liquidator provided for a *pari passu* distribution to creditors.[23]

In most other cases too, national courts were anxious to guarantee somehow that the equal treatment, equal protection of creditors would be a non-avoidable principle.

Still, especially during the last years, certain countries allow—by law—that this principle be contravened. A clear example is that of the "master agreements", standard contracts of financial institutions that document derivative, repo and other types of financial transactions worth trillions of US dollars in value. As it is stated, "[t]he laws of most developed financial markets make sure that these – purely contractual – arrangements are enforceable despite the fact that the liquidation arrangements made under master agreements somehow contravene the *pari passu* principle, much as in the case of security interests."[24]

The insolvency law provisions that guarantee the enforceability of master agreements are called in USA, "safe harbor" rules. The value of that special protection is questioned by many,[25] since it extends unjustified privileges to financial institutions and their cost is borne by society.

Furthermore, some countries provide for different treatment of creditors, either by legislation, like Argentina, out of fear and the need—as they feel it—to protect the local economy and the domestic creditors; or via the courts, like USA, especially in reorganization cases. Reasons for the latter are easily offered, seemingly pragmatic, in reality rather cynical and favoring the big players; nevertheless, it is clearly a disrespect of a very important principle that since bankruptcy law's genesis was reigning.

Thus, it is stated, that "[t]he ability to treat legally similar creditors differently allows the American courts to tailor the chapter 11 procedure to match the scope of the court's power. The procedure is thus "just right", neither too narrow, nor so broad as to be unworkable."[26]

---

[21] Most interesting is also the fact that in some laws there is a sort of discrimination towards some claims which, because of their specific qualities, do not receive an equal treatment with the ordinary claims, so that sometimes they are called "antiprivileged".

[22] Paulus (2017), p. 481.

[23] *Re Swissair Schweizerische Luftverkehr-Aktiengesellschaft* [2010] BCC 667, 671.

[24] Paech (2016), p. 855.

[25] Mooney (2014), pp. 247–251.

[26] Couwenberg and Lubben (2015), p. 740.

Is this principle reigning in international insolvencies too? Should it reign, should it be a *par conditio omnium creditorum*?

Yes,[27] is the obvious answer of those who believe that this is the most important target that international insolvencies should aim to.[28]

However, the problems arise when one questions oneself which system can guarantee that.[29] Creditor protection in general is steadily diminishing. Rescue procedures have often side effects for the creditors. Some pre-pack procedures[30] do not involve creditors at all. Some others, like the 363 sales, of U.S. law, often have as result significantly lower returns for unsecured creditors.

Forum shopping—not the good one, if there is such[31]—could always be a temptation for the debtor or/and the [secured] creditors who would want to take advantage of a national law that would seemingly favor them.

National legal systems that permit and often favor private pre-pack agreements may attract the above interested persons, by "promising"—often unreasonably[32]—bigger gains.[33] In these cases, one can hardly speak about equal treatment of creditors, since most often, if not always, secured creditors and cooperative debtors reach agreements in their favor[34] privileging the first and reducing the cost for the second,[35] so that unsecured creditors remain without any protection.[36]

The fact also that these procedures, even somehow transformed, are being transplanted in other national laws, does not really calm down the fears about the disrespect of a principle that once was and that should still be the reigning principle in insolvencies and in international insolvencies.

---

[27] Moustaira (1992).

[28] Garrido (1998), p. 79.

[29] Vattermoli (2013), p. 156.

[30] In pre-packs, a distressed company and its creditors reach an agreement about the company's assets prior to appointing an administrator out-of-court. The administrator then implements the agreement. Pre-packs give, as a rule, a high level of control to secured creditors, see Nocilla (2017), p. 68.

[31] See *supra*, Sect. 2.7.

[32] LoPucki and Doherty (2007), p. 1, had found that, from 2000 through 2004, reorganizations of large public companies under Chapter 11 of the U.S. Bankruptcy Code had yielded more than twice the returns of Section 363 sales. Denying that, Murphy (2011), p. 113, argues that using a different valuation model, the differences in returns are statistically insignificant. However, this is not a solid argument in favor of Section 363 sales. If there are slight or no differences, why choose a "procedure" not guaranteed by a court?

[33] Jacoby and Janger (2014), p. 862.

[34] Mooney (2015), p. 754.

[35] Roe and Tung (2013), pp. 1258–1262.

[36] Wood (2011), p. 446.

References

Baird DG, Picker RC (1991) A simple non-cooperative bargaining model of corporate reorganizations. J Leg Stud 20:311–349

Block-Lieb S (2017) The UK and EU cross-border insolvency recognition: from Empire to Europe to "Going It Alone". Fordham Int Law J 40:1373–1412

Couwenberg O, Lubben SJ (2015) Corporate bankruptcy tourists. Bus Law 70:719–750

Dammann R (2017) Umsetzung des EU-Richtlinienvorschlags vom 22.11.2016: Vorschläge zur Einführung eines präventiven Restrukturierungsverfahrens. In: Paulus CG, Wimmer-Amend A (eds) Festschrift für Dr. Klaus Wimmer. Nomos, Baden-Baden, pp 162–186

Eidenmüller H (2016) Was ist ein Insolvenzverfahren? Zeitschrift für Wirtschaft Recht:145–150

Eidenmüller H (2017) Contracting for a European insolvency regime. Eur Bus Org Law Rev 18:273–304

Eidenmüller H, van Zwieten K (2015) Restructuring the European business enterprise: the EU commission recommendation on a new approach to business failure and insolvency. Eur Bus Org Law Rev 16:625–667

Ganter HG (2017) Von der Beständigkeit rechtspolitischer Richtungsentscheidungen – Der Kampf für und gegen ein vorinsolvenzliches Sanierungsverfahren. In: Paulus CG, Wimmer-Amend A (eds) Festschrift für Dr. Klaus Wimmer. Nomos, Baden-Baden, pp 187–218

Garcimartín F (2016) Universal effects of European pre-insolvency proceedings: a case study. In: Parry R, Omar PJ (eds) Reimagining rescue. INSOL Europe, Nottingham, pp 77–90

Garrido JM (1998) Some reflections on the EU bankruptcy convention and its implications for secured and preferential creditors. Int Insolv Rev 7:79–94

Goldenber Serrano JL (2010) Consideraciones críticas respecto al denominado principio de la *par condicio creditorum*. Revista Chiena de Derecho 37:73–98

Jacoby M, Janger E (2014) Ice cube bonds: allocating the price of process in Chapter 11 bankruptcy. Yale Law J 123:862–947

Johnston JB (1991) The bankruptcy bargain. Am Bankruptcy Law J 62:213

Landfermann H-G (2017) Die Befriedigung der Gläubiger im Insolvenzverfahren – bestmöglich und gleichmäßig! In: Paulus CG, Wimmer-Amend A (eds) Festschrift für Dr. Klaus Wimmer. Nomos, Baden-Baden, pp 408–445

LoPucki L, Doherty J (2007) Bankruptcy fire sales. Mich Law Rev 106:1–59

Madaus S (2014) The EU recommendation on business rescue – only another statement or a cause for legislative action across Europe? Insolv Intell 27:81–85

Madaus S (2017) Restrukturierung mit Insolvenzprinzipien und Insolvenzverfahren mit Restrukturierungsziel? Eine Betrachtung der Grundannahmen des Insolvenz- und Restrukturierungsrechts. In: Paulus CG, Wimmer-Amend A (eds) Festschrift für Dr. Klaus Wimmer. Nomos, Baden-Baden, pp 446–474

Mooney C Jr (2014) The bankruptcy code's safe harbors for settlement payments and securities contracts: when is safe too safe? Texas Int Law J:245–267

Mooney C Jr (2015) The (Il)legitimacy of bankruptcies for the benefit of secured creditors. Univ Ill Law Rev:735–764

Moustaira EN (1992) The equality of creditors in international bankruptcy law [in Greek]. Ant.N. Sakkoulas Publishers, Athens

Murphy J (2011) Bankruptcy Avant-Garde. Am Bankruptcy Inst Law Rev 19:113

Nocilla A (2017) Asset sales and secured creditor control in restructuring: a comparison of the UK, US and Canadian models. Int Insolv Rev 26:60–81

Paech P (2016) The value of insolvency safe harbours. Oxford J Leg Stud 36:855–884

Paulus CG (2017) Gedanken zur Effizienz der Insolvenzordnung. In: Paulus CG, Wimmer-Amend A (eds) Festschrift für Dr. Klaus Wimmer. Nomos, Baden-Baden, pp 475–487

Pulgar Ezquerra J (2016) Corporate restructuring: the European recommendation and the Spanish model. In: Parry R, Omar PJ (eds) Reimagining rescue. INSOL Europe, Nottingham, pp 119–137

Roe M, Tung F (2013) Breaking bankruptcy priority: how rent-seeking upends the creditors' bargain. Va Law Rev 99:1235–1290

Thery A (2016) Crossroads in EU harmonization on restructuring and insolvency: towards a market-based system or one where "The Senior takes it all?". In: Parry R, Omar PJ (eds) Reimagining rescue. INSOL Europe, Nottingham, pp 139–147

Tollenaar NWA (2017) The European Commission's proposal for a directive on preventive restructuring proceedings. Insolv Intell 30:65–81

Vallender H (2017) Harmonisierung des Insolvenzrechts in der EU schreitet voran – Zum Kommissionsentwurf einer Richtlinie für ein vorinsolvenzliches Sanierungsverfahren. In: Paulus CG, Wimmer-Amend A (eds) Festschrift für Dr. Klaus Wimmer. Nomos, Baden-Baden, pp 537–554

Vanmeenen M (2016) Pre-insolvency arrangements: the Belgian experience. In: Parry R, Omar PJ (eds) Reimagining rescue. INSOL Europe, Nottingham, pp 161–173

Vattermoli D (2013) Par condicio omnium creditorum. Rivista trimestriale di diritto e procedura civile:155–183

Wood A (2011) The decline of unsecured creditor and shareholder recoveries in large public company bankruptcies. Am Bankruptcy Law J 85:429–450

Chapter 9
Conclusions

9.1 Could We Consider the Existing International Texts as Successful?

The Hague Conference on Private International Law had tried many decades ago, to create an International Bankruptcy Convention. It had been discussed in the Conference of 1904 and at the Fifth Session of the Hague Conference 1925 it was one of the issues to discuss. It was the first time the British government sent a delegation to The Hague to discuss the possibility of a diplomatic convention on uniform rules of private international law.[1]

Delegates from 22 European countries attended the 1925 Hague Conference on Private International Law. The Conference covered several topics however the British delegation had come to participate only in deliberations on a convention on bankruptcy law.

At the conclusion of the third day of deliberations, the British delegation left[2] after having entered a statement, remarking, first, the following[3]:

> Owing to the differences which appear to exist between the English Bankruptcy law and those of other countries in regard, for example, to such matters as the relation back of the trustee's title (*report de la faillite*) and the extent to which property acquired by the debtor subsequently to the bankruptcy vests in the trustee, it seems doubtful whether it would be practicable for Great Britain to be party to a convention under which the effects of a bankruptcy declared in one country are extended to the other country ipso facto and without qualification.

[1] Block-Lieb (2014), p. 1.

[2] After that, UK did not return to the Hague Conferences for nearly 30 years. Also, UK was not involved in negotiating any international instrument concerning insolvency law until it adhered to European Communities and started participating in the negotiations on the draft European Communities Convention in the 1970s, see Block-Lieb (2014), p. 1 note 2.

[3] Block-Lieb (2014), p. 13.

E. Moustaira, *International Insolvency Law*,
https://doi.org/10.1007/978-3-030-04450-3_9

The British delegation submitted a different proposal, according to which "there would be a concurrent bankruptcy in the second country, in aid of that in the first, the administration under which would be coordinated so far as practicable and all creditors treated on an equal footing."[4]

This position shows that probably are right those who claim that UK followed only an "imperial universalism", that is, a universalism "restricted" in the territories that in the past were under its control and after their independence had anyway adopted a legal system with many similarities to the UK's legal system.

The following day, the German and the Spanish delegations submitted their own declarations, in favor of "*le grand principe de l'unité et de l'universalité de la faillite*", rejecting implicitly the British delegation's proposal.

The final report on the revised draft—which never became a Convention—noted that while it [the draft] did not follow the principles of unity and universality in bankruptcy "with absolute logic", it was predominantly universal in its focus.[5]

Since then, there have been more efforts to harmonize either private international law (jurisdiction, choice of law, recognition and enforcement of judgments), as it has been above presented. Some of these efforts have failed and some have been considered successful.

"These texts are an advance on what existed before their development", it is argued, and they have become the catalyst for further legal steps to be taken. Their "success" sheds light to the need for incremental reform in insolvency law,[6] it is added.

When States are participating in a harmonization process, they become more familiar with the issues at stake and their difficulties, with the result that they often become more willing to adopt the solutions that are being proposed.[7] However, things are never—and may never be—perfect, there are always obstacles in the way to the harmonization of laws, mainly because of the different choices that each State does, regarding the regulation of the issues that are being the focus of the harmonization process.

According to many jurists, the harmonization of national substantive insolvency laws may have even better results in cross-border insolvency cases, since the applicable law, whatever that would be, would offer the same solutions. But would it? To my opinion, it would be doubtful, since legal mentality influences a lot the interpretation of texts: different legal mentality, different interpretation, therefore, different results.

In any case, the efforts towards the harmonization of certain sections of insolvency law are still in movement. Some of them focus on harmonization of substantive rules and others focus on harmonization of conflict of law rules. The results of these efforts are not always binding international instruments. Still, it is always

[4] Block-Lieb (2014), pp. 13–14 and note 73.

[5] Block-Lieb (2014), p. 15.

[6] Block-Lieb and Halliday (2007), p. 853.

[7] Clift (2011), p. 141.

useful for jurists and their countries to try to understand each other's legal culture, legal mentality, so that no one may impose to the other solutions not compatible to their legal culture, to their legal mentality.

9.2 Is the (Re-)Design of Insolvency Systems an Answer to International Insolvency Proceedings' Problems?

Would academic research contribute to a "sound" and adaptable to local uses and traditions re-design of national insolvency systems?[8] Should they work together with insolvency specialists or, at least, consider the latter's experience or would it better that the two categories work separately and that the governments or their agencies assess the respective results/answers and, based on them, try to re-design their insolvency systems?

Should governments try to harmonize the national insolvency systems? And if research into the literature shows "an aversion to the very use of the "H" word",[9] why should or would one keep on thinking about or trying to achieve such a harmonization?

9.3 Is the Perspective of an Extended International "Cooperation" Feasible?

National laws differ substantially in defining the classes of creditors in an insolvency proceeding and in the allocation of value to each one of them and that is one of the main reasons why countries/courts are reluctant to apply foreign law in these issues.

Defendants of the [modified] universalism are convinced that the common to all countries fundamental goals of insolvency law, that is, maximizing value for all creditors and guaranteeing a fair allocation that would not be contrary to the public policy of the court's country,[10] can only be realized in a single collective insolvency proceeding that will be recognized everywhere[11]—or, at least, in a main insolvency proceeding and secondary proceedings referring to the first.

It is reasonably argued that that was the main reason bankruptcy law is federal law, in USA: the founders of the country realized that, to create a single national market, bankruptcy law should be uniform national law.[12]

[8] Mason (2015), pp. 216–217.

[9] Fletcher (2015), p. 190.

[10] Westbrook (2018), pp. 1475–1476.

[11] Westbrook (2006), pp. 324–325.

[12] Schulman (1995), pp. 99–105.

Modified universalism is said to be "universalism adapted to the political realities of differing laws". Its results are as close as possible to those of an absolute universalism, that is, of one single insolvency proceeding that would be recognized everywhere.[13]

Control by a court is necessary for the purposes of insolvency law to be reached.[14] The court will be able to apply insolvency law properly in a cross-border case only if it is able to prevent losses that would result from individual actions by creditors in other parts of the world. The court will also control the allocation of the remained value "in an orderly and fair way."[15] Private agreements are not really guaranteeing the reach of the above purposes.

A worldwide stay of individual actions, ordered by the court opening the insolvency proceeding, would only be possible if its recognition by the other countries where assets and creditors are found were absolute. It depends on the recognition of the jurisdiction of the court opening the insolvency proceeding; however, the court would not have the power to impose a stay everywhere in the world.

In certain common law countries, such as USA, the courts have the possibility to issue an order that forbids persons that are subject to their personal jurisdiction from acting individually anywhere in the world. It is argued that that is a case of an "indirect global stay", since it applies only to persons subject to the court's personal jurisdiction, however it restricts their individual actions everywhere in the world.[16]

Again, let me repeat that the differences in legal mentality are not so easy to bypass and reach a common point of understanding international insolvencies' problems and the way(s) to resolve them.

References

Block-Lieb S (2014) Turnaround: reflections on the present day influence of negotiations on international bankruptcy at the fifth session of the Hague Conference on Private International Law in 1925. Brooklyn J Corp Financ Commer Law 9:1–19

Block-Lieb S, Halliday T (2007) Incrementalisms in global lawmaking. Brooklyn J Int Law 32:851–903

Clift J (2011) Developing an international regime for transnational corporations: the importance of insolvency law to sustainable recovery and development. Transl Corp 20:117–144

Fletcher QCI (2015) Spreading the gospel: the mission of insolvency law, and the insolvency practitioner, in the early twenty-first century. In: Parry R, Omar PJ (eds) International insolvency law: future perspectives. INSOL Europe, Nottingham, pp 179–197

Mason R (2015) Insolvency specialists and government enquiries: a unique opportunity to contribute to the public good. In: Parry R, Omar PJ (eds) International insolvency law: future perspectives. INSOL Europe, Nottingham, pp 199–219

[13] Westbrook (2018), pp. 1477–1478.

[14] Westbrook (2004), p. 795.

[15] Westbrook (2018), p. 1479.

[16] Westbrook (2009), pp. 17–18.

Schulman DJ (1995) The constitution, interest groups, and the requirements of uniformity: the United States Trustee and the bankruptcy administrator programs. Nebraska Law Rev 74:91–136

Westbrook JL (2004) The control of wealth in bankruptcy. Texas Law Rev 82:795–862

Westbrook JL (2006) Multinational financial distress: the last Hurrah of territorialism. Texas Int Law J 41:321–337

Westbrook JL (2009) Multinational insolvency: a first analysis of unilateral jurisdiction. In: Norton annual review of international insolvency, pp 11–32

Westbrook JL (2018) Global insolvency proceedings for a global market: the universalist system and the choice of a central court. Texas Law Rev 96:1473–1496

MIX
Papier aus verantwortungsvollen Quellen
Paper from responsible sources
FSC® C105338

If you have any concerns about our products,
you can contact us on
ProductSafety@springernature.com

In case Publisher is established outside the EU,
the EU authorized representative is:
Springer Nature Customer Service Center GmbH
Europaplatz 3, 69115 Heidelberg, Germany

Printed by Libri Plureos GmbH
in Hamburg, Germany